P9-BBQ-034

"IF YOUR DESK ISN'T CLUTTERED, YOU PROBABLY AREN'T DOING YOUR JOB."
—HAROLD GENEEN

MANAGING

"You can't run a business on 'theories.' Like fads and fashions, they come and go."

"Management *must* manage means that you *must* get results."

"You read a book from the beginning to the end. You run a business the opposite way. You start with the end, and then you do everything you must to reach it."

"Knowing and understanding the numbers is the key to the mastery of any business."

"The worst executive disease is not alcoholism . . . it's egotism."

MANAGING

"Refreshing . . . MANAGING is recommended for its business insights, its straightforward look at the way things work, and the devotion with which [the author] handles the subject."

Newsday

"Sensible advice from the legendary practitioner of superior management"

Publishers Weekly

"An interesting history of the conglomerate of all conglomerates"

Library Journal

Managing

HAROLD GENEEN
with Alvin Moscow

AVON
PUBLISHERS OF BARD, CAMELOT, DISCUS AND FLARE BOOKS

AVON BOOKS
A division of
The Hearst Corporation
105 Madison Avenue
New York, New York 10016

The Doubleday & Company edition contains the following Library of Congress
Cataloging in Publication Data:

Geneen, Harold.
Managing.
Includes Index.
1. Management.   2. International business enterprises—Management.
I. Moscow, Alvin   II. Title.   HD31.G395   1984   658'.049

First Avon Books Printing: September 1985

*To all those who aspire, in whatever endeavor,
to rise above the level of mediocrity*

CONTENTS

PREFACE   ix

INTRODUCTION   by Alvin Moscow   1

ONE   *Theory G on Management*   15

TWO   *How to Run a Business*   33

THREE   *Experience and Cash*   51

FOUR   *Two Organizational Structures*   83

FIVE   *Management Must Manage*   109

SIX   *Leadership*   131

SEVEN   *The Cluttered-Desk Executive*   155

EIGHT   *Not Alcoholism—Egotism*   171

NINE   *The Numbers*   187

TEN   *Acquisitions and Growth*   205

ELEVEN   *Entrepreneurial Spirit*   233

TWELVE   *The Board of Directors*   255

THIRTEEN   *On Caring: A Summing Up*   275

FOURTEEN   *Envoi!*   291

INDEX   295

PREFACE

BUSINESS IS MANY THINGS, the least of which is the balance sheet. It is a fluid, ever-changing, living thing, sometimes building to great peaks, sometimes falling to crumbled lumps. The soul of business is a curious alchemy of needs, desires, greed, and gratifications mixed together with selflessness, sacrifices, and personal contributions far beyond material rewards. It serves the aspirations of many men and women and is the source of physical security and well-being for all of us.

To my mind, the process of conducting business is fascinating, demanding, and creative, worthy of being classed with the higher arts, worthy also of the greatest personal commitment for self and society, and yielding the greatest satisfactions. I have experienced all of this—and I know.

It has always been my contention that no one has a corner on brains. The greatest feats in business, as in virtually all of life, are performed by very ordinary, normal men and women. Not geniuses. Peak experiences of ordinary, normal people create leaders in business and elsewhere.

So if it befalls an ordinary man in his career to come upon and recognize one or two basic truths about a portion of life as we live it, it behooves him to offer back to others what he has learned.

It was with that in mind that this book was written. The pages that follow are offered with the hope that they may engender some enlightenment and truths about business, based upon my own experience.

Harold Geneen

MANAGING

INTRODUCTION

by Alvin Moscow

GENEEN!

The name is recognized and known throughout the modern business world far beyond the borders of the United States, for he is said to be the greatest business manager since Alfred P. Sloan, Jr., the management genius who revamped, restructured, and revitalized General Motors into what it is today.

For seventeen years, Harold Sydney Geneen was lord of the realm at the International Telephone and Telegraph Company, commander in chief of the most complex corporation in the world, operating in every major country not behind the Iron Curtain, employing at its peak more than 375,000 men and women of every race and religion on the face of the earth, producing a variety of products and services that defied the ordinary man's imagination.

In a sense, he accomplished what Sloan did fifty years ago, but he did it in a far more complex time and against greater adversity. Geneen's accomplishment was ITT. When he was hired as president and chief executive officer in 1959, the International Telephone and Telegraph Company was a thirty-nine-year-old corporation that manufactured telephone and telegraph equipment, operated several telephone companies in Latin America, and built communications networks for the U.S. Defense Department. With most of its operations abroad, the company had taken quite a beating in World War II. In the postwar years, it struggled to rebuild its overseas business and to find a new niche in the burgeoning United States economy. By and large, it failed. Colonel Sosthenes Behn, the company founder, died in June 1957, a bitterly discouraged man. By modern standards, the company seemed old-fashioned, outdated, stagnant, adrift.

Two years later, when Geneen came aboard, ITT's sales were $765.6 million, with a slim profit margin of only $29 million, and $15 million of that came from other than operating income, including the sale of its headquarters building in lower Manhattan for $3 million. In 1977, when Geneen stepped down as chief executive, ITT's annual sales had reached $16.7 billion, with earnings of $562 million. He had bought, merged with, or absorbed some 350 different businesses in eighty countries, and fashioned them into 250 different profit centers.

Geneen described this new creation as "a unified-management, multi-product company." Under his direction, ITT not only built highly sophisticated telephone and telegraph equipment and operated telephone companies, it also baked breads and cakes, rented cars, built houses, operated hotels, wrote insurance, published books, manufactured pumps and valves, automobile spare parts, lawn products, electrical equipment . . . And these were not tiny, insignificant companies strung together to make one large company. They were billion-dollar companies in their own right, growing bigger and more profitable under the ITT aegis. Continental Baking's Wonder bread and Twinkies were number one in their fields, Avis Rent-A-Car was number two, of course, in its industry, Sheraton Hotels became the second-largest hotel chain, Hartford Insurance Company rose to fourth in the casualty insurance business, and no one could find a company which produced more industrial pumps and valves than did ITT. Geneen called it a unified-management, multi-product company. Everyone else called it a conglomerate—the largest, most profitable international conglomerate in the world.

At its peak, ITT was the ninth-largest industrial company on the Fortune 500 list. In 1977, when he relinquished the chief executive's spot, two of the major oil companies had moved ahead, so that ITT became the eleventh-largest. But of the ten ahead of ITT, six were oil companies with their tremendous resources, two were the Goliath auto firms of General Motors and Ford. That put ITT in the rarefied atmosphere of General Electric and International Business Machines. Down the list, outstripped by ITT, were such familiar names as U.S. Steel, Procter & Gamble, Dow Chemical, Union Carbide, Eastman Kodak, RCA, and Westinghouse Electric.

Unmistakably, Harold Geneen had made it all happen. He did it in such a big, bold way and in so short a span of time that he was regarded in many quarters with suspicion and concern. Popular opinion in the United States, or at least a large segment of it, held that there must be something malevolent behind such rapid success. Novels, movies, and television plays portrayed heads of large international corporations as power-mad fiends who were working nefariously and unscrupulously to take over the world. There were congressional investigations of the power wielded by conglomerates, antitrust suits against ITT, and a variety of charges and accusations made against Harold Geneen. None of them resulted in any corrective action, for the airing of the charges revealed that there was nothing to correct. Nevertheless, perched upon the pinnacle of ever-increasing corporate profits, he became a popular target for all those who believed that in every armor there must be a chink.

Through it all, Harold Geneen remained something of a mystery man. He did not appear in public often. He seldom made speeches. He did not join committees. Even within the business establishment, he was thought of as a maverick, something on the order of "the General Patton of industry." He thought for himself and dared to do the unexpected. In Europe, however, where there is far less suspicion of business success than in the United States, and where ITT did almost half of its business, Harold Geneen was regarded with outright awe. In Western European countries, he was often referred to as "the Michelangelo of management."

Almost all those who have worked closely with the man describe him as a genius, which he vehemently denies, and a true master of professional business management, which he does not deny. For countless young men and women on the bottom rungs of the business ladder, Harold Geneen was seen as larger than life, a man to emulate. He had worked his own way up. He was no inventor or entrepreneur. He had not discovered oil, a computer microchip, or instant photography. He had not launched a new product at the beginning of an era and ridden the crest of its wave to riches. He did not even own his own company. He was, simply, a manager who had taken over an ill-managed, stagnant telephone company and had turned it around, reshaped it, and rebuilt it into the largest, most complex, modern, diversified multinational corporation in the entire world. Even though he was the highest-paid executive in America at one time, still he was a hired hand who had to answer to a board of directors which employed him.

Nor did he start out with any particular advantages over others. He began as an errand boy, knew adversity, attended night school for eight years before earning his degree, and went to work as an accountant. The implication was clear to other would-be business successes: If Geneen could do it, so could you. In that sense, he became a hero, a legend in his own lifetime. Heroes are a rare breed today and there are few in the realm of business. If you run your finger down the list of the Fortune 500 largest industrial corporations in America, you would have a tough time even naming the heads of those companies, much less their accomplishments.

In financial circles and the Wall Street community,

Geneen was viewed with mixed feelings. In the beginning, when he was reshaping and rebuilding ITT, some
analysts said it couldn't be done, that his complex mix-
ture of companies and products would all come crashing
down. Other conglomerates did crash, but ITT prospered
and grew. The undeniable statistic which impressed Wall
Street more than anything else was the steady growth of
this complex company. Under Geneen, ITT increased its
earnings over the year before for *fifty-eight consecutive
quarters*. That's fourteen and a half years. In corporate
America that record is unparalleled.

The business community began calling ITT "the Geneen Machine." It made money. In his seventeen-year
reign, ITT failed to make an 11 percent gain over the previous year's earnings only twice, in 1974 and 1975, and
that was largely because of the oil embargo, the energy
crisis, and steep fluctuations in the exchange rate of the
American dollar.

How did he do it? How could ITT, with its more than
two hundred different profit centers and products, make
increased profits of 10 to 15 percent in good years and
bad, despite recessions, tight money, economic upheav-
als, and political vicissitudes? How could he do it when
other companies of similar size were increasing their
earnings by 1, 2, 3, or 5 percent at a time when there was
no inflation to help them. ITT's management was scrutinized and analyzed probably more than any other company among the Fortune 500. Some described it as
"management by objectives," others called it "management by meetings," others singled out its tight centralized financial controls, still others said it was simply the
man, Geneen; while some simply refused to believe the
figures. Explanations did not suffice. Other corporations
appeared to be doing the same things as ITT; they had
their own management by objectives, regular meetings,
review and analysis procedures, and centralized financial
controls. Some of them even had tough, hard-driving
bosses who said the same things that Harold Geneen

said. And yet, somehow, they did not achieve the steady bottom-line results that ITT did year after year. One could only conclude that those on the outside did not really know what those on the inside at ITT knew: Hal Geneen.

I met Harold Geneen in the spring of 1980 through the introduction of Richard Curtis, the literary agent who conceived the idea of our collaboration on a book. Geneen, who had retired as ITT chief executive in 1977 and stepped down as chairman of the board in 1979, was very active in his retirement. He was doing what he had done at ITT, buying companies, reorganizing, refinancing, and reshaping them, but this time as an independent venture capital investor. We met at night, after the regular business day, on four successive evenings, discussing the potential subject matter of this book. We skimmed through his career, his education, the early influences on his life, the history of ITT, his views on management, the economic/political history of the United States during his fifty-year working career, and a variety of other subjects. Then we agreed to allow it all to "incubate" while I finished work on another book.

A year later, in April 1981, we went to work together. From all the material at hand, we agreed to try to write, not a history or a memoir, but rather a book on business management based upon what he had learned, had done, and had accomplished. It turned out to be a happy collaboration which took two and a half years. Our working pattern remained the same. We would meet after his normal business day and work from six to eleven o'clock, sometimes to midnight, sometimes on weekends. Our tape-recorded sessions, which must run to millions of words, were dutifully transcribed by Catherine Farago, his administrative assistant, and his secretary Marie Serio, both of whom worked long into the night.

In the process, I received a profound education. It changed a good deal of the way I thought about and perceived everything around me. Early on, I was struck with how much of what Harold Geneen was saying about managing a business was equally applicable to all of life—the way one should approach a problem of any kind, the way one should pursue a goal, any goal, the way one should deal with other people, and on and on. Harold Geneen, on his part, searched back into his past to trace the origins of his thoughts and philosophy on business and life. Much of what he did at ITT was based upon instinct and intuition as much as upon logic and experience, and that came from what he had learned from his mother, from his school days at Suffield Academy, from old bosses and peers with whom he had worked. We tried to get all of that into this book. In the process, he found that he had become much more articulate in describing what it was he had been doing all of his life. Like most men who lead very active lives, he had never before had the time or inclination to look back.

The Geneen concepts which form the heart of this book may seem simple, but they are deceptively simple. And I think they will reverberate in your life, as they have in mine and in others who have read the manuscript. I had heard or read about many of them before, but never in the context and with the impact that Harold Geneen gives to them. They contributed to the way this book was written. "Decide what it is you want to do, and then start doing it," was Geneen's philosophy. And it proved to be true. Once we decided what it was we wanted to do in this book, the steps we had to take revealed themselves to us, one by one, and we were on our way. We knew where we were going. I came to understand the aura of those long General Managers Meetings he held at ITT through the long work sessions we had on this book. There were times when Geneen and I started out feeling tired at the end of a day and then became more and more excited and alive by the time we concluded around midnight. Oftentimes we discovered things neither of us had thought about when we had started on the agenda for that meeting.

In order to round out my understanding of the management of ITT, Geneen suggested that I see some of the men with whom he worked closely there. He drew up a list. When it became rather long, he divided it into an A and a B list. The A list had the names of 132 men on it. I met with about fifty of them, including the top headquarters management of ITT, several members of the board of directors, a few subsidiary company managers, and some outside people.

They described Harold Geneen with great fondness, most of them expressing a deep appreciation for the impact he had had upon their lives and their careers. A portrait of the man emerged. Of his many attributes, most agree that his high energy level, natural enthusiasm, and quick mind are what make him extraordinary. He does everything at high speed and without tiring. He walks fast, drives fast, eats fast, thinks and talks at incredible speed. He leaps from idea to idea, pausing only to inquire, "Do you follow me?" But he is a good listener, too, ever curious to learn something new. That makes him, unlike so many other men of power, easy to talk with. He is a man who is down to earth, even earthy. His emotions are close to the surface, hardly ever repressed. He laughs easily and often, for he enjoys his way of life and he likes people. He is curious and eager to learn anything new to him. He may not suffer fools gladly, and he is often short on patience with those who do not live up to his expectations. He gives free vent to his anger or frustration when the occasion warrants it. He has been known to hurl across his forty-foot office inanimate objects that refuse to work as they should. But in his relationships with his fellow human beings, he is very human. He may complain when a job is not done well or on time, but he takes great care never to demean a man personally, especially a subordinate. When touched by someone's personal misfortune, he can be extraordinarily kind and compassionate.

He likes his work. Above all else, he works hard. He sets a clear example for all those who work with him: To keep up, they too must work hard. The ethic of hard work, doing your own homework, permeated the ITT ranks of management. Ten to twelve hours was a normal workday for Harold Geneen and his headquarters staff, and many, if not most, workdays were longer. On weekends or business trips, Geneen carried his work with him in two, three, or more oversized, custom-made leather attaché cases, each weighing some forty pounds.

Geneen ran ITT with tight, centralized financial controls, a large headquarters staff to keep him informed, and, above all, face-to-face meetings with the managers of ITT's profit centers worldwide. The General Managers Meetings had the most impact upon the top management of the company. Once a month they met with "Mr. Geneen," who, they knew, had gone over their monthly operations reports with his unerring eye for the erring detail. In an open meeting, attended by some 120 managers in Europe or the 130 managers in the United States, Geneen would ask questions based upon their reports. He went over the major problems of each company, which were "red-flagged" in the monthly reports. But he also looked for "inefficiencies" because he believed all large corporations, like ITT, were inefficient. They competed in inefficiencies. Their job as managers was to make ITT less inefficient than its competitors.

Geneen's intense probing for answers in an open forum was Socratic. One question led to another. He demanded facts and opinions backed up by facts. Some executives had to struggle to adjust to Geneen's bare-faced questioning of their decisions and actions; others thrived on it. For all who survived, it was a tremendous learning experience. Not only did these highly paid, powerful company managers have to give close personal attention to the details of their business affairs, but they had to learn to rein in their pride and egos and to focus on the intellectual challenge that business problems present in the cold reality of day. Geneen looked at past performance primarily to solve the questions of the future. He was forever urging ITT's managing directors to try something new, to expand existing operations, and to venture out into new marketplaces with new products.

In essence, Harold Geneen was an unstinting teacher, running a school for business managers. Unlike at graduate business schools, however, at ITT they were dealing in real-world problems with real money. Geneen's extraordinary enthusiasm was highly contagious. He inspired men with his enthusiasm for their projects. They often left his presence with a revitalized eagerness to try something new, to experiment, to get on with a job overdue, to work a little harder in order to achieve something worthwhile. They knew that no one worked longer hours at ITT than Harold Geneen.

He was demanding, but he had earned the right to be tough and demanding. He was accused of being harddriving, impatient, and tough on his subordinates, but the accusations came from men who had left the company because they could not, or chose not to, keep up the pace. Those closest to him observed that he had little patience with "phonies" who, for one reason or another, chose to "wing it" rather than do the work required of them. But he had "unbelievable patience" with people who sincerely were trying hard to do their best. "He was like a teacher who did not want to waste his time on the bad students, but could not give enough time and help to his good students," according to one of his executives.

His enthusiasm and complete involvement in the work at hand almost always transcended the element of time. He was hardly a clock watcher. When working in his New York office, he would break for lunch when he had time for it, anywhere from noon to four o'clock. A meeting with his staff at the end of the day might go on to eleven or midnight, with or without a break for dinner, depending upon the seriousness of the agenda. Geneen's hunger pangs often were not strong enough to interrupt his concentration upon a business problem. Rand Araskog, who succeeded him as chief executive of ITT, tells of the night he and his wife showed up in evening clothes for dinner and the theater, only to become involved in a business discussion which went on past midnight, the social part of the evening completely forgotten.

All the top executives of ITT remember favorite anecdotes about working with Geneen. A senior vice president tells of arriving home in the suburbs even later than usual after a meeting with Geneen at New York headquarters. His long-suffering wife raised her head from the pillow and asked, "What time is it?"

Sheepishly, he replied, "Five A.M."

"You're crazy," she sighed, and fell back asleep.

Geneen's meetings always ran long. At the end of one of those meetings in Brussels, when he and key members of his staff had adjourned to a nearby restaurant to continue their discussions at two o'clock in the morning, Geneen asked, "What special quality are we looking for in ITT executives which will differentiate them from other company executives?"

"Insomnia!" said Tim Dunleavy, then an executive vice president.

On another very late occasion in a restaurant, after a managers meeting, the overhead lights began to flicker off and on. "Hal, it's late," said one colleague, "even the lights are getting tired."

"Only the lesser lights!" he shot back, and picked up where he had left off.

These are the stories that ITT men, those who are still there as well as those who have left to head other companies, tell with a touch of pride. They are badges of honor. They reveal not only Geneen in action but also something about themselves. The men were also part of the legend. They worked hard and late, too, and they too succeeded.

As one former ITT group executive summed it up:

"Hal Geneen taught us to aspire higher. We really did not know what we had in us until he showed us, and then we could say, 'By God, we can do it.' Geneen was very much like Vince Lombardi, the coach of the Green Bay Packers, a tough taskmaster but a great leader, and, you know, it's true what Lombardi said: There's no sweeter feeling than being exhausted after a victory."

Harold Geneen brought a new quality of professional management to ITT. Under his unique leadership, the company became known, fondly, as Geneen University. The executives and managers who served under him graduated to become premium "products" on the executive job market. They were highly sought after by other companies and by the professional executive recruiters. Charles Revson personally handpicked Michel Bergerac, then president of ITT-Europe, to succeed him as head of Revlon, luring him away from ITT with a $5 million contract. CBS hired Charles Ireland from ITT to become its president, succeeding the legendary Frank Stanton. Crucible Steel took John C. Lobb away from ITT to become its executive vice president. Colt Industries made George A. Strichman its chairman, and he was succeeded in later years by another key ITT manager, David Margolis. Robert M. Flanagan moved on to become chairman and chief executive of Western Union. Edward L. Hennessy, Jr., became chairman and CEO of Allied Chemical; Robert L. Kirk, chief executive of the Vought Corporation; Joseph A. Rice, president of the Irving Trust Company. Others took what they had learned under Geneen and applied it to entrepreneurial ventures of their own.

And they all did spectacularly well. Glenn Bailey in his first year as president of the Keene Corp. raised sales from $2 to $53 million. Gerhard Andinger, as the new chairman of Esterline, doubled sales there to $35 million in a few months. On and on it went, ITT managers and staff executives spreading what they had learned throughout American industry.

By the time Harold Geneen retired, the number of ITT managers who had moved on to top positions in other American companies had grown to a remarkable 130. They have formed an elite group of alumni with a private listing of members, their current positions and phone numbers, so that Geneen graduates can keep in touch with one another as they move around and usually up in the business world.

Many keep in touch with the old master. Some have written him that the intense years they spent with him at ITT have turned out, upon reflection, to have been the happiest and most thrilling of their lives.

I feel fortunate to have shared with them a portion of Harold Geneen's practical wisdom in my special three-year course with him. His principles of good business management apply to aspects of all of our lives. They have an astonishing universality.

So, welcome to Geneen University.

ONE

Theory G on Management

THEORY G: *You cannot run a business, or anything else, on a theory.*

THEORIES ARE LIKE those paper hoops I remember from the circuses of my childhood. They seemed so solid, until the clowns crashed through them. Then you realized that they were tissue thin and that there was little left after the event; the illusion was gone. Yet we keep going back to the circus and the theater for the magic of illusions. We are always buying nostrums of some kind, those patent medicines sold with exaggerated claims, even in business, where we call them concepts, because we are always looking for simple formulas that will solve our complex problems. Almost anything that can be fitted into a neat little package and given an attractive label will be swallowed like a sugarcoated pill. Business theories are like that.

In more than fifty years in the business world, I must have read hundreds of books and thousands of magazine articles and academic papers on how to manage a successful business. When I was young, I used to absorb and believe those theories and formulas propounded by professors and consultants. They told you how to increase productivity, sales, and profits while keeping your management staff, your production line workers, and your shareholders prosperous and happy. Their reasoning was always solid and logical, the grains of wisdom true and indisputable, the conclusions inevitable.

But when I reached a position in the corporate hierarchy where I had to make decisions which governed others, I found that none of these theories really worked

17

as advertised. Fragments here and there were helpful, but not one of those books or theories ever reduced the operation of a business, or even one part of a business, to a single formula or an interlocking set of formulas that I could use. Even the fragments I took from books had to be applied with care and judgment in the real world of business.

In fact, in all my years at work, I have never come across a chief executive who tried, much less succeeded, running his company according to any set formula, chart, or business theory. On the other hand, I have met many men who never finished high school or read a business theory who, to my mind, had the art of running their own businesses down cold. How did they do it? They lived with their businesses. They grew up with them. They applied their own God-given common sense to dealing with more and more complex realities of the business world, and they learned as they went along. Some, I have to admit, moved up the ladder of success so fast, and their companies grew so large, that they lost contact with the heart and soul of the very business they founded. Then, almost inevitably, their sales would flatten out, their earnings diminish, and the slow spiral down would begin. In many cases, the turnabout came when the founder or the man in charge, awed by his own success, shifted his attention from the business he knew so well to the so-called higher philosophy of world economics or the broader burdens of the sociological problems of his community, state, or nation, which he knew hardly at all. He delegated to others his business responsibilities while he went out to make speeches, head community projects, and participate in a host of outside activities. Without demeaning his contributions to the community, in my opinion he would have served his community or nation better if he had stuck to his primary responsibility: running his business successfully and providing economic security to his employees and to his community. But outside community activities supplied him with a personal ego gratification which he thought he could not get from sticking to his job. Ego gratification is one of the worst traps devised to ensnare the successful businessman. I have seen it happen again and again and yet I've never seen it theorized about at Harvard or in *Fortune* magazine. On the other hand, I have no doubt that most of the chief executives who delegate their business responsibilities to others while they go out to help save the world, leave behind full instructions and personal formulas for carrying on the business; yet, somehow, those formulas and theories of management do not survive in their absence.

One of the latest in the long list of theories on successful management is the current "Theory Z" or "The Art of Japanese Management." Those happen to be the titles of two of the more popular books on how we should revise our ways and methods in American business in order to overcome the competition of the Japanese. And they have been augmented *ad infinitum* by hundreds of magazine articles and academic studies that try to tell us of the magic formula for success developed by our wily competitors in the Far East.

Long before "Z" we had the Theory X and Theory Y philosophy of business management, promulgated by Professor Douglas McGregor, of the Massachusetts Institute of Technology. The beauty of Theory X and Theory Y was that they so neatly encompassed all of business management. Everyone in business schools studied them because once you thoroughly understood these theories, it was intimated, you could proceed fearlessly through the maze of the business world. All companies were run according to Theory X or Theory Y.

Theory X held that no one really liked to work or wanted to work any harder than he or she must, nor did he or she want any more responsibility than was absolutely necessary to do his or her specific job. Given that premise, a Theory X company was structured along a strict line of command. Each level was told explicitly what it must do, when it must do it, and how it must be done. The classic example was the Army. In theory at least, the general gives his orders to the colonel, who tells the major what to do, and the commands are passed down the ranks to the lowly enlisted men on the firing line. In a Theory X company, one cannot talk directly to anyone two or so levels above his station. Instead, he salutes his superiors and obeys orders.

Theory Y is based upon the premise that people, at no matter what level of responsibility, innately want to work as best they can; they want to expand their skills and productivity and are bored and stymied by the strictures of a Theory X type of organization. On the basis of this formula, the management of a Theory Y company should strive for an egalitarian type of operation, with workers being given a share in the decision-making process. Most modern managers today opt for Theory Y and try to instill a cooperative feeling of teamwork within their organizations—at least they say they do.

The trouble with these neat theories, however, is that no company that I know of is run in strict accordance with either Theory Y or Theory X. Not even the Army. If you know anything about the true roles of sergeants and second lieutenants in the field, you would know that leadership depends upon the man more than the rank. When the chips are down, where you have a strong lieutenant, he will lead; where you have a weak one, the sergeant will make the crucial decisions. That's the way it works in the business world. The crucial decisions, in reality, are made by the men and women who have the self-confidence to lead, whether they are in the Pentagon or in prison, in the executive suite or in the company cafeteria. All organizations, large and small, military or civilian, reflect the personality and character of the man or men who lead them. Even that oversimplifies the complexity we find in real life. I have known managers who prefer to be told what to do, men who do not want responsibility for making crucial decisions which might jeopardize their careers, and once they are given precise directions, perform their assigned tasks with care and diligence. I have also known managers who are self-starters and perform best only when they have shared in the decision-making process; in fact, they resent being given orders. Both these types of managers were working for the same company. If you were the chief executive, how would you run that company—by Theory X or by Theory Y? Or would you use your common sense and act according to the circumstances at hand?

Theory Z, with its intimations of Oriental Zen philosophy, attempts to explain why and how the Japanese system of business management is superior to our own. It starts off with some obvious facts: The Japanese are outproducing and outselling us in all sorts of products—automobiles, cameras, television sets, radios, electronics. The balance of trade between our two countries has been heavily in Japan's favor over the past few years and threatens to get worse. Conclusion: They must be doing something right that we are not doing. So Theory Z focuses upon the differences.

In Japan, the large industrial corporations treat their employees with the loving care of a concerned parent. They guarantee them lifetime employment and security; they require them to sing songs and exercise together before the day's work begins; they give their most skilled young men (and some women) ten years of diversified management training before assigning them to key roles in company management; they foster cooperation among the workers and management; they favor decision-making by the group with shared responsibilities and rewards; individual self-aggrandizement is frowned upon. In return, the Japanese worker toils at his or her job with a devoted loyalty to his or her company that is equal to his or her love of family and country. The three seem inextricably intertwined. As the company prospers with ever-increasing production, the workers prosper, their families prosper, the nation prospers—all working for the greater common good.

On the other hand, American corporate life is characterized by just the opposite: relatively short-term employment, rapid promotions and dismissals, individual decision-making and responsibilities with commensurate rewards and punishments, specialized careers, and a sense of personal loyalties rather than corporate loyalties.

As portrayed, the American scene appears gray, bleak, and stressful in comparison to the rosy, serene, and caring atmosphere of the Japanese workplace. I doubt if the contrast is, in reality, all that great. Even so, would we Americans really want to trade our heritage of personal freedoms and individual opportunity for the ingrown paternalism, humility, and selflessness of the Japanese? Could we, even if we wanted to? The Japanese way of life, so different from ours, is based upon a culture centuries old, and it was upon this deeply ingrained culture that its modern industrial management was fashioned because it could be developed no other way. We in this country had a somewhat similar kind of corporate paternalism at the beginning of our Industrial Revolution. But we have long since chosen wisely to do away with such company controls over the lives of employees. The freedom of the individual to move from company to company, to go wherever he will, to learn and to grow and to earn what he can, according to his own merit, is what made this nation the greatest industrial power in the world, not excluding Japan. I have to ask: What's wrong with that?

The underlying fallacy of Theory Z and of most of the reports given to us from observers who have traveled to Japan to see their factories in operation is that the Japanese are outproducing us in the world marketplace because the structure and management of their businesses are better than ours. I think the high contrast of our cultures tends to cloud the real issues. If the wrong questions are asked, one is likely to come away with the wrong answers. In the early sixties, when ITT was viewed as a showplace of modern American business management, a group of Japanese executives visited our headquarters in New York and asked our comptroller, Herbert Knortz, "Could you please show us the ITT computer room, where all the decisions are made?" Herb showed them the computer room and tried to explain that ITT's corporate decisions were not made by computer. But he was not at all sure, he told me, that they went away convinced.

American observers in Japan could have Japanese customs explained to them and could witness the group discussions, singing and cheers, and smiling faces in the factories there, and they would note the differences from the American scene, but I wonder if they saw where the management decisions were made. I would venture to guess that the Japanese financial controls, quality controls, production schedules, marketing surveys, and all the rest are not very much different from our own. I would suspect that the pragmatic Japanese managers view the marketplace, survey their own capabilities, and proceed to try to fill the needs and wants of customers around the world—very much as we try to do.

The Japanese do undersell American manufacturers at a variety of levels and for a variety of products—all for reasons which are not based primarily upon the structure, system, or efficiency of their management. I am not saying Japanese managers are not efficient. They are. I am saying that the Japanese management *system* alone does not account for the Japanese edge in world competition. They undersell us for mundane, but real, reasons. Japanese labor costs are far below ours; their factories, built there after the devastation of World War II, are newer, more modern, and far more efficient than ours. It costs them $1,500-$1,800 less to build a car than it costs us. They can afford to invest some of that margin in quality controls that Detroit manufacturers apparently felt were not possible for them up to now. Beyond lower costs, Japanese industry reaps the benefits of all the help their government can give them; because their small island nation is utterly dependent upon its export market, Japan's government and its powerful national banks work hand in hand with Japanese corporations to develop products that will sell abroad and bring wealth into the country. They have a national industrial policy. We do not.

In contrast, American industries have operated over the past fifty years in a virtual adversary relationship with the American government. It has been a long, long time since the United States government has actively helped American companies sell their goods overseas. The laws and regulations of this nation have been designed to rein in the free enterprise of American business. But we were never as dependent upon exports as other nations. Since World War II, when we emerged as the wealthiest and only unscathed industrial power in the world, we have lived off the fat of the land, paying the highest wages in the world while cutting the demands upon the productivity of our labor force; we allowed our factories to age and become obsolete; and, ultimately, we as a people grew slack and flabby.

Theory Z touches on none of this. Nor does it take into consideration that America has been losing its competitive edge over several nations other than Japan. Hong Kong produces textiles and women's clothes which are not only cheaper than ours but of superior quality. Korea builds oceangoing ships that we cannot equal in price or quality. Western European nations are now engaged in some very good research which will result in new products for the marketplace and make them competitive with the best we or Japan can produce, and in the not too distant future.

All is not lost, however. I sense that the sleeping giant, his nose tweaked, is arousing. Despite the temptations, it is significant that we have not tried to ward off foreign competition by imposing tariffs or restrictions upon Japanese automobiles and electronics, or upon any other foreign imports. This should signal to the world that the United States has accepted the challenge from abroad and intends to compete on the open market. We can see the first signs of this in the automobile industry, which has been hurt the most by Japanese competition. In the past few years, we have seen more innovations and improvements in the American automobile than we have had in the past few decades—because Detroit has had to compete, whereas it did not have to before. The steel industry, too, shows signs of waking up. Our electronics industry is competing at full tilt, aware of and alert to the pace and demands of high technology.

How and to what degree the United States meets the challenge of open competition on the world market remains to be seen. The problems involved will define the right questions that have to be answered and the answers we find will define the steps that have to be taken. But if we are to maintain our standard of living without giving up our individual freedoms, those answers will have to come not only from American management but also from American labor and from the American people through their government. I do not envision a future in which American working men and women will turn to the Japanese style of corporate paternalism, starting each working day singing songs in praise of General Motors, ITT, or any of the old component parts of the Bell System. No Theory X, Y, or Z will give us simple answers to complex problems.

Like fads and fashions, business theories tend to come and go. They are the talk of the town one year, gone and forgotten the next. Remember all those time-motion studies so popular after World War II? Industrial psychologists and business consultants invaded factories and corporate offices to measure and analyze every motion and step involved in each specific job on the assembly line and in the steno pool. Then they wrote the specifications on how each and every task should be performed for maximum efficiency. It was all supposed to be scientific. In essence, the time-motion studies were designed to make people as productive as machines (and just as unimaginative). Academicians wrote long, esoteric treatises on the new postwar advances in applying science to industry. The millennium never arrived. The new time-motion standards of performance were eroded over the years by labor contracts and became enshrined in company manuals as minimum acceptable standards of productivity rather than high. Today, those thoroughly outmoded time-motion studies serve for the most part only as a reminder of what had once been considered efficiencies. Even so, time-motion analyses applied only to low-level, repetitive work which could have been structured much more simply by an intelligent supervisor at the site of the job, without all the hoopla of pseudoscientific overkill.

At ITT, several years back, I was presented with one of the then newest management theories to come out of the Harvard Business School on how to orchestrate the cash flow of a multidivisional corporation. That was the theory of "cash cows" and "stars," whereby you were to carefully analyze each of your profit centers and label them according to this formula: A "star" was a division that had a high growth potential with a high margin of profit; a "cash cow" had high earnings but low growth potential; another had high growth but low margins; and the "dog" had low growth and low earnings. With that structure, you managed your company by taking the earnings milked from the "cash cow" and feeding it to the "star," so as to enhance its high growth, high earnings potential. You might even nurse along your high growth, low earnings division in the hope of turning the corner. As for the "dogs," you simply chose your time and got rid of them.

Sounds great in theory? I could not accept it. Not only would such a formula not work, it would violate everything we had built up in twenty years at ITT, which was the belief in one-team management, all moving together as fast as possible toward a single, agreed-upon set of goals. If that formula of "cash cows" still appeals to you, as it does to many managers, ask yourself: Who would want to work for a company or a division labeled "cash cow" whose earnings were ladled out to someone else and which had no hope of future growth? Instinct tells me that a sound, money-making division with obviously good management should be encouraged and expanded, not milked for the benefit of a so-called "star" whose ascendancy is not ordained in the heavens. As for the "dogs," to my mind it is management's responsibility to figure out why they are "dogs" and what can be done to turn them into greyhounds. I've never believed in selling off management's failures. If a company or a division must be sold, I want to build it up first so that I am selling a greyhound, not a mutt.

There is a formula, too, for categorizing personnel so that you can place them in managerial positions appropriate to their characters and personalities. The two variants are "brains," to be able to make reasonable decisions and know what to do, and "courage," to be able to act upon decisions. So you place each individual in one of these categories: "brains and courage," or "brains and no courage," or "courage and no brains," or, finally "no brains and no courage." The rest is easy: You fire the man with no brains and no courage; you put the man with brains and no courage in a staff position; you put the man with only courage in a mundane line job; and you give the toughest, best assignments to the man endowed with brains and courage. That's another theory that may sound good but in the practical world of business is next to useless. The men and women with whom I have worked have been whole, rounded, complex persons with a wide variety of good and bad qualities. I could never fit them into any convenient psychological pigeonhole. The only way I knew how to judge people at ITT was by the test of performance: I put a person on a job and I observed how he or she managed. Brains and courage were only part of the answer. Equally important were his or her judgments, actions, attitudes, efforts, objectivity, and a host of other qualities. Even then, one could never be completely certain. Preset formulas simply did not come into any of my judgments on people.

All these theories and formulas are part of what is usually called modern scientific management. Tens of thousands of young and eager men and women are graduated from business schools every year with the title "Master of Business Administration." Steeped in the aura of scientific management, they go forth into the world with theories, formulas, and checklists with which to run a business, backed up with the vicarious experience of handling case histories upon which those formulas worked so well. If they are bright enough, these "Masters" soon discover that such formulas do not work in the business world as well as do those immutable formulas used by chemists and physicists in the laboratories. The simple truth is that business is not a science. It follows no immutable laws; nor is it as predictable as machines. With startling accuracy, a machine can cut a piece of steel to ten thousandths of an inch, and do it every time. You can pour raw materials into one end of an automated assembly line and get a finished product out of the other end. But the assembly-line worker is not a robot, nor is the foreman or the superintendent of the plant. And in business, with all its automation, it is still the people, with all their faults and frailties, that provide the mortar which holds together the building blocks and bricks of business enterprise.

To be sure, logic, reason, techniques, and acquired skills can help anyone find his or her way in handling the various facets of business, whether it be marketing, sales, accounting, financial controls, or whatever. These are the tools of management, to be used skillfully as practical applications warrant. Too many people rely too heavily upon theories and rigid formulas because they are looking for an easy, structured approach to business decisions. But a structured approach is probably most important as a means of gathering in facts. After you get the facts, then you have to throw away the structure and act upon those facts. Your decisions in business have to come from within you, as an amalgam of everything you have ever learned applied to the facts of the situation or problem at hand. In short, you cannot run a company, a division, or a department with a checklist of things to do or by slavish devotion to a theory devised by the most brilliant professor at a business college, because business, like all of life, is much too vital and fluid to be wholly contained by any checklist, formula, or theory.

At ITT, we used as many, if not more, of the tools of so-called scientific management as any company in the world. We had giant computers at work around the clock, telexes that clacked out reports from our far-flung subsidiaries around the world. We had weekly and monthly and yearly reports that filled shelves and shelves of bookcases. We had an enormous staff of experts to analyze the figures that poured into our headquarters. But we never fooled ourselves. We never believed that any or all of this made our management of ITT scientific. All the computers, reports, surveys, and staff analyses provided us with only one thing: information—factual information and, sometimes, misinformation. When it came time to make a decision, I would ask one, two, or several people, "What do you think?" From the interchange of ideas, one sparking the other, based upon the facts at hand, we would reach a decision, for better or worse. We learned as we went along; our bank of experience grew richer; we became quicker and more sophisticated in handling more complex problems; we became more self-confident of our abilities. But we never reduced the art of management to a formula. We could never be sure we were right on any one, specific decision.

Over a half century has gone by since I began making business decisions, and if I were forced to try to sum it all up, I would have to say that the best way to run a business with the best hope of eventual success is to do it as you would cook on a wood-burning stove.

How do you cook on such a primitive stove? Because you know that you cannot control all the elements of fire, wood, air flow, etc., you keep your eye on everything at all times. You follow the recipe to an extent, but you also add something extra of your own. You do not measure out every spice and condiment. You sprinkle here, you pour there. And then you watch it cook. *You keep your eye on the pot.* You look at it and check it from time to time. You sniff it. You dip your finger in and taste it. Perhaps you add a little something extra to suit your own taste. You let it brew a while and then you taste it again. And again. If something is wrong, you correct it. Whatever you do, the most important thing is to keep your eye on it. You don't want it to be ruined when you are off doing something else. When it is done to your satisfaction, you're right there to take it off the stove. In the end, you will have a pot roast or a lamb stew that is the very best you could possibly make, a joy to your palate and a tribute to your ability as a cook. It will taste far better than any slab of meat you cook automatically by pushing buttons on a microwave oven. That is how you would cook on a wood-burning stove when nothing is preset. And that is the frame of mind to take into the art of conducting and building a successful business.

This is all by way of an opening to the chapters that follow. They are based upon what I have learned and adopted as useful in the pragmatic world of business. They are practical, but I am not sure they deserve to be raised to the level of principles. I do know they should not be misconstrued as a formula or guide to business success. They are, as you will see, more on the level of what your grandmother might tell you if you asked for her favorite recipe.

Many people, young and old, have asked me from time to time for the secret of my success in business. Usually I avoided giving any answer. Now I can reveal it: The secret of how to succeed in business or in life is that there is no secret. No secret at all. No formula. No theory.

With that caveat, I am prepared to give you a complete course in business management. I can do it in just three sentences, if you'll be good enough to go on to the next page.

TWO

How to Run a Business

A THREE-SENTENCE COURSE ON BUSINESS MANAGEMENT: *You read a book from the beginning to the end. You run a business the opposite way. You start with the end, and then you do everything you must to reach it.*

WHEN ALL IS SAID and done, a company, its chief executive, and his whole management team are judged by one criterion alone—performance. Lost and long-forgotten are the speeches, the luncheons, dinners, conventions and conferences; the public causes endorsed and supported; all those supposedly key contacts with important people. What remains is the record of the company and its performance. What did the company and its management do in comparison with similar companies? How well did it perform in the economic environment, good and bad?

Performance is not limited to one quarter's or a year's earning statement. Performance is something that is built into a company for the long haul. It is something that says that a company can repeat what it did last year and continue to grow at a certain pace year after year after year. This kind of growth and accomplishment over a protracted period of time in an ever-changing business world is what I have in mind when I think of performance. It is what running a successful business is all about.

This was the attitude I brought with me when I came to ITT in 1959 and, perhaps more than anything else, it shaped the way I tried to run the company. I started out with no preconceived notions of building a conglomerate such as ITT became. Certainly, the screening committee

35

of the ITT board of directors which selected me issued no such instructions. All they asked of me was that I take over this company and give them "satisfactory results." That was all that I promised them. After all, satisfactory results are the basic objectives of all business activity. It was left to me to determine what would constitute satisfactory results at ITT. Then, of course, the board of directors would pass judgment upon my judgment. It was as vague as all that.

No doubt, I was hired as president and chief executive officer of ITT because of the reputation I had earned as executive vice president of Raytheon, a company of engineers dealing mostly in electronics and defense contracts. I had been hired by Raytheon to institute some financial controls and modern business management—in short, to "make money" for a company which had had dismal earnings. In my four years there, the earnings trebled, the stock moved from $14 to $65 a share, and the all-important earnings per share advanced from about 50 cents to $2.00.

I accepted the new position with alacrity, without any long-term employment contract; in fact, without any contract at all. For me, the ITT assignment was the culmination of thirty-three years of working for somebody else. It would be my first opportunity to run a company as I saw fit. Although I may have had some personal difficulties with Charles Francis Adams, the Boston blue blood who headed Raytheon, I have always felt grateful to him for giving me my first opportunity to go beyond the advisory role of staff work and to be a "line man." As executive vice president, second in command at Raytheon, I had responsibility over the whole company. Before that, I had been limited, at least to an extent, to financial matters as comptroller of other companies.

I came to ITT knowing perhaps less than nothing about the company, for what I had read and been told about ITT turned out to be largely incorrect.

Years before, when I had been hired as comptroller of

Bell & Howell in Chicago and told to report for work on the following Monday, I had obtained the keys to the office and permission to look over my new office during the weekend. Armed with a bottle of milk and sandwiches, I spent Saturday and Sunday, from 8 A.M. to midnight, reading through every paper in my office files. On Monday morning, when I faced my new boss, the irascible president of Bell & Howell, who had fired the previous comptroller out of hand, I was thoroughly prepared: I knew more about the company's varied problems than the last comptroller did. But at ITT it was different.

I was hired by ITT sometime in April, but instructed not to report to work until precisely the morning of June 19. That was my predecessor's sixty-fifth birthday, his day of retirement. He did not want to see me before that date. A West Pointer, General Edmund Leavey was a firm believer, it seemed, in military protocol. I learned later that General Leavey had been appointed president of ITT upon the death of the company's founder, Sosthenes Behn. Being at that time only two years from retirement, Leavey had been told that his primary task was to find and to develop someone to take his place as a permanent president for the company. After two years, General Leavey recommended himself. The board thought otherwise. It appointed a five-man search committee from among its members and within a short time I was offered the presidency of a company more than twice the size of Raytheon.

Because my appointment had been announced to the public, I was invited to sit on the dais at the annual stockholders' meeting that May. But since I was not to take office until June 19, I was told to keep my mouth shut and not to answer any stockholders' questions, even those addressed to me.

So it was that on the morning of June 19, 1959, I came to the old International Telegraph Building at 67 Broad Street in the financial district of New York and presented myself to General Leavey in the penthouse office of the president. It was the first time I had been in the building. General Leavey sat ramrod straight at the large ornate desk of the legendary Sosthenes Behn. The European-style office was certainly impressive, with large oriental rugs on the floor, a stone fireplace on one wall. It was elaborately furnished. An enormous crystal chandelier swayed overhead as the wind outside caught the top of the building. The changing of the guard was formal and correct. General Leavey shook my hand, introduced me to his immediate staff of eight or nine, I shook their hands, they left, the general and I exchanged some pleas-antries, and then he presented me with the keys to the desk and to the office. He gave me his home telephone number and asked me to phone him if and when I needed him and then he walked out. I did not see the man again for two years, and then it was strictly a social occasion.

I sat at the desk of Sosthenes Behn and reflected upon the man who had started it all. He had bought a small, primitive telephone company in Cuba in 1920 and had built and fashioned it all into a worldwide telephone op-erating and manufacturing company that stretched from Australia to Japan to South Africa and to Europe and back again to South America and the United States. A strong and highly individualistic man, he had devoted thirty-seven years of his life to ITT, and though he had been dead two years, the character of Sosthenes Behn was stamped indelibly upon this office and throughout the worldwide company.

As I sat there in his office, I was aware of that old fear and trepidation. It came upon me at the start of every new beginning in my career and I recognized the feeling for what it was. And yet I knew that I never could say no to a new challenge and live with myself afterwards. The fear was in my heart, a normal sense of uncertainty, but men-tally and intellectually I was eager to start again. This was my first command, my first opportunity as the chief executive officer of a company. I did not know precisely what I could or would do in this new assignment, because

I did not know very much about the company, but I also realized that I had paid my dues, that I had worked my way up through the management of different types of companies in both light and heavy industry, and I felt that I was as prepared as any man to do what had to be done at ITT. I was, in short, eager to plunge in.

The first week or so, I devoted most of my time to studying the company's financial statements and reports, division by division, unit by unit. As an accountant by profession and an old-fashioned bookkeeper at heart, I had always believed that the numbers were the bare bones of a corporation. The numbers, coming in from units of the company all over the world, identified the assets of ITT, the sources of its income, the cash flow, where the money was going. More than that, the relationship among the numbers was for me like reading between the lines of a book. I could visualize the operations from unit to unit, the thrust or lack of thrust of the divisions. In my mind's eye, I could see the men writing the reports I read. I got a sense of the general health of the company, the performers and non-performers, the problem areas. Then I started asking questions. I called in various executives in the home office and went over with them the various financial statements. Little by little I came to know the men involved in this company that Sosthenes Behn had fashioned over the years in his highly individualistic way.

In that first year, there was the expected jolt to the company of having a new man come in from the outside and take charge. There was the usual politicking for position with the new boss. There were two or three top executives who were very unhappy that one of them had not been chosen to lead. There were some immediate decisions to be made. But, above all, it was the internal financial reports which were important and, to me, something of a shock.

ITT was not what I had expected from reading the various Wall Street reports of security analysts. I had been

led to believe, as had most of the public, that ITT was
doing very well domestically, particularly with military
electronics. Shortly before I came upon the scene, it had
been announced that ITT had been awarded a major,
multimillion-dollar contract on the communications system connecting all Army bases worldwide. That was in
addition to the well-known work of ITT in building the
global communications systems for the Air Force, the
Strategic Air Command, and for other military uses.
Nevertheless, ITT had a very low return on its overall
sales and assets, which led security analysts to believe
that ITT must be losing money on its overseas operations.

Exactly the opposite was true. I was surprised to learn
that even with all those military contracts, which added
up to three quarters of all ITT's domestic sales, the domestic operations were yielding only about 15 percent of
the company's profits. Eighty-five percent of our earnings came from the telephone and telegraph operations in
twenty-four foreign countries, most of it from Western
Europe. Not that those earnings were so great either. Net
profits hovered at the 3 percent mark.

The company was lopsided. It was an American company with 113,000 employees abroad and only 23,000 in
the United States. Worse, virtually our whole management team was at home and not where the work was
being done: fifteen vice presidents with offices at 67
Broad Street and one, only one, coordinating all the work
abroad.

That one man was Henry Scudder, a tall, distinguished, soft-spoken fellow who dressed and acted like
an international diplomat and spoke with a trace of a British accent. He was a tireless, dogged worker. Over the
next six months, Hank Scudder was to lead me on a tour
of all, or almost all, of ITT facilities in Western Europe,
South America, Australia, and the Far East.

Returning to America only for the monthly board of directors meetings, I spent most of those first six months

visiting the company's plants, meeting the managing directors, their top staffs, walking through the factories, seeing and touching the products we produced, lunching with bankers, some customers, some government officials. They all wanted to get a look at the new man running ITT as much as I wanted to blend together impressions of the men running the companies with the reports they had turned in to headquarters. It was the age before the jet plane and, among other impressions, I gained a healthy respect for the job Sosthenes Behn had done traveling by ship and train to the outposts of the ITT empire. I also sensed the deep loyalty that these managing directors in England, Germany, France, and elsewhere felt toward Colonel Behn and toward ITT. After all, each of these companies was run entirely by men who were native to the countries in which they were located and yet they were all working for American stockholders.

It took a while, as we toured the ITT plants in Europe, before Hank Scudder opened up to me. In his most diplomatic fashion, he acknowledged honestly that he felt that his major contribution to the company over the past several years had been to keep the various cardboard vice presidents who occupied the New York office from upsetting the European operations. He maintained a staff of about twenty people in New York to accomplish just that: to arrange things so that certain vice presidents in New York never had to go to Europe on other than ceremonial or social visits. Not one office or even one desk was assigned in any of the European companies to a New York executive. Hank Scudder traveled from country to country, from company to company, meeting with managing directors in hotel rooms. He and he alone went over their problems, approved or disapproved their budgets, their plans, their capital expenditures, and whatever. The foreign managing directors liked it that way. They conducted their own businesses virtually as they wished; they worked through Hank Scudder and sent their earnings and reports back to America.

While I could appreciate the appeal of such an arrangement, it certainly was no way to run a company. One of the most obvious drawbacks was that such independence from the home office allowed the European companies the freedom to compete more fiercely with one another than they competed with rival companies. As I visited and talked with the managers it became evident that the personal and emotional hostilities of World War II had carried over well into peacetime. These men shared nothing with one another. Each company had its own elaborate research and development facilities, and they were all doing essentially the same work. It was as if each one was inventing the wheel over and over again. Worse, they designed their telephone switching and other equipment so that they were not interchangeable. They each made the same kinds of consumer products and competed throughout the European market with one another. It was waste on a terrible scale.

As the months went on, I discovered there were many things that had to be ironed out between the European and American managements. They had different products, different kinds of markets, and a wholly different attitude toward competition than we did in America. I felt that there was room for higher markups and profits in Europe than our companies were getting. I tried to convince them of the need for a higher turnover of inventories and receivables and better use of their available assets. But traditions and habits, even in professional management, are hard to break.

At least some of them are. At our very first European General Managers Meeting, held in an overcrowded Paris hotel meeting room, I made a long, detailed presentation of the need to introduce certain modern American management methods into the European companies. At the end, I asked for questions. Not one man there raised his hand. At lunch afterwards, I asked about that and it was explained to me that at the last such meeting, chaired by Colonel Behn more than two years ago, one man had questioned the old colonel and not long afterwards he had been fired. No one had dared to ask a question since then.

Another director confided to me that perhaps in my ignorance as an American I had committed a social faux pas in addressing them by their first names. That, he explained, was simply not done in Europe until one was invited to such familiarity. After lunch, I told the group firmly that this was an American company, that we were all of one family, and that we would follow the American custom of using first names, and that, furthermore, as one family we would henceforth be open and candid with one another. Questions were always welcome and answers were always to be candid and honest.

The changeover was not instantaneous. But it came. Over the next two years, they were all calling each other by their first names and it helped bond these diverse and independent men together in a single enterprise. English became the official language at ITT and those who could not speak it in the beginning learned. In our early meetings, the European managers told me in one way or another, usually on a one-to-one basis, that they were well aware that the European earnings were carrying the whole company and that not until the American side of the company could show that it could equal the Europeans in earnings did we have the right to preach to them. They honestly preferred to do things their European way—at least until we Americans could prove that we knew best.

It was a point well taken. I had concentrated my first efforts on the European operations because that indeed was the major source of ITT's income and profits. I knew I had to back our winning horse in Europe before I could turn my major attention to the lame American side of the ITT equation.

In the back of my mind during these first six months, as I commuted between Europe and New York, was the bottom line that I was fashioning for the goal of ITT. I was well aware of its ultimate importance. It was the "end" to which all my efforts at ITT would be directed, an "end" to which I would commit myself without reservation. It would serve also as a measure by which my own performance could be measured at ITT. I had long believed that the primary role of a chief executive was to serve as a management team's quarterback and show his team where the goalposts were and how best to get there, and finally to lead the way down the field.

Because most measurements of performance are in terms of improvement, I set my goal at ITT at a 10 percent annual increase in earnings per share. That was my "bottom line."

How did I arbitrarily reach that decision? First I looked to see what similar companies were doing in that economic climate. The rate of inflation then was about 2 percent. (If the inflation rate had been 10 percent, as it later became, then a growth rate of 18 percent would have been comparable.) Other companies, such as RCA and Westinghouse, were lucky in 1959 to grow at a per share rate of 5 percent. Most of them were doing about 3 percent.

For me, a growth rate of 10 percent a year, every year, represented what I called a "stretch target." In a mature company the size of ITT, everyone would have to stretch all of his efforts to increase his previous year's earnings by at least 10 percent. Of course, in a multi-divisional company such as ITT, some units would have a goal of more than 10 percent, while others could not make that 10 percent. In reality, we talked of increasing earnings by 15 percent, if possible; but the bottom line for the whole company, adding up the performances of each unit, had to be 10 percent. In short, we "stretched" for 15 percent and would settle for nothing less than that 10 percent. That was the bottom line.

In the beginning, to a large extent, this goal was misunderstood by a great many of the Wall Street analysts and financial reporters. They thought all of my efforts were directed to producing a one-year 10 percent growth in earnings. They overlooked the "quality of earnings" that I insisted upon within ITT. The performance I sought was a 10 percent annual increase that could be repeated year after year. Almost anyone can push earnings into one year and expenses and costs into another year for a dramatic one-shot performance. Inside ITT, all of our managers understood that they had to grow 10 percent per year in a manner that would ensure the continuance of that same or better growth in future years. That meant that they would have to allocate some money this year for research and development, developing new products, finding new markets, and such, so as to ensure growth for the following year. That was an integral part of our planning.

I went over this time and again with the press. I told them that our goal was to increase our earnings from 10 to 15 percent a year "under any conditions." That meant, I explained, that in good years it would be relatively easy to reach that goal, and in bad years we would have to work like hell. But the goal was the same.

And it worked out that way. For fifty-eight consecutive quarters, fourteen and a half years, ITT increased its earnings, which was reflected in its earnings per share, by between 10 and 15 percent. In those years, I used to say ITT was a "lockbox" stock. That meant that shareholders, large and small, could put our stock on the bottom of the safe-deposit box and not have to look at it again: it would take care of itself. We made our 10 to 15 percent growth each year, in spite of the recessions of 1959–60 and 1968–70, until the OPEC worldwide oil bust and panic of 1974, coupled with the foreign exchange collapse that year, stymied our rate of growth.

But, from the beginning, the beauty of setting a realistic, firm objective—or, as I said, starting out with the end—is that it will in itself begin to define what it is you have to do to reach that end. If you want to reach Z, you have to get to Y, and to get to Y you have to achieve X, and so on. Each goal defines the actions you must take to reach that goal. Each in itself becomes a bottom line. Thus, in any business, there are many bottom lines, things that you *have* to do in order to succeed.

Thus at ITT, to achieve the 10 to 15 percent increase in annual earnings which I had set as my bottom-bottom line, certain major goals had to be achieved first.

• I needed to restructure the company from a loosely held, sluggish holding company into an integrated, well-managed entity.

• In order to achieve that and the growth I envisioned as possible, I needed first of all to overhaul the management team at the headquarters.

• To do that, I needed to attract to ITT the very best corporate managers and staff. I wanted men who not only were professionally capable and competent but also had the inner drive to thrive on the fast pace, long hours, and innovative thinking necessary to accomplish my idea of a bottom line.

To attract these kinds of men, in presenting to the board of directors a comprehensive plan of my objectives at ITT my foremost request was a proposal that ITT pay a management salary scale generally 10 percent higher than the rest of the industry, plus a generous bonus system which would reward our executives according to their annual performance. The board approved the plan immediately. Executive search firms were hired to find the managers we needed; the consulting firm of McKinsey and Co. was engaged to work out our salary schedules and bonus and stock option plans.

Aside from a new management team, the most glaring need of ITT, if it were ever to succeed, was to bolster and boost the earnings of our domestic operations. With 85 percent of our earnings coming from abroad, ITT could fairly be viewed and perhaps shunned by American stockholders as a foreign company. To make ITT truly international, I told our board of directors, I wanted to set out upon an acquisition program designed to increase ITT's domestic earnings from 15 to 50 percent of our income. Moreover, I wanted our domestic earnings to be large enough to cover our stockholder annual dividends. There was a real danger in the economic climate of Europe. Any number of those countries could decree that foreign earnings could not be sent back to the United States. If that ever occurred, ITT would be hazardously exposed to sheer disaster on the American stock market. In fact, just that had once happened shortly after the end of World War II. Our foreign earnings were cut off and ITT almost went bankrupt. It was saved by some courageous bank loans.

To increase our domestic earnings, we had to increase our domestic equity by acquisition. In order to do this, we had to get our own existing house in order, here and abroad, so as to position ourselves favorably to be able to afford these acquisitions.

To increase our earnings, we had to consolidate and unify our rather large European holdings and to increase their margins of return. The European companies, although providing us with the bulk of our earnings, were lagging far behind their competition in Europe, particularly Philips and Siemens. In fact, because of the large postwar market for our products and the low labor costs in Europe, there was some danger—even recognized over there—of those companies being bought out by their competition.

To accomplish that, one of the earliest decisions made was to create an ITT-Europe, which would serve as a headquarters for all those operations. There were many problems. They did not involve business management so much as they did national attitudes and different personality quirks of the managers in Germany, France, England, Belgium, the Netherlands, and elsewhere. We chose to put our headquarters in Belgium, not because of its central location in Europe or because Brussels was the seat of the Common Market. We chose Belgium because it was neutral ground. Frenchmen and Englishmen who would not agree to be ruled from an ITT headquarters in

Germany would go to Belgium. Germans who would not go to Paris or London would agree to meet in Brussels.

One of the most difficult problems to solve in postwar Europe was how to persuade managers of the French or British companies to follow the lead of the Germans or Italians, or vice versa, and how to convince the companies in the smaller nations to go along with the decisions made by the bigger companies without feeling dominated. Our early meetings sounded something like United Nations meetings of have and have-not nations. We solved this one with the idea of establishing what we called our Strategy and Action Boards. They were set up along product lines, consisting of the leading producers of a given product along with one or two of the smaller producers. The decision of the Strategy and Action Board on any one product line was binding upon all other European companies.

Since most of the smaller companies depended one way or another on one or more of the larger companies for parts and other products, this seems to solve the rivalry problems. Decisions were made by three or four persons rather than eight or nine, and since different national companies served on different product strategy boards, national rivalries were assuaged. These Strategy and Action Board decisions finally worked their way down the ranks and served as a working start to unified European operations. Over the years that I was at the helm of ITT (from 1959 to 1977), it accomplished its goal of becoming a unified organization with pride in its combined accomplishments. During that period, ITT-Europe increased its sales from some $300 million to more than $7 billion.

And so it went, with one bottom line defining the tasks that needed to be done to reach the next bottom line until we reached the desired "end." It was like peeling an onion to get to its core. As you unwrap one layer of skin, you come upon what is underneath, and peel that one away. You learn as you go along.

One of the first things I learned in those early days was that when I responded to a question or request from Europe while sitting in New York, my decision was often different from what it would have been had I been in Europe. In New York, I might read a request and say no. But in Europe, I could see the man's face, hear his voice, understand the intensity of his conviction, and the answer to the same question might be yes. So, early on, I decided that if I and my headquarters team intended to monitor and oversee the European operations, I owed it to the European managers to be there on the spot. So, again, to accomplish what I had set out to do, for seventeen years I went to Europe with my senior staff for one week every month, except for August and December, when vacations and Christmas holidays intruded. It became our policy to deal with problems on the spot, face to face.

In those early days, I also discovered that we were spending so much time planning for the next year and the next five years that our units were not making their current quarterly earnings. They were falling prey to the old trap of saying, "Oh, don't worry. I didn't make it this quarter, but I'll make it up before the end of the year." I found that realistically it did not work that way. If you did not make your earnings for the first quarter, as I told them, you would not make it for that year. You had to make your first quarter's budgeted earnings, then the second quarter's, then the third, and, if you did that, somehow the fourth quarter always took care of itself.

I also issued the shortest memo on record at ITT, which said: "There will be no more long-range planning." The men recognized the humor and the seriousness of that memo. It put a stop to those elaborate five-year plans which were made at the expense of quarterly earnings. Later, of course, when we could afford the time, we did lots of planning, but we never lost sight of the current quarter or year.

The overall principle worked in practice. You read a book from the beginning to the end. You run a business the opposite way. You start with the end, and then you do everything you have to do to reach that bottom line.

Another, even simpler way to put it is: You decide what it is that you want to do, and then you start doing it.

It never ceases to amaze me how many people can give this lip service and then not follow through. It is the follow-through that is all-important.

THREE

Experience
and Cash

In the business world, everyone is paid in two coins: cash and experience. Take the experience first; the cash will come later.

IN THE DEPTHS of the Depression, when I was in my early twenties, I discovered a particle of practical wisdom that guided me for years. It was, in fact, handed to me by an exciting professor named Hoopingarner at New York University's night college, which I attended off and on for eight years to earn my bachelor's degree in accounting and finance. Professor Hoopingarner was an academic theoretician—and much more. Long before the advent of executive search recruiters, Professor Hoopingarner earned his living primarily by helping to find capable executives for one of the large insurance companies. At NYU, he taught applied psychology. Not once, but many times, the good professor expounded this advice to his class:

"If you want to succeed in business, it is essential that you get yourself into the top 20 percent of the people in your chosen field, no matter what field you pick or fall into."

His advice struck me as reasonable. He had not stipulated the top 5 percent or the top 10 percent and that in itself was reassuring to me at the time. After working a full day, I almost always arrived at my NYU night classes tired, if not exhausted, and I had to struggle to keep up my grades. But I thought I ought to be able to achieve the professor's target.

His reasoning went like this: If you were in the top 20 percent of those working at your level, then in bad times when people were being laid off, you would keep your job and be gaining experience. When good times came along, you would move ahead rapidly because of the level of experience you had acquired.

Soon after I had adopted that "top 20 percent" as my standard, I had occasion to add some thoughts of my own to it. I answered a classified want ad of an engineering firm called Day & Zimmerman in Philadelphia. A kindly old man at the reception desk wished me luck as I went in for my interview.

"How'd you make out, son?" he asked when I emerged from the inner office. I told him that I did not get the job because they had said that I did not have enough experience.

"Well, you'll never have enough experience until one day, young fellow, you'll have enough experience." And he paused, looked me in the eye, and added, "But then you'll be too old."

That comment nagged me for years. It meant that if I was going to get experience, I'd better get it in a hurry, before I became too old.

I was young then and, in a way, lucky. The Depression forced me from job to job and I was ever doing something new. Merely putting in time on a job, doing repetitive tasks, is not the "experience"of which the good Professor Hoopingarner spoke. Experience is a process of discovering and learning something new, which somehow leads to a growing cumulative capability. You have to go out and consciously seek that kind of experience. You have to reach for it. You have to pummel your brain, if necessary, to come up with something better, something novel, something different from the old way of doing things. That is creative experience. Even failures, as long as the ventures are creative, add to one's storehouse of experience. As someone long ago once told me, "What you got when you got what you didn't expect—is experience."

Over the years, this attitude toward work as a creative

experience became an ingrained way of thinking for me, and it served me well. I have always tried to find some way of doing things better than I had before, and over the years it has given me an enthusiastic outlook on almost everything.

Only now as I look back can I see some of the elements which instilled in me this compelling urge to improve upon my own performance, to outdo what I had done before. Some of my earliest memories go back to 1915 when I was five and returned with my mother to visit my grandmother in Bournemouth, a seaside town not far from London, where I was born. My mother had been a singer of light opera and still a teenager when she married my father, an impresario who directed touring concerts. They had come to the United States when I was one year old. Through the years my father tried his entrepreneurial hand at a variety of ventures. He produced concerts, records, plays, and even one movie. He ran restaurants and he invested in real estate. Many of these enterprises had been highly successful; some were not, but he was always optimistic. I still retain a vivid impression of that visit to my grandmother's quaint house with her little garden in the rear, the monkey puzzle tree in the front yard, the golf course at one end of the street, and the big red ON HIS MAJESTY'S SERVICE mailbox at the other end of the street. One particularly wild episode of that visit remains with me to this day. My youngest uncle dared me to climb an awesomely high cliff overlooking the ocean. I did it with fear in my heart. But I did it.

Sixty years later I returned to that street in Bournemouth. The big red mailbox was still there. The small house was still there with its garden unchanged. The monkey puzzle tree had grown much bigger. The golf course was the same. But my fearsome high cliff had shrunk to more modest proportions. And so has been my experience down through the years: Every new job, every new major undertaking has seemed at first to be a high, dangerous cliff—until I surmounted it. Then, in retrospect, it did not seem that tough at all.

When I was five, my parents separated and my younger sister and I were sent off to a convent boarding school, chosen by my mother, where the discipline was strict and the nuns loving. I can still picture in my mind Sister Joseph, who more than once whacked my outstretched hand in punishment, not for any infraction of discipline, but because I had misspelled a word. It instilled in me, I think, a serious appreciation of my responsibilities as a student; certainly I learned to do my homework.

Because my mother had resumed her singing career, I generally returned home only for the Christmas vacations. In the summertime, my sister and I went to camp. Thus, I was often alone in an empty school during the Easter and Thanksgiving holidays. But that never bothered me. I have a vivid memory of myself at age six, sitting at a desk alone in a large empty classroom reading a book. The Mother Superior came by and, concerned over my apparent loneliness, asked me what I was doing. I told her simply that I was reading a book. She smiled at me sympathetically. Perhaps I noticed pity in her expression. What remains with me is the feeling that she was wrong, that I never felt uncomfortable about being alone. I thought that I could always find something to do, even at that tender age. Perhaps the isolation back then taught me to be independent, to be able to think through my small daily problems, and to achieve a sense of self-confidence.

At the age of eight, I transferred to Suffield Academy, a fine college preparatory school, in Suffield, Connecticut, where I was to remain until I was sixteen. My mother had made a very good choice. Suffield was a small, typical New England town of four or five thousand people and had no public high school of its own, and so the town's boys and girls of high school age attended the Academy along with the boarding students. Even among the boarding students, we had a hefty sprinkling of scholarship students. A completely democratic, community atmosphere prevailed in the school in those days. We wore no uniforms or fancy clothes; there was no elitism, no discerning the rich from the poor. Yet within that academic freedom there was a discipline and a value system and a reverence for life that I absorbed, which would stand me in good stead all the days of my life. We were indoctrinated with the belief that you got only what you earned, that you were not entitled to anything more. I received a fine classical education and, more importantly, a wonderful feeling of being at ease in a world that consisted of a school, a town, and a loving community where I came to know many different kinds of people, visiting their homes and receiving, in effect, a small-town upbringing.

In the beginning of my junior year, when I was fifteen, I decided that I had had enough of summer camps. That summer of 1925, I returned to New York and got a job as an errand boy for a lithograph company on West Fortieth Street. Still wearing short pants, I lugged heavy lithograph plates around the city, traveling to the outer reaches of Brooklyn by subway on the old Canarsie and Bensonhurst local subway lines, often working to eight and nine o'clock at night. The sharpest memory of that summer was a crisis and furor over a lost piece of copy that I had delivered to the printing room. A major client was furious. I was called into our manager's office to explain what I had done with the papers involved. I explained and he agreed that I had left the documents in the proper place. He thanked me and sent me back to work. For many years, that man's polite and fair treatment of me remained in my mind as a lesson.

It was in my junior year at Suffield that my father went broke in a speculation on Florida land (in what became known as the Florida land bust of 1926). Since coming to the United States fifteen years earlier, my father had had his ups and downs as an "investor," but this venture wiped him out. I finished my last two years at Suffield waiting on tables and working in a local bakery. As a waiter in a boarding school, I ate better than I ever had before. The only thing I had to give up was some after-noon play outdoors because of my after-school work. I was graduated with my class and presented with a diploma—unsigned. The headmaster assured me privately that the diploma would happily be completed when my out-standing tuition and boarding bills were paid. It was a number of years before I was able to retire that debt.

Instead of going to college, I went to work as a page on the floor of the New York Stock Exchange. I got the job through the recommendation of one of my father's friends, Dean Wellington Taylor of New York University, who urged me to attend night college while I worked. I remember him questioning my desire to study accounting. He suggested that with my quick mind and eager interest in so many things, I would probably find accounting a rather limiting field. But even at sixteen I had seen enough of booms and busts in my father's life and their effects upon my mother. I thought I wanted something more stable and secure. But college, even night school, would have to wait until I earned some money.

I spent six years on the floor of the stock exchange, the money capital of the world, first as a page and then as a floor clerk successively for two or three brokerage firms. They were glorious, learning days. I soaked up reams of information from the financial "blue sheets," the "yel-low sheets," and the annual reports on the leading com-panies of the nation. I learned the exchange symbols of every stock listed and I knew where to find most of the brokers and stock specialists on the floor of the ex-change. Wall Street legends from Whitney to Baruch to Jack Bouvier and others became real live people to me. Fortunes were made and lost in those roaring twenties. And then came the crash of October 1929.

On that tumultuous day, October 29, one broker whom

I represented spent most of the day lying in the smoking room with failing nerves and I rushed about, handling his orders for him. The market went wild and down, down, down. But of all the doom and gloom tales told of that day, I remember best the story of one specialist who, on the morning of the twenty-ninth, forgot to execute a batch of buy orders. I believe it was for American Sugar. By that afternoon, when he discovered the orders in his back pocket, American Sugar had fallen precipitously. However, by law, the customer was required to buy the shares at the opening, higher price, as ordered. The specialist made a fortune that afternoon by pocketing the difference. They said he retired on the spot.

Then there was a little man who used to stand by the ticker machine near me. For two years prior in 1929, that man would sell short, insisting the market was overbought, and he would watch the stock prices go up, and then rush in to cover his short sales. All the while, he would wag his head and say that wise men should sell short, not buy. He had lost some $18 million in those two years of soaring bull markets, or so I had been told, and I admired his courage of conviction. When the market finally tumbled, as he had long predicted, he not only recovered everything he had lost, but in the next sixty to ninety days he too had made a fortune.

As the Depression deepened and more and more men around me lost their jobs, my salary was cut from $25 a week to $20, then to $18. I saw great fortunes being wiped out, other fortunes being made. I watched companies going bankrupt, others struggling to survive. I saw a great change take place upon the economic landscape of the country. While hardship abounded everywhere, I came to recognize the inherent resilience of men under dire circumstances. One day in 1931, for example, the floor brokers held a yachting party. They came in that day wearing their yachting caps, with their lunches in brown paper bags, and they spent their lunch hour sailing to Sandy Hook and back on the New Jersey Central Railroad ferryboat, reminiscing about their lost yachts.

For a lad from sixteen to twenty-one, those were important, impressionable years. Nevertheless, somewhere along the line, I realized that I did not want to devote my life to the stock market. To me at that age, it seemed like a gigantic gamble. As much as I studied the scene on the exchange, during good times and bad, I could not discern how anyone could know what the stock market would do. Speculators were betting on the fortunes of the various companies and winning or losing. It seemed to me at the time that they were doing nothing really productive. My time came in late 1931 or perhaps early 1932. I was let go by Landsberg Brothers. The firm could no longer afford a floor clerk.

My savings from those six years of work, something just under $200, were tied up, literally, in the Harriman National Bank at Fifth Avenue and Forty-fifth Street. I had chosen that bank because it advertised that it stayed open late (until 10 P.M.). But when the crash came, it was one of the earliest banks to close. I searched diligently for another job, but try as I might, I could not find one. I lived sparingly in a rooming house for about six dollars a week. To preserve that shelter, I had to cut down on my eating. I decided upon bread and taffy. Bread cost something like five cents a loaf and the Loft Candy Company had an enticing sale: a pound of taffy for nine cents. If you bought one, you got the second pound for a penny. I had figured it out "scientifically." The bread would provide the bulk, and the taffy, with all its sugar, would provide the energy.

Finally, after two weeks, I landed a job as a door-to-door book salesman at $15 a week plus commissions. I carried around a large Gladstone bag full of popular novels, which, when I weighed it on a penny scale, came to sixty pounds. At the time, I weighed no more than 125. But I cherished that first pay envelope at the end of a week's work, for I remember walking out of that building with about $25 in my pocket and stopping at the first cafeteria I saw. It was one of a chain called Silver's, and in the window was a paper sign: *Liver Steak—37 cents.* That was probably the best meal I have ever eaten. The taste of it remains with me now.

I stayed with that job through the summer of 1932, earning between $25 and $30 a week, knowing there was no future in it for me, and falling into bed every night thoroughly exhausted. My days were full but not grim. I was young and healthy and eager and full of hope. Then I paid a call on a good friend of the family, Eugene Parsons, who had recently moved from the position of advertising manager of the Chicago *Tribune* to publisher of Bernarr Macfadden's New York *Graphic,* one of the worst scandal sheets in the era of yellow journalism. Gene Parsons took me to lunch at Chumley's, a Greenwich Village hangout with good food and drink, for he must have known that I was in need of a hearty square meal. There I screwed up enough courage to impose upon the family friendship. I asked him for a job on the *Graphic.*

Predicting a greater career for me in the future, he offered this advice: "If you're going to be a concert pianist, you cannot practice on an old, broken-down piano. The *Graphic* is not for you."

He advised me to go into broadcasting: it was a growing, profitable, and expanding field, especially in advertising, and he told me how to go about it. Following his advice, I presented myself to the receptionist in the office of the president of NBC. I told her that it was very important that I talk to him on a confidential matter and that under no circumstances would I impart my important message to anyone else. It did not work. Perhaps they had heard that tale before. I never got past the receptionist.

So Gene Parsons wrote a note to the advertising manager of the New York *Telegram,* an afternoon newspaper which had just then merged with the New York *World,* and I was hired, along with two hundred other aspirants, to sell classified real estate ads at a salary of $15 a week, plus 10 percent commissions. The newly merged *World-Telegram* had just launched a sales contest to woo the classified advertisers in the morning *World* to the new evening paper. The two salesmen out of the two hundred who had sold the most ads would be given permanent jobs on the paper.

Assigned to a territory on the outer reaches of the city in Queens and in the bordering communities on Long Island, I made my rounds by subway and on foot. I remember well my first stop to sell a real estate ad to a big advertiser in Jackson Heights. I had walked a long way to reach him. I hesitated a long while before entering his office, fear in my gut. But I walked in, drew a deep breath, and blurted out, "Would you like to take out some classified this week in the new *World-Telegram?*"

"No!" he shouted at me.

"Thank you very much," said I, beating a hasty retreat, thankful that the ordeal was over.

As I walked back to the subway, it did not take much imagination to realize that that was no way to sell advertising. So I picked up a book on the tactics of selling, which said:

Never make your sales pitch right away. Offer the client a cigarette, sit down, and talk to him about the advantages of your product.

Listen to what he says. Don't interrupt him (which was difficult for me).

Pick out his main objection or doubt and focus your sales talk on that.

Finally, before you leave, don't forget to ask for the order.

Another book on selling was far more important to me, for it has guided me in business far beyond the aspects of salesmanship. Written in 1918 by Norval Hawkins, the first sales manager of the Ford Motor Company, it was called *The Selling Process: A Handbook of Salesmanship*

Principles. It made a lasting impression upon me. To be a good salesman, essentially, you had to be a good man. It was not the clothes or the sales pitch which made one a good salesman; it was the man himself who gained the confidence of the customer. Hawkins said that a successful salesman had to be as clean as a hound's tooth in body, mind, and spirit. He had to be honest and straight.

There really was no great skill required in selling classified real estate ads. It consisted of ringing lots of doorbells and inviting people to advertise their vacancies and in 1932 there was no shortage of vacancies. I did plenty of walking and rang plenty of doorbells and talked to all sorts of building managers and superintendents, working to eight or nine o'clock every night, but I was young, interested, and hungry in those days. The first week, I got my $15 salary and about one dollar in commissions. The second week, my commissions went up to five dollars. I was learning. By the third or perhaps fourth week, I collected $70 and thereafter I never earned less than $100 a week. And that was mighty good money in those days. Yes, I got one of those two permanent jobs on the *World-Telegram.*

One of the first questions asked when I was hired was: "Do you have a car?" If so, I could have all of Queens, Long Island, Westchester, Connecticut, New Jersey, and Staten Island as my very own territory. "Yes," I replied, and went home to borrow money from my mother. I bought a Model A Ford and took a three-day course on how to drive it. For two years, I sold classified ads, met and dealt with a wide variety of men, and learned the lessons of fierce competition. I could see my losses, the ads I did not get, in the rival newspapers. I began to think, at age twenty-two, that I was finally out in the real world.

I had dropped out of night school because of the long hours involved in selling classified ads, but after a year my mother prevailed upon me to return to New York University. I remember her advising me, "You don't want to grow old and gray and look like so-and-so, selling ads until they throw you out. You've got to have a profession.'' For two weeks, I holed up at home and studied all the required books for five courses, then took a solid week of examinations, and was given credit for the year's work that I had missed. Of course, I had to pay NYU the tuition fees for all those courses I had not attended. I also found another job as a floor clerk on the stock exchange, where the hours were shorter and more regular.

The following year, 1935, after gaining some proficiency in accounting, I went to work as bookkeeper for a small closed investment company called Mayflower Associates, headed by Joseph McConnell, a mining engineer from Denver. In the three years I was there, the company distinguished itself as a major finder of oil fields and other properties, and I learned a good deal from Joe McConnell. In fact, as a $22-a-week bookkeeper, I made my first financial investment with him. He had returned from a field trip to Louisiana with several suitcases full of stock which he had bought, giving him a large ownership of an oil exploration company which, at the time, derived its principal income from muskrat trapping. I bought a number of shares at 75 cents per share and when the company struck oil I sold out at $1.50. Joe closed down Mayflower to devote his full attention to his investments. The muskrat-trapping company became the great Louisiana Land and Exploration Company. If I had held on to my stock, I might have become a millionaire without working another day in my life. Nevertheless, at the time I was delighted with a 100 percent profit on my first investment.

However, when Mayflower was closed down, I went over to its auditors, Lybrand Brothers, a public accounting firm, and applied for a job. I remember telling Norman Lenhart, a partner in the firm, what a great accountant I would be for his company. I asked for $22.50 a week, which I had been getting at Mayflower, adding that I would not accept less than $18.50 a week.

"We don't pay our people $18.50," said Mr. Lenhart, as my heart sank. "Our minimum salary is $35, and you're hired."

My job was temporary and seasonal and I was promptly assigned to help in the audit of Floyd Odlum's Atlas Corp. of Journal Square in Jersey City, which had become notorious and highly profitable in buying up bankrupt and near-defunct mutual funds and companies. Atlas Corp. owned a grab bag of securities representing hotels, barge lines, frozen foods, utilities, as well as a wide variety of other assets. The job was conspicuous, most of all, for its overtime. We worked on that audit until ten o'clock at night, five and sometimes six days a week, and in the final three weeks until three or four o'clock in the morning. Considering that I had to take the tube back to New York, sleep at home, and return to work at 9 A.M., I think I slept about two hours a night those last three weeks. When the audit certificate was signed, I requested an audience with Mr. Lenhart.

"What's on your mind?" he asked.

"Well, I haven't had but nine hours' sleep all week and I can't help worrying about this job," I said. "I just want to know whether I am permanently on the staff or not, so I can go home and get a good night's sleep." I got the job and a good night's sleep.

As a public accountant, moving from one company to another, doing audits, I enjoyed the work and the training and the associations involved. Public accounting taught me analytical approaches to business problems, objective reasoning, and the highest order of discipline in making factual presentations. I learned a great deal about how businesses were run by studying their internal financial reports. Public accounting, it seemed to me, was much more substantial than life on the stock exchange. And yet, it too was not quite satisfying. I had the feeling of a bystander. Just as on the stock exchange, I sensed that I was missing out on the constructive, active side of business. On the stock exchange, I was aware that behind all the numbers and symbols were these great companies and huge factories and plants which were producing automobiles, homes, industrial machinery, and all sorts of things we lived with. I wanted to do something with them or about them, rather than stand on the sidelines and help place the bets. Later I would learn of the importance of the stock market in the growth and well-being of the companies. But then, I could only see that the industrial companies of America were producing products and goods, and the stock market was something akin to a gambling operation. As a public accountant, I was closer to the production lines, but I was just adding up and checking the numbers, not helping to produce anything.

I worked for Lybrand Brothers for six years, during which I took the examinations and became a certified public accountant, and then the Japanese bombed Pearl Harbor. I went down to Church Street in New York and volunteered for the Navy, with the understanding that I would get a commission as a second lieutenant. I had just turned thirty-two. But when I put on my glasses to read or sign something, having passed the physical, I was promptly dismissed. They told me that I could hardly navigate a ship if my eyeglasses fogged up at sea. The Army gave me a more complex but not different runaround. At just about this same time, which was not more than a month or two after the United States joined World War II, I learned that the American Can Company, for which I was doing audits, was going to build one or two torpedo factories as its part in the war effort. I immediately applied for a job.

The next four years, working for Amertorp, a new division of American Can, were a whirlwind of activity, tension, learning, and sheer hard work for me. But it was great! It was everything that I had hoped for. From the very beginning, I was immersed in the vital work of starting from scratch and building two naval ordnance plants, one in a clay pit on the outskirts of St. Louis and another on a golf course in Forest Park, outside of Chicago. We were to build aerial torpedoes. The country had been shocked by the sinking of the British dreadnought *Prince of Wales* and another ship off Singapore in an attack by Japanese aircraft firing torpedoes. At the time, the Allies had no aerial torpedoes at all.

In charge of contracting and finance for this new group, I helped arrange to have as many as six hundred people working in a naval torpedo station in Newport, Rhode Island, copying blueprints of what we would make in our two ordnance plants. Then I traveled by train to St. Louis to help in setting up our first plant, contracting for building supplies and equipment and getting the necessary contract approvals from government agencies. All sorts of people from various parts of the country poured into St. Louis to provide the expertise needed for our first torpedo plant. We were strangers to one another in a strange environment, trying to do something that no one there had ever done before. Our deliberations often dissolved into arguments, personality conflicts, and shouting matches.

Then C. G. Preiss, the senior vice president of American Can in charge of construction, would drop in on us, invite everyone to a huge cocktail party and dinner. We would all yell and sing and get happy and then return to work the next day, eager to work together with a feeling of camaraderie. But under the strain and stress of the job, the amiability and cooperation would wither away day by day, and we would be at each other's throats again within two weeks. C.G. would appear on the scene again, invite everyone to a party and smooth out the ruffled feathers, and back to work we would go, happy and cooperative once more.

I asked him about this one day and he explained, "When you have a lot of strange bulldogs in a ring together, you've got to keep shaking them out so that they can work together."

He was a great leader of men, this C. G. Preiss, a gung-ho, down-to-earth, stocky, powerfully built man who was in his fifties at the time, and he had about him an aura of class and courage; no one doubted his leadership, and no one would dispute that he also was one of the boys. He endeared himself to us one day when he stood up to a full admiral who was giving us unnecessary problems, calling him to his face an "elevator starter." He would plunge into our problems, help us solve them, and somehow inspire us to work even harder than the week before.

With tremendous energy, we all worked full out building those two plants. Under C.G.'s leadership, I, for one, learned how to get things done and how to get people to fulfill their responsibilities. Problems were there to be solved and you did not rest comfortably until they were solved, not if one wanted to retain a feeling of self-respect. Work became the most important aspect of our lives. Even family life became secondary. We all pitched in to get the job done, for we felt inspired; we were part of the war effort; our work meant something to us and to our country. And this spirit, I think, spread across the nation during the exigencies of wartime. People pitched in and worked; victory or defeat was at stake. American productivity more than doubled during those war years and it was American productivity that won that war, as much as anything else. If we could ever recapture that spirit now, I am sure that American industrial power would once again become the envy of the world.

Personally, I worked almost around the clock five and six days a week, routinely spending four nights a week on sleepers, traveling between St. Louis, Chicago, Washington, and the home office in New York, reporting the work of our plants to the home office and to Washington. In eight months, we built our first naval ordnance plant in St. Louis and in another four months the Forest Park plant was finished and in production. We were mass-producing aerial torpedoes, and later deck torpedoes, all of them precision-made.

I was most pleased that my job went beyond that of

comptroller for the two plants; I got into production problems. At one time I was in charge of setting up controls for waste products and scrap on the production line. One department head gave me the most trouble, insisting that keeping records on scrap would slow up his crew's "real" work. I could do nothing with him. But then he was promoted and put in charge of the plant's scrap and waste materials. His whole point of view changed. Scrap and waste metals became his most important concern. He became a bulldog on channeling scrap parts back into the production line. It was another lesson learned for me, at least.

As the war drew to a close, it became evident that the plants would have to be dismantled, and so a small group of us began to draw up plans for converting torpedo plants to some kind of peacetime production. We had two excellent factories, a wonderful group of workers, and management personnel ready to go. The government would allow American Can to underwrite the costs of conversion and even initial losses by drawing from the 75 percent excess profits taxes the company had paid during wartime. In fact, the government was encouraging companies to follow this course. We worked up the figures on converting the plants to the manufacture of sewing machines, flat irons, appliances, or any number of products which would be sorely needed in the postwar years. But the top management of American Can was conservative. They sold one plant to the government and closed down the other one for later conversion to a canning plant. They decided to stick with cans and containers.

I was offered and happily accepted a peacetime job with American Can as an assistant comptroller. But first I had to wind up the financial affairs of the torpedo plants, accounting for profits and losses, the government inventories, and the liquidation of unneeded or unsold assets.

When I finally returned to the home office and reported for work, I found myself listed as an "expense clerk." The salary I had been promised, which was a cut from the $10,000 I had been earning, had been cut further. I went in to see my new boss, the comptroller of the company, and he explained that this was all temporary. "I have something very big in mind for you. Just be patient," he advised. It did not make sense to me, and after some judicious inquiries, I discovered that he had been making the same promise to others. I did not think he was treating me fairly—or honestly. Nor did I know what to do about it.

One did not switch jobs in those post-Depression days without a great deal of soul-searching, but this was my first lesson in not accommodating myself to an unsatisfactory environment. The only thing to do in such cases was to change the environment. Fortunately, while browsing in a bookstore I came across a book, *Pick Your Job and Land It*, which seemed to call out to me. It told me that in the quest for the right job one should go where the trouble was, go to a company that was in trouble or one that was growing, for that was where one would find the greatest opportunity to advance. It told me to send out only original application letters, no carbons. It even recommended the then remarkable Hooven duplicating typewriter, which made a tape that typed the same letter over and over again. After consulting Moody's stock directory for likely companies, I sent out more than three hundred letters. I got six or seven replies and from those interviews I got four job offers. Then and there I decided that I never had to fear being out of a job again.

Because I wanted to work in the Chicago area, I picked Bell & Howell, a young company which made cameras, optical equipment, and precision instruments. My salary was $11,000 a year, more than I had been promised at American Can, and I was the comptroller of the company.

When I informed American Can of my imminent departure, I was summoned to the president's office, and there Mr. Black proceeded to give me a twenty-minute lecture about the mistake I was making in leaving such a great company as American Can, the great opportunities I would be missing, etc. I heard him through and thanked him for his pep talk, adding, "But you should give this talk to a man who is coming into the company, not to one who is leaving it." I didn't say a word about the promises that had been made and not kept. I had already made my decision to move.

At the war's end in 1946, Bell & Howell was a small, growing, exciting, well-managed company, founded and headed by Joseph McNab, who ran it with an iron hand. Charles Percy, who later would become a U.S. senator from Illinois, was the executive vice president. From the start, Percy and I worked closely together in instituting the latest modern methods of management and trying to keep up with the rapid postwar growth of Bell & Howell. Its research and development laboratory was excellent, and Percy and I were constantly involved in figuring and refiguring costs, prices, and profit margins in a fast-moving technological business. We also spent considerable time redesigning the plant, tearing down walls and building new ones, squeezing ever more activities into our available space.

Joe McNab was a self-made man, and during the war he had built up the company from practically nothing, making precision lenses for the government, so that now it was poised for conversion to peacetime products. He was an irascible, highly volatile boss who, I had been warned, did not hesitate to fire any subordinate who did not live up to his expectations. It was he for whom I spent a weekend cramming for our first meeting. McNab turned out to be a hard taskmaster, but fair. He also had some idiosyncrasies which he imposed upon his staff. He was, for instance, the only man in the company allowed to use a blue pencil. He never signed his name, but whenever you saw a blue pencil mark upon a document, you knew that was an order from Mr. McNab. He also automatically cut all lawyers' bills in half. He did this by drawing his blue pencil line across half the bill and sending it down to me. I knew to pay only half of the bill. Of course, in time, the lawyers caught on and doubled their normal bills, so that both parties were satisfied with the amount paid.

Toward the end of my first year there, I had my first major run-in with "Ol' Joe" and I knew my job was at stake. He was very unhappy with the restrictions set upon our pricing of our products by the Office of Price Administration, established to curb soaring postwar prices on scarce peacetime items. The prices allowed were set by a rigid formula based upon costs, labor, and overhead. Unfortunately the OPA formulas did not properly provide for such indirect expenses as engineering and general research and development, of which Bell & Howell had quite a bit. Word came down to me that Mr. McNab wanted me to fill in the OPA forms in such a way that we would get the price increases we needed on certain camera models.

There was no way I could do that without fudging the figures. And so I said. Word came back that Mr. McNab did not care how or what I did. He needed and wanted those price increases.

So I presented myself to him in his office, unannounced, and told him, "I will not fill in your figures or anybody's figures incorrectly. But I'll tell you what I will do. I'll go to Washington and I'll plead our case under the hardship provisions of the OPA."

He grew red in the face, muttered some words I could not understand, and I beat a hasty retreat before he could say yes or no.

In Washington, it took me a week to get what I considered a reasonable and honest answer. I did not know if he would be satisfied with it, but I phoned him and announced that we had won an 8 percent increase on all our prices, across the board, rather than an increase on one or two of our product models. His thanks came in the form of a grunt before he hung up on me.

When I returned to the plant, Mr. McNab never acknowledged in one way or another what I had done. But I never had one bit of trouble with him after that encounter. Bell & Howell was for me a happy place to work. It was small enough so that you knew your colleagues personally and did not have the burdens of corporate bureaucracy. As chief financial officer, I got into many things which had nothing to do with accounting. For instance, I thoroughly enjoyed working out several innovative changes in our costing and pricing approaches, which allowed us to take on contracts we might otherwise have turned down.

I was in my fifth year at Bell & Howell when Joe McNab died of cancer in 1950. He left behind a letter of instructions, a sort of last testament, in which he said that Chuck Percy should be made president and that I should be kept on at all costs as the financial head of the company. And so it was. Not long afterwards, I was married and set about buying my first home, and I asked for a raise in pay. I was given an increase of $1,000 a year, which brought me to an annual salary of $14,000. Chuck Percy was drawing down something like $70,000. Considering the division of work, I thought that unfair. I realized that if I hoped to move up in the corporate world, I would have to move on.

I found Jones & Laughlin, of Pittsburgh, the fifth-largest steel-producing company in the nation, where I was taken on as vice president and comptroller at $40,000 a year. Leaving Bell & Howell was not easy, emotionally. Strong doubts and misgivings besieged me right up to the evening that I left the plant. It had been my first real postwar job, a happy, good place to work, with responsibilities that had challenged my abilities. Looking back from the parking lot to the light still burning in my office, I wondered whether or not I should turn back. But I could not turn back. No one can turn back, not successfully. One makes a decision to go forward, for better or worse, and you go forward, with the feeling and faith that if you succeed at one task, you have every reason to believe you will succeed at your next, bigger one. There are no guarantees, of course, but the risk must be taken, if you are going to live with yourself thereafter.

I did go back to Bell & Howell some years later—for a visit. Many of my old colleagues were still there, the same faces but a little older, a little quieter, a little more set in their ways, and, I thought, a little sadder than when I had known them.

Jones & Laughlin held a special fascination for me. It was a slice of heavy industry. During the war, when I had traveled by train in and out of Chicago, I had never failed to wonder what went on in those huge steel mills and sprawling factories in Gary and the Chicago environs. Now I would find out.

J&L was just such a plant, with mills and blast furnaces spread over a wide acreage by the side of the Ohio River. There was dirt and grime and grit everywhere, and the constant roar of blast furnaces and heavy machinery at work. The products were enormous, those long, wide coiled sheets of finished steel rolling out of the huge machinery. It was awe-inspiring. And yet, when I went to work as comptroller, I found out that what went on inside these giant companies was the same as in the small plants, only on a larger scale. The finished product was more massive, costs were greater, aggregate sales were larger, but the problems were similar. They involved people, morale, teamwork, productivity, costs—the same things that go into making any company run well or poorly.

One factor was different, however. Men in a steel mill worked under constant hazardous conditions. The awareness of physical danger in those mills produced a common bond of full and diligent performance on the job, as far as safety was concerned. People's lives depended upon it. And that bond went further to form a sense of family and caring among the men that is seldom seen in corporate life.

The steel industry in those days in the early 1950s was not a happy industry. The malaise that the steel industry suffers today began back then. Steel was underpriced; the companies were besieged by union wage demands; the companies did not have the capital needed to invest in new plants; replacement costs were excessive in relation to the price steel would bring. The handwriting was on the wall. Many could not see it at the time, and those who could see into the future seemed powerless to do anything about it.

When the industry united in refusing higher wage demands of the United Steel Workers Union, President Truman seized the mills, granted the wage demands in a new contract, then handed the steel mills back to their owners. When the industry raised the price of steel by $8 a ton to cover the increased labor costs, there was a hue and cry from the government and the public that the increase would price new automobiles out of the reach of people. I personally checked what that increase would mean in the increased price of a car. Two tons of steel went into the making of an American car. Sixteen dollars more! And in the automobile showroom, the average American cars were being offered with some $500 in optional equipment, which consumers were gobbling up without complaint. When I proposed that we point this out in a public announcement, which would exonerate the steel industry, Admiral Ben Moreel, the chairman and chief executive of Jones & Laughlin, calmed me down, saying, "We can't do that—the automobile industry is our best customer."

Even in the best of times, steel is a highly cyclical industry, and when demand is high, the industry cannot work very much over 80 to 90 percent of capacity without getting jammed up, and when demand dips low and the blast furnaces are banked, the high overhead costs of those huge mills remain constant. The steel industry, producing one product, steel, was at the mercy of the market. There were always troubles and problems and crises, and they served to bring me out of the accounting office and into the plant. Most of my work seemed to entail persuading foremen and supervisors to institute controls upon their work, so that they could check and control the costs of their particular operations. The point I would make over and over again would be that I was there, not to spy on them, but to help them in their own jobs. I would help make them more efficient, help make their work easier for them. Little by little I succeeded. But it was a long haul. If we could not raise prices enough to make a fair profit, we had to cut costs.

In search of some new ideas, I wangled an invitation to a six-day inspection tour of the management systems used at General Motors, where Alfred P. Sloan, Jr., in his genius fashioned the first highly successful decentralized company with centralized management control. I returned to J&L and had to fight long and hard in the executive suite to institute some precepts I had learned at GM. One in particular involved pooling the maintenance men of Jones & Laughlin so that they could work where they were needed and when needed. We first had to take an inventory of all the maintenance men and their jobs in each of the departments. And in so doing we found plenty of waste. In fact, we discovered one maintenance man who for twenty years had done no work at all and had gone undetected. He simply picked up a pail at one plant, carried it across a bridge to another plant, sat down out of sight all day, carried the pail back at the end of the day, and went home. We fired him. But all in all, the pooling of maintenance men saved Jones & Laughlin several million dollars a year, every year.

But it was a losing battle. Jones & Laughlin was a tradition-bound, rigid bureaucracy of a company, as were most of the steel companies. You could address questions or suggestions only to the man above you. There were many good, imaginative men in the middle ranks of management, but their ideas were apt to die on the intricate ladder of management. I fought many a battle and lost.

What it finally came down to was that Jones & Laughlin could solve its problems and save itself only by getting out, at least in part, of its dependency on steel. We had to diversify. One instance, out of many, involved a plan to go into the manufacture of the chemical by-products of our coal-tar-processing plants. We sold those by-products at five cents a gallon, as I remember it, to the Barrett Division of Allied Chemical, who in turn processed them and sold the result for some forty cents a gallon. I worked out a full presentation, suggesting that J&L build a chemical company, refine its own coal-tar by-products, and go on from there to build up its own chemical division. Among other things, the development of a chemical company would bring new men and new ideas into J&L. It never came about. The top management of Jones & Laughlin could not see it. They were steel men, proud of it, and they would stick to their trade. Several other plans for diversification, which I either initiated or supported, were turned down. Suggestions seemed to get nowhere at J&L. Years later, U.S. Steel did diversify into chemicals, and other steel companies, under pressure, did buy into other industries in order to keep afloat. Jones & Laughlin never did diversify sufficiently, and the company came upon bad times and was eventually acquired by James Ling.

In 1956, after five years with J&L, still in search of new management techniques with which to help our ailing company, I attended with the company's blessings the advanced management course at the Harvard Business School. While there I heard that the Raytheon Company had just lost their financial vice president and was looking for a replacement. I met with Charles Francis Adams, the president and chief executive of Raytheon. A descendant of the Adams family which had produced two Presidents of the United States, Charles Francis Adams was a fine figure of a man, a famous yachtsman, and a Boston blue blood. In our first talk, I persuaded him that I was not the stereotyped accountant-comptroller, and that my real interests lay in managing a company with the modern techniques of management and financial controls. It turned out that I was precisely the kind of man Adams needed at that particular time. He hired me as executive vice president of the company. It meant that for the first time in my career I would make the big leap from staff to line, responsible for production and all that it entailed. As the good Professor Hoopingarner had predicted back at NYU, I had gained the experience in my chosen field and the "cash" did come afterwards. My salary was $100,000.

I more than earned my keep that first year. Raytheon wanted to withdraw from a joint venture it had with Honeywell in a small company called Datamatic, which was trying to build one of the early large computers for the military. Raytheon had already lost some $13 million in the research and development phase and now more millions were being demanded. The Honeywell agreement, however, provided that if either of the partners chose to withdraw, it would greatly dilute that partner's share of the venture. Given the assignment to get Raytheon out of the deal, I met with the chief executive of Honeywell and insisted that the only way Honeywell could get free and clear control over the venture was to buy us out for our full investment. Otherwise, I told him, we would be obliged to sell our shares in the computer company to the public. Then if the project failed as a Honeywell-controlled subsidiary, the embarrassment to Honeywell would be widespread. It was almost complete bluff. But Honeywell was persuaded to buy us out for our full investment. I saved Raytheon $13 million and lots of headaches. Charles Francis Adams was very happy with my performance. Honeywell went on to lose almost $200 million before it turned the corner on computers.

Raytheon in those days was a fairly small company of

brilliant engineers and little top management. Almost its entire business was with the military, as Raytheon specialized in radar, missile guidance systems and navigational instruments. The company was growing fast in military contracts, but the operation was disorganized, so that it was not showing the amount of profits commensurate with the size of its military business. On the other hand, Raytheon had been rather unsuccessful in its commercial areas. Thus it was almost entirely dependent upon one customer, the U.S. government.

When I joined the company, Raytheon consisted of ~SAIC~ separate divisions, all of which reported rather haphazardly to Mr. Adams through four or five group executives. Mr. Adams himself had a staff of men whom I felt seemed more oriented to saying what pleased their boss than to the true facts of various problems. My entry into this arena caused a sort of tug-of-war between Mr. Adams' staff and myself. They would come to me and relay "orders" that they said came from Mr. Adams; they furthermore insisted that I relay my reports to them and through them to Mr. Adams. The situation continued for quite a while, until in utter disgust I walked into Mr. Adams' office one Friday afternoon and outlined the problem to him in no uncertain terms:

"Either I am running this company or they are. We both can't do it. I want to report directly to you and get my orders directly from you and not from them. So, you think it over. And let me know on Monday morning."

On Monday I was made chief of operations, and though the tug-of-war continued, I was able to restructure the organization of Raytheon so that each division manager was given greater autonomy over his own operation but was also given the responsibility for the profit-and-loss record of his own division. I set up certain standards for accounting for the costs involved in each project, so that profit margins were closely monitored.

The management problem at Raytheon, as I saw it, was that its research and development department was staffed with brilliant engineers, the division managers were competent, enthusiastic men, but some of the group executives to whom they reported and the headquarters staff men were less inclined to get into the financial details of their divisions' performances, and this constituted a bottleneck in the forward thrust of the company's progress. I could not very well change these men. So I worked around them. I called for monthly meetings of the entire top management, including not only the group executives, but also the division managers. In that way I could talk to all of them at once, so that without ruffling any egos, I could discuss company plans and problems directly with the division managers. They were the men who were doing the work, understood the nitty-gritty of the business. I needed to learn from them the engineering problems they faced and to organize them on the techniques of management control, particularly in the financial aspects of their undertakings. It worked marvelously well. Our margins of profit grew fatter, the men earned well-deserved bonuses, the company prospered and its stock soared. The men, almost all of them engineers, found a pride in financial success which I like to think equaled their pride in their engineering feats.

As part of my job, I conducted security analysts through our plant, explaining our operations and our plans for the future, and while the stock of Raytheon advanced handsomely as the company became more widely known to the public, there was some talk of my becoming president of Raytheon and Mr. Adams moving up to chairman of the board. Rumors and counter-rumors spread rapidly through the company and into the financial world. One heard that I was going to become president of Raytheon or that Mr. Adams had decided I would never become president of Raytheon. It bred discord in the company. I decided I needed to know what was on the man's mind. So I walked into his office and explained that the rumors were hurting the morale of the company, that I had no intention of rushing him upstairs, but that I would appreciate knowing what my future was with Raytheon. Could we have an understanding that someday, whenever he chose, I would become president of the company? He stared at me coldly without saying a word for what seemed like an eternity. Then he said, "I never make any commitments of any kind to anyone. It's against my policy."

I considered that an answer in itself.

Toward the end of 1958, I began quietly looking for another job. The opportunity presented itself six months later.

International Telephone and Telegraph was looking for a new president.

In negotiating with the search committee of the ITT board of directors, I did not ask for the security of a long-term contract, as is now the common practice. I did not even ask for a contract. Nor did I get one. I accepted the compensation offered: $125,000 a year. There were no bonuses or stock options promised. I would have to prove myself all over again at ITT. Professor Hoopingarner had neglected to tell our class at NYU that beyond a certain point in one's career, cash is not all that important. One returns again to the value of the experience offered by the job, the challenge to test one's own mettle, and also the fun, the enjoyment, the pride, and the sense of self-fulfillment that hard work can offer.

FOUR

Two Organizational Structures

*Every company has two organizational struc-
tures: the formal one is written on the charts;
the other is the everyday living relationship of
the men and women in the organization.*

AN ORGANIZATIONAL CHART delineating the structure of
a company is absolutely essential to any enterprise larger
than a small family business. When you get up to the Fortune 500 companies, with their tens of thousands of employees and an annual business volume of billions of
dollars, then the business structure charts get more and
more complex. But no matter how big or small the business, the organizational charts are designed to do the
same task: to tell who is in charge of what and who reports to whom. They are needed to facilitate the free flow
of information so that people can communicate with one
another in an orderly and logical way.

The formal structure of a company is almost always
designed in the shape of the familiar pyramid, with the
labor force on the bottom supporting the whole structure,
and with the various layers of supervisory management
spread out one on top of the other, on up to the top. That
structure defines the regular chain of command. Information flows up the chain and orders flow down. Everyone
knows his or her own place and responsibilities in the
hierarchy. Logic and order are supposed to reign su-
preme.

While there is logic and reason to it, the system never
satisfied me. It has in it all the seeds of bureaucracy
which have plagued the military service, the government, and most of corporate America. In some of our

largest companies it can take as long as six months for a decision to be made. Everything must work its way up through the chain of command and back down again. Managers often become paper pushers. Reports stack up, recommendations are made warily, decisions are delayed, actions are not taken. The company stagnates. I have seen it happen again and again at various companies where I have worked. The rigidity of the management structure, almost as much as the men themselves, stymied and lost many fruitful ideas.

Without a formal structure and chain of command, there would be chaos. With it, however, there is the danger that each box on the organizational chart will become an independent fiefdom, with each vice president thinking of his own terrain, his own people, his own duties and responsibilities, and no one thinking of the company as a whole. What tends to happen is that one man says, "My job is to do this, and that's all I know." The next man says, "My job is to do that and I don't know anything about his . . ." And so it goes, with memos traveling from one letter tray to the next, until someone higher up plunges in and tries to get the two men to work together on a common goal.

Worse than that, however, it seemed to me that as vital information makes its way up the chain of command, it is cleansed and summarized each step of the way, so that the man or men at the top only get an *idea* of what is going on below. They do not really know. The men on the line know what is going on and the divisional vice presidents know what is going on, but of necessity, the senior vice presidents summarize their knowledge in their reports, so that at the top, the chief executive, more often than not, knows only what his four or six group executives report to him. He relies upon these men. He has to rely on them because they supposedly know, far more than he does, what is going on below.

The system works as long as every executive in the chain of command does his work well. When one of these key men fails and a crisis looms, the chief executive often does not really know enough about the situation to judge what he should do about it. Most likely, all he can do is fire the man who failed and put someone else in to take over. If need be, he'd explain to his board of directors, "Here's the situation. It's not my fault. I relied on Joe Smith, usually a good man, and he disappointed me, and so I had to fire him."

What happens then? Word gets around that if you fail, you get fired. So men, who would not have otherwise, begin to cover up their mistakes. The longer they can hide any mess confronting them, the longer they can keep their jobs. What happens? A problem grows into a crisis. If the crisis is not recognized in time, it can become a catastrophe. I've seen it happen. You read about it in the financial pages of the newspapers every week, if not every day. Crises and catastrophes do not pop up overnight. They are the results of problems that have been covered up and festering for a long, long time.

Not only problems, but good, innovative ideas are often overlooked in a bureaucratic channeling of information in a large, complex company. There are always some executives who do not want to risk their jobs by proposing something that might fail. So they send those bright and bushy-tailed ideas back down the line for more study or they reject them out of hand. They never get up to the inner sanctum of top management. What happens? Eventually, the bright young men of middle management stop making suggestions. They stick to the work assigned to them and forget about trying to be bright. Or they quit and seek better opportunities elsewhere. The top man, in his executive suite, never knows what he has missed. The company never lives up to its full potential. No one really recognizes the fundamental problem of too close adherence to the formal structure of the company.

That was pretty much the system that was in place at ITT when I got there in 1959. I recognized it from my past experience and immediately set about changing it. I announced loudly, clearly, and often that I wanted *open communications* throughout ITT. Many chief executives say that, but they follow through only to limited degrees. At ITT, it took years to get a new system in place which would cut through the formal structure so that the managers of our autonomous subsidiaries would think of ITT as one company, one team, one group of management men heading in the same direction. We set up a system of monthly reports from our operating divisions, and we augmented our headquarters staff so that we had expert and experienced staff people to check on all facets of our work in telecommunications, electronics, consumer goods, engineering, accounting, legal, marketing, whatever. Our basic and primary policy then became a system in which any staff man could go anywhere in the company and ask any kind of questions and get any kind of answers he could and he could report his findings straight to my office. The only proviso was that he had to inform the manager involved exactly what he was doing before he sent his report upstairs. He did not need his superior's permission to send the report, but he could not act behind the man's back. He had to give the manager involved a chance to correct the situation. If they could agree on a solution, it got no further. If they could not agree, their dispute would be settled at the headquarters level. I wanted anyone with an idea for improving the company's performance to be able to send it up to my office. I also insisted that every report had to be signed by the man who wrote it. His superior could initial the report and add his comments. But if I had questions, I wanted to talk to the man who wrote the report, not to his superior who might have signed it. I really wanted to know what was going on in the company. I thought it was essential.

These staff men out of headquarters cut through the structured rigidity of the formal organization, monitoring each of the subsidiaries. The accounting staff man monitored the profits, the engineering staff monitored the engineering department, and so on with marketing, personnel, legal, etc. The staff people worked very closely with the men out in the field, and they made their reports and recommendations, and they were held equally responsible for whatever went well or poorly in the unit they were monitoring. Actually, if a conflict arose between staff and operations men, one of three things would happen: The operations man would persuade the staff man that he was wrong because he did not understand the facts; or the operations man would admit he was wrong and agree to correct the situation; or, occasionally, the operations man would admit he was wrong but wanted to continue doing things his way, even after the intercession of the president's office (and eventually he would lose his job). In time there developed a common bond between, say, the engineering staff man at headquarters and the chief engineer down at a particular subsidiary. They learned to work together for the common good of the company, for the staff man did help in lending a knowledgeable outside viewpoint on the operating engineer's problems, and the staff man helped in persuading headquarters to approve the subsidiary's requests for funds. This did not happen overnight; it took time. Conflicts in thinking did occur between headquarters staff and operating men, but different points of view never hurt. Eventually, the operating men came to look upon the headquarters staff as "outside consultants" who could be relied upon to help when needed.

In addition to this regular staff, we added a new staff position. We had at the time twelve to sixteen senior staff men designated as product line managers. Each of them roamed over complete product lines, representing the competition! He was monitoring the competitive ability of an ITT subsidiary in the marketplace. Every salesman, manager, engineer, or member of an operating team is so used to thinking well of his own product it is hard for any of them to recognize anything but the faults of his competitors. The product line manager was paid to look cold turkey at an ITT company and its competition and raise questions as he saw fit. It was a very difficult position for any man, being a product line manager at ITT, but he was worth his weight in gold in balancing the human factors involved in recognizing the realities of what was happening in the competitive marketplace. He had no authority to order the operating manager to do anything. But he could raise questions that had to be answered. He introduced a healthy attitude toward the competition, that it had to be considered honestly and responded to speedily. The product line managers succeeded only by persuading our line managers that they were not out to get them personally; that they were there to help them; that the ideas they presented were in fact salutory, effective, and workable. The product line managers were free of the responsibilities of budgets and performance. They had in effect a license to speculate on what could be done differently and better. They were free to be imaginative and creative. All they had to do was to sell their ideas to the line managers and work with them for the improvement of the company. If they could not agree, once again, the differences in opinion would be reported, aired, and settled at the headquarters level.

In line with open communications, another major innovation introduced at ITT was my edict that the comptrollers in each and every division of the company would submit their financial reports directly to headquarters in New York. There was an immediate hue and cry from the division managers that I was turning their financial chiefs into spies for the home office. It did not matter, they said, that their comptrollers gave them a copy of their report and that they could dispute any portion of that report. They wanted complete control over their domains and the absolute loyalty of their financial men. But I wanted an independent check on their activities by comptrollers who would be personally responsible for the figures they submitted to headquarters. It is all too easy to fudge or cover up the facts with numbers as well as with words. The temptation is always there. Even without conscious lying, different men honestly interpret events and situations differently. Company or division managers can exaggerate anticipated sales or underestimate costs or whatever and the men under them will go along because their jobs depend upon it. I wanted the comptrollers to feel free of that pressure and be able to give the home office their honest opinion. If the division manager and his comptroller could not agree, we would settle it at a higher level after a full and open hearing.

The fundamental and basic job of management in any company is to manage. I've said that hundreds and thousands of times during my career. Management manages by making decisions and by seeing that those decisions are implemented. And the only way management can do that successfully is to have full access to the facts of any situation affecting the welfare of the company. Top management, headed by the chief executive, is in effect the fulcrum of the company. Pressures for performance are exerted upon him from the top and from the bottom of the organization. The shareholders, who own the company and who are represented by the board of directors, want ever more profits and progress and a better return on their investment. They always want more, and they should want more. From the other end, the men and women who are manning the production line want higher wages, better machinery, better working conditions, and more help from management. They cry out that there is a limit to what they can be expected to produce under the given circumstances. With pressures from both sides, the crunch comes in the office of the chief executive. He and his management team must balance the demands which come from the top and from the bottom and satisfy both sides, fairly. That is why the free flow of information is so essential in any business enterprise, for it is only by knowing the realities of one's own business and the realities of the marketplace that management can hope to manage satisfactorily.

At ITT, information flowed into our New York headquarters from the managers of each and every division or profit center of the company in the form of annual budgets and business plans, followed by their monthly operating reports. The budgets, which contained the business plans for the following year, were drawn up in February and March, reviewed and revised at the local level, and then reviewed and revised at headquarters. We sat face to face with each and every managing director and his own senior staff, division by division, unit by unit. The plans and budgets were discussed and revised and agreed upon in the last quarter of the year, and then they served as the benchmark of performance for the following year. Each division manager and his own management staff had negotiated an agreement with headquarters on his budget and business plan for the following year. He had made a firm commitment to ITT. His subordinates down the line had made their commitments to him for the integral parts of his budget. He would hold them to their word as we would hold him to his commitment—or know the reason why.

We planned in detail for the four quarters of the year ahead. Our two-year, three-year, and five-year plans were far more sketchy, and less important. Some capital improvements, such as new plant and heavy equipment, had to be laid out three and five years in advance. But in principle, I did not believe in long-range planning. No one is wise enough to see five or ten years into the future and plan for it with any sensible certainty. We prepared carefully for the year ahead, we outlined what we thought the year after that might bring, and then we sketched in the follow-ups for the future. We certainly began projects that would take five or even ten years to complete. But I did not put much stock in a strategy that called upon ITT to begin doing something five or ten years into the future. Management has enough to do in planning for one year ahead. The budgets and business plans for all our divisions, bound in loose-leaf books, occupied more than thirty feet of bookcase shelves. But those books were the bible we lived by.

The monthly operating reports from each and every profit center contained all the pertinent data on sales, earnings, inventory, receivables, employment figures, marketing, competition, research and development, problems being faced and problems anticipated, and, finally, expectations for the remainder of the year. Managers were obliged to put everything that affected or could affect their operations into their monthly reports, including the economic or political situation of the countries in which they operated. Beyond that, the division comptrollers made their monthly financial reports to our chief comptroller, Herbert Knortz, at headquarters. We also had a steady flow of reports from our headquarters staff (specialists in engineering, accounting, research and development, and so forth) who operated in their specialized areas with the line people. Then we received reports on particular situations from our product line managers. This stream of information poured in to headquarters from all over the world.

These monthly reports, which usually ran from fifteen to twenty pages each, were scrutinized by our headquarters staff in each of their areas of expertise, and were read and reviewed by me and my top management team in the office of the president. As ITT grew larger and more complex each year, my staff and the office of the president grew larger. In the beginning, for at least the first ten years, I handled the presidency of ITT alone because I had a horror, based on past experience, of administrative assistants. With no authority of their own, they somehow presumed or were presumed to speak for the chief executive. I'd seen administrative assistants issue orders, subtly or not, without the knowledge of the men they were assisting. I preferred to have my communications come directly from me, or at least from company officers who shared the responsibility for the matter at hand. However, as the sheer increased size of ITT dictated, we did go to an "office of the president" that gradually grew from three to five executive vice presidents—Tim Dunleavy, James Lester, Richard Bennett, Lyman Hamilton, and Rand Araskog. Nevertheless, even with three or five men assisting me in the office of the president, I refused to subdivide the workload or the basic source of the company's top decisions. I read each and every one of those monthly reports from our operating divisions, and I also insisted that each of the five executive vice presidents read every report so they too would have an overall, indepth knowledge of all of ITT operations. We worked as a team in the president's office on the simple premise that six minds are better than one in attacking any single problem or series of problems.

As ITT continued to grow at an annual rate of between 10 and 15 percent, the stream of information that poured in to our headquarters became a gushing torrent. We had at one point 250 separate and distinct profit centers, each sending in a manager's monthly report, a comptroller's report, and specialized reports on particular situations. By the late 1960s, ITT had grown into the ninth-largest industrial company in America, with only the five major oil companies, General Motors, General Electric, and International Business Machines bigger than us. We had some 375,000 employees in 115 countries worldwide and a staff of more than 2,400 executives in the United States and another 1,600 in Europe and we were manufacturing and selling an enormous variety of products, ranging from highly sophisticated communications systems to breads and cakes and car rentals, hotels, auto parts, parking lots, lawn seed, industrial equipment, cosmetics, and financial and insurance services. We were generally recognized as the largest, most complex multinational company in the world. How did we, as a management team, keep up with this enormous flow of complex activities? How could we maintain our control over this vast company and continue to grow year after year as we had done before? I pondered this question year after year, and the best answer was always the same: We had to work harder. That meant, of course, better and better information and better and better group decisions.

On paper, the structure and organization of ITT was not very different from that of most large corporations in the United States. But an organizational chart is really only a piece of paper, a static dumb thing, that identifies a chain of command of people and functions. True management begins only when you put all these people together, functioning together, in a vital, human interrelationship so that the company performs as a single team, driving onward toward the goals set by the chief executive. These human interrelationships, in all their facets, are what differentiate one company from another. On paper, one company can appear to be exactly like another, and in reality be completely different. The important policies, decisions, and activities of a company are those which deal with people, not functions.

ITT differed from most other companies in the size, scope, and style of the management meetings we held every month. Our top management team from headquarters met face to face with the managing directors of our profit centers in Europe and then in the United States to go over their operating activities for the previous month. Other companies hold meetings and review their business activities, too, but those are almost always small committee meetings at a given level, with reports and recommendations sent up to a higher committee, resulting in management by committee. Management in most companies is compartmentalized by committee decisions. Proposals go up the chain of command and decisions come down, usually with bureaucratic sluggishness. At ITT, we cut through two or three levels of upper management, so that my management team and I could talk and deal directly with the men on the firing line, the men who were responsible for the performance of their divisions and profit centers.

As noted before, soon after I came to ITT I saw the advantages of meeting face to face with our European directors, rather than trying to solve problems over the transatlantic telephone or telex systems. The look on a man's face, his tone of voice, his body language made a difference in the decisions I was making. We started out in Europe in small, smoke-filled hotel rooms, but as the company expanded and built its own European headquarters in Brussels, the monthly General Managers Meeting usually consisted of 120 to 150 managing directors. Every month I flew to Europe with about forty headquarters staff, and we sat down together and went over the monthly operating reports. The pertinent figures from the comptrollers' reports and the managing directors' reports were flashed on giant project screens in three corners of the room. Everyone on the headquarters staff had read every monthly report to be reviewed. We were informed. In going through the two large brown leather-bound loose-leaf books of reports, I made it a practice to jot down my queries in red ink and turn down the corner of the page to mark any item I wished to query at the meeting.

One by one, we would go through each of the monthly reports. Not only I but anyone else at the meeting could say anything, question anything, suggest anything that was pertinent. Each man had a microphone in front of him. With the figures on the screen, we could all see how each profit center measured up to its budget commitments, its last year's performance and whatever, in sales, earnings, receivables, inventory, etc. When problems arose, as they always did, we could deal with them and perhaps even solve them on the spot. Some problems involved the interfacing of two or more companies, particularly in Europe in those early days, when there was considerable wasteful overlapping of duplicate activities.

The managing directors of these companies were right there in the same room to iron out their differences. Often, we would deal with a problem of one company that was similar to if not a replica of a problem faced by several other companies. Men learned by listening to the woes of others. It was at times almost group therapy. Often, the manager of one company could suggest a solution that worked for him that would help another manager with a similar problem in his company.

We sat around a large U-shaped table, covered in green felt, facing one another, and I asked questions based upon the notes I had made on their monthly operating reports. Why were the sales down? Was he sure of the reasons? Had he checked it out? How? What was he doing about it? What did he expect in the month or two ahead? Did he need help? How did he plan to meet or outdistance the competition?

Oftentimes, as we explored a situation, we found that the reason for a problem was not as expected, but something entirely different. I did not come to those meetings with all the answers. We explored and we tested out alternatives. The minds of many men dealt with the problem at hand. When I felt the man needed help, I assigned a team of staff men to help him. And I explained that we were all there to help the man in trouble; we were all one team, one company, and I was interested in solving the problem at hand, not taking action against the man personally. In the early years, many of the managing directors who represented giant-sized subsidiary companies and were accustomed to independence, resented the imposition of "outsiders" from headquarters on their domains.

"Look," a manager would say in effect, "I've been running my company for years and I know what has to be done. I want you to leave me alone. It's my responsibility. If I fail, you can fire me, but let me do it myself."

"That's not a satisfactory answer," I would reply. "If

you fail and I have to fire you, there's no way that I can take a twenty-million-dollar mistake out of your severance check. On the other hand, if you solve this problem, no matter how much help you need or get, you will be solving it and you will get the bonus at the end of the year for fulfilling your budget commitments."

It took a while—years—before the effect of this policy took hold and it was accepted by the managing directors of the subsidiary companies of ITT. Some men could not abide what they considered an attack upon their abilities, and they left the company. But most of the men came to recognize that all the monitoring of their activities that I instituted was for their benefit as much as for mine. It was all part of our fundamental policy of open communications. When we found any manager in trouble or "over his head," my "action assignments" were for his own benefit. They discovered that we were interested in solving problems, eliminating inefficiencies, rather than passing judgment upon the man or men involved. In time, I came to assign as many as five different teams of staff specialists to work on a particularly thorny problem.

Out of all this we hammered out our company policies, because we tried to solve problems in such a way that they never came up again. We began to recognize the similarity of business problems that arose repeatedly and we became, as time went on, more and more sophisticated in our solutions.

One of our basic policies at ITT, which grew out of our experience in these meetings, was: *No surprises!*

Ninety-nine percent of all surprises in business are negative. No matter how adept we were as a management team, mistakes would be made, the unexpected would happen, problems would arise. But the earlier we discovered and dealt with the unexpected problem, the easier it would be to solve. We might not catch all of them at an early stage, but if we dealt with 95 percent of these situations early enough, we would have the time and energy to handle the few big problems that got through our net.

So, very early on, I demanded that all our company managers put all their significant problems into their monthly reports. I wanted no cover-ups, no surprises. Then one day a company manager told us of a massive strike he had on his hands. How long had the strike been threatened? Three months. Why hadn't he warned us in his monthly report? He had. Where? On page 18, hidden in one line of a paragraph in the middle of the page. So I amended the policy. Managers were to put all their significant problems in their monthly reports on a "red flag" page at the beginning of the report, and *keep putting them in* with "red flags" until the problems were solved.

In my first few years at ITT, I read so many wishy-washy, equivocating, vague reports that I became exasperated in my search for the meaning of what I was reading. I lectured interminably to executives on the line and on the staff on how important it was for headquarters to understand what was being recommended to us for a decision and also *why* the recommendation was being made and also *who* was responsible for the recommendation. So, in no uncertain terms, I sent out a memo on what I expected in a report:

Effective immediately, I want every report specifically, directly and bluntly to state at the beginning a summary containing the following facts in this order.

1. A clear short statement of the action recommended.

2. A brief summary of what the problem really is.

3. The reasoning and the figures where necessary for clarity and perspective to understand the basis of the reasoning and judgment areas leading to this recommendation.

4. A brief personal statement by the writer expressing any further personal opinion, his degree of confidence and any other questions that he has in this respect.

Obviously, to make this kind of direct, clear-judgment statement, one must first do hard "crisp" thinking and adequate homework. Otherwise, we will get a continuation of vague, general statements and reports which indicate no clear position, or basis for any taken by the writer. In the future this kind of "indefinite" statement and report will be subject to review with the author, and action will be taken on this point alone.

Indeed, in the early years as the executives in the company came to know one another better and better, a great deal of time was spent in my reading a line or two of a report and demanding to know what the writer of those lines meant. If the man knew and was reluctant to put the facts out in the open, my questions would force him to admit what he was trying to hide. If the man did not know or understand his own lines (which was often true because he had not written them), then my questions, doubly embarrassing, would force him to do his own homework.

It took me a while to convince our managers that I was sincere in telling them that there was no shame or humiliation in being wrong or making an occasional mistake. Mistakes are a facet of business, and should be treated as such. The important thing was to face up to one's mistakes, examine them, learn from them, and go on about one's business. The only real mistake was being afraid to make a mistake.

I have long believed that one of the primary, fundamental faults with American management is that over the years it has lost its zest for adventure, for taking a risk, for doing something that no one has done before. The reason behind this change is the mistaken belief that professional business managers are supposed to be sure of themselves and never make a professional mistake. In school, one gets an A only if one gets 90 or 95 percent of the answers right. But in business, I would give an A to a manager who was right 83 or 87 percent of the time. He would certainly beat out the average manager, who is right 45 to 55 percent of the time. More important than the score, however, is the mental attitude of the executive when he faces a decision. I wanted the ITT executive to be imaginative and creative. He could be that and succeed only if he was also objective about the facts of the situation at hand. I came to see that an objective view of the facts was one of the most important aspects of successful management. People go wrong most often when their decisions are based upon inadequate knowledge of the facts available.

Time after time in those early ITT management meetings I would question a man about his facts. Where did he get them? (Usually from some other man.) How did he know they were correct? *Were* they facts? So I wrote a memo about "unshakable facts."

Yesterday we put in a long, hard-driving meeting, mostly seeking the facts on which easy management decisions could be then made. I think the most important conclusion to be drawn is simple. There is no word in the English language that more strongly conveys the intent of incontrovertibility, i.e., "final and reliable reality," than the word "fact."

However, no word is more honored by its breach in actual usage.

For example, there are and we saw yesterday:

"Apparent facts."
"Assumed facts."
"Reported facts."
"Hoped-for facts."
"Facts" so labeled and accepted as facts—i.e., "accepted facts"—and many others of similar derivation!

* * *

In most cases these were not the facts at all.

In many cases of daily life this point may not be too important. But in the areas of management momentum and decisions, it is all-important! Whole trains of events and decisions for an entire management can be put in motion in the wrong direction—with inevitable loss of money, time, and morale—by one "unfactual fact," accepted by or submitted by YOU—however unintentional.

The highest art of professional management requires the literal ability to "smell" a "real fact" from all others—and moreover to have the temerity, intellectual curiosity, guts and/or plain impoliteness, if necessary, to be *sure* that what you do have is indeed what we will call an "unshakable fact."

That is the kind of "fact material" we have to deal in. And, as a member of the team, it is the *only* kind you can accept or submit—as our management team has to rely on each member exercising the *greatest* care in this respect as to the material he submits for the team's common use.

So let me invite you and at the same time insist that you now become a "connoisseur of all these kinds of facts" so that you can then tell a "genuine snapping turtle" from the others—and so that you learn to force to the surface and deal only with *"unshakable facts"* in the future.

You will hear a lot more of this term *"unshakable facts"* as we go forward—it is a never-ending discipline and one that we need.

So, good luck with them—and start now—IS IT A FACT? but more important, IS IT AN UNSHAKABLE FACT?

P.S.: No matter what you think, try "shaking it" to be sure.

P.P.S.: Send this message down the line.

* * *

The message did go down the line, right through the managerial ranks, because what we demanded of our managing directors they demanded of their own people at the division and unit levels. The only way a subsidiary company manager could prepare himself for a General Managers Meeting was to demand of his own people that they inform him fully of everything going on in their company. The effect was not immediate. One cannot command a discipline. But over the years, more and more, there developed at our General Managers Meetings in Brussels (for the European companies) and in New York (for the U.S. companies) a discipline of adhering to factual objectivity in dealing with the realities of our business problems. Out of that grew an intellectual integrity that became the pride of working for ITT.

Meeting one week a month in Brussels and one week a month in New York, year after year, we all got to know one another well. The same men—the top forty or so executives from headquarters, our group executives, and the managing directors of all 250 ITT subsidiaries—came together face to face at least once a month, and we interacted in a significant way. They came to know me personally, to know what I expected of them and what they could expect of me. I came to recognize how their minds worked. Some people have a bias this way and some have a bias that way. Some were more imaginative than others, some more logical than others, some were very conservative in their thinking, others were overoptimistic, some more reliable than others. One can learn such things only by face-to-face interaction, not by reading reports. Sitting in a meeting and talking with people, seeing them think aloud, answering questions, solving problems, you get an idea of their capabilities. Moreover, once you knew a man and his idiosyncrasies, you became much more adept in interpreting his written reports. You knew the man, as members of a family know one another instinctively from the years of interaction and talk at the dinner table. You learn how to weigh what each particular man tells you in his reports or at a meeting. You learn the extent to which you can trust and rely upon him, and that, in itself, is usually as important as what he actually reports to you.

In a way, I suppose, our meetings were a complex version of the personal dynamics involved in running a small family business. We talked and we argued and we solved problems and we came up with new ideas. <u>The key point was that no one was afraid to talk.</u> There was a zeal in finding new facts, new inventions, new alternatives. Out of this cauldron of ideas, facts, and proposed solutions, answers were found that were in no one's mind when he came into the room. Everyone there was generally on an equal footing, regardless of the size of the company he represented, seniority, or pay scale. No one would dare say that his ideas were better because he earned more money than the next fellow. Anyone who tried to fudge the facts, evade the significant question, or bluff his way through a presentation at one of our meetings was soon exposed, not only to me but to the others at the meeting. Anyone who tried to score with a personal attack upon another man also was readily exposed for what he was before his peers. We were there to learn from one another, help one another, work as a team, and we took pride in our ability to solve any and all business problems better than our competitors could. We constantly sought to find some improvement over what anybody else had ever done. To do that, we probed for something that was beyond the obvious answers. We figured that our competition could find the easy answer; we wanted to go him one better. We could and we did. The figures showed it. Year after year, ITT was forging ahead of its competitors in product line after product line.

Everyone talks of the importance of "team spirit" in a business, and in a very real way, ITT worked as a team. In our annual budget meetings, we laid our game plans in anticipation of what the competition might do, and in our monthly management meetings we huddled and agreed upon what we would try to do in our next play. We could change parts of our game plan on the spot and go ahead. We could try new things and alter those ideas in our next huddle. We could act and react fast. And it worked and we knew we were number one. We came to believe, and would fight to sustain that belief: we were the best business managers in the world. We could and did merge with new businesses, take in new players and make them part of our team, and forge ahead in the worldwide marketplace bigger and stronger than we had been before.

Those General Managers Meetings brought highly diverse men together. In one room we had highly skilled professional men in the law, accounting, engineering, marketing, government, interacting with experienced and capable business managers from every major country in Western Europe. In Europe, we had men from different countries dealing in the same product lines, telecommunications, electronics, industrial products. In the United States, we had men from the same country who dealt in a wide variety of different products and different marketplaces. If you think of a giant human memory bank in operation, each of those General Managers Meetings had an average of 120 highly competent men, each with more than twenty years of business experience from all parts of the world and in different product lines. That's 2,400 years of business managerial experience on hand for each of our meetings. And we had two of them, every month.

As we listened to the points of view of one another each of us became more sophisticated in our own knowledge of the marketplace, world economics, world trade, international law, engineering, and, of course, the techniques of business management. Moreover, we were all on one team. We became, in effect, a working "think tank,'' a problem-solving mechanism in business management.

Not only did we learn and get help from one another, not only did we achieve speed and directness in handling our problems, but our meetings often were charged with such dynamism and enthusiasm that at times we worked with a feeling of sheer exhilaration. Generating new ideas that were not on anyone's agenda, we came up with new products, new ventures, new ways of doing things.

Our normal GMM meetings ran from ten in the morning to ten at night. In Europe, they often went on past midnight because we could spend only a limited number of days there. Our budget and business plan meetings almost always ran on past midnight. We did not watch the clock. We worked on and on until the task at hand was completed.

Now, if you add up the days and weeks spent in those meetings, you will find that we spent three weeks in February and March on our preliminary, rough business plans and budgets for the coming year, and then twelve weeks at the end of the year reviewing and agreeing on those plans. That's fifteen weeks. One General Managers Meeting in Brussels and one in New York, a week each, ten months of the year, and you had another twenty weeks. That's thirty-five weeks of time. Add four weeks for vacation and holiday time, and you have thirty-nine weeks. That left a scant thirteen weeks of ''other'' time in which to run the company. How did we do it? We did it in overtime at night and on weekends and whenever we could, for it was truly at our meetings, and the face-to-face meetings down the line in our subsidiaries, that we ran ITT.

Where does all this appear on the organizational structure charts? ITT appears to be structured just like all the other companies of similar size and yet we were vastly different. We were different in the human, living, everyday relationships and interactions of the men and women of ITT and those who worked for other corporations, and I would say 80 percent of all that occurred in our face-to-face meetings of management.

FIVE

Management Must Manage

Management must manage!

Management must manage!
Management MUST manage!
MANAGEMENT MUST MANAGE!
How many times do I have to tell you?

It is a very simple credo, probably the closest thing to the secret of success in business, in professional life, in almost everything you undertake. The strange thing is that in one form or another everyone knows it, and somehow they forget it all the time. Or they think it too simple to be real.

Defining our terms, "management" is the team of managers who operate a business, an enterprise, or whatever. "Manage" means to get something done, to accomplish something that you, or the team of managers, set out to do, which presumably is worthy of your effort.

"Must" means *must*. That is the active word in the credo: "must."

Business managers set up a business plan and budget designed to produce satisfactory earnings by the end of a given fiscal period. A business plan is a target you "shoot for." But to "want" to achieve certain year-end results is not enough. Managing means that once you set your business plan and budget for the year, you *must* achieve the sales, the market share, the earnings, and whatever to which you committed yourself.

If you don't achieve those results, you're not a manager. Oh, you may have the title and it may say "Managing Director" or "Vice President" or "Sales Manager" on the door, but in my book you're still not a manager. Things may be happening out there, for better or for worse, but you are not making them happen. You're not managing them. It's not that you're a mediocre or a bad manager. You're not a manager.

Consider, for example, three college students, of generally equal intelligence and ability, who want to go on to a graduate school of business administration and become successful, well-paid business executives. The first boy, Cal, figures he will get a B average because he had always done that well before. He attends all his classes, hands in most of his homework assignments, and does what is expected of him. When he gets the flu before final exams one year, his average slips to just above a C. But that wasn't his fault, he says. He figures he will average them out with A's the following year. But something else happens. He misunderstands one question on his exam and brings home a C. One thing or another seems to happen to thwart his most sincere intentions. He graduates with a B-minus average and with a little luck he may make it into a B-minus business school.

The second would-be executive, Al, decides he wants to go to one of the twelve top business schools and for that he needs an A average or something pretty close to that. When he pulls down his first B, he begins to put in three or four hours a night studying, rather than one or two. In his second and again in his third year he slips to one B among all the other A's. He feels chagrined, but he does not know what more he can do about it. So he decides three or four A's and one B each year is not so bad, after all. In his senior year, he receives two A's, one B, and one unexpected C. Then he makes his twelve applications and crosses his fingers. He hopes for the best. Whether or not he will get into one of the top schools now depends upon his competition as much as upon his own grades.

The third boy decides that he wants to go to the Stanford or the Harvard Business School and no other, and for that he will need straight A's. Let's call him Hal—somehow the name has a nice ring to me. He knows in his gut that he must get straight A's. He studies three, four, or five hours every night so that when he goes into an exam he will be confident that he knows his subject. In his senior year, with a straight-A average, he gets into trouble with one subject, advanced accounting. At the end of the first quarter he is struggling for a B. He studies harder. Midyear, he still has a B-minus average in that subject. What can he do? He does some outside reading, beyond his assignments. He still cannot master that subject. He appeals to his professor for help. The professor, however sympathetic, has no time for him. What can he do? His friends, Cal and Al, scoff at his concern. One B in four years is not so bad. But Hal has set his heart upon his goal. He *must* get that A in advanced accounting. He swallows his pride and finds a graduate student to tutor him; he burns the midnight oil; he thinks things through; he works hard. And, of course, he gets his A; he gets into the school of *his* choice.

In my estimation, the first two boys were not managers. Cal just drifted along. Al did set out to achieve certain goals and was sincere in his efforts, but he allowed events to overtake him. Whatever success either boy might find would depend upon what is generally called "luck." If no one else did any better, they might scrape through. The third boy, Hal, *was a manager before he even reached business school*. Instinctively, he had grasped the essentials of good business management, not because he worked so hard at his studies, but because when one action failed, he tried another, and then another . . . until he achieved his goal. That's managing.

If and when Cal, Al, and Hal take their places in the business world, they undoubtedly will fit into the notches of management already carved out by men like them. Cal will lope along with low standards of achievement; Al will become a conscientious plodder with little imagination; and Hal, bless him, will scale the heights at companies like ITT.

In the business world, everyone is always working at legitimate cross-purposes, governed by self-interest. Customers plead for lower prices; suppliers demand higher prices; unions press for higher wages; stockholders want more and more earnings. The competition is trying to market a better product at a lower cost. Your job as a manager is to manage all of that, and more, and to finish the year with results that satisfy those cross-purposes as well as the goals you set for yourself and your own company. In business there always will be problems and your job as a manager is to solve them. If you try twenty-two ways to solve one problem and still fail, then you must try the twenty-third way. But your attitude should be: "I'm going to stay here all night if I have to, but I'm going to solve that problem."

Though I've done it often and recommend it at times to others, spending all night in your office is not the essential point; solving the problem is. Results are important in management. If you can solve your problem with two winks and the wave of a hand, well and good. You work through the night only because it takes you that long to find an answer that will solve the problem and satisfy you. The results will show up on your P&L sheet at the end of the quarter and at the end of the year. "Management must manage" means that you *must* get those results!

Almost no one in business will argue with that attitude, but it is perfectly obvious that a lot of people in corporate life talk that way but do not act that way. Middle management reports to top management: "Sorry, chief, we couldn't pull it off, but we came close, and let me tell you what we ran into . . ." And so the report goes up the ranks from this division and that division, and the chief executive reports to his board of directors: "I'm awfully sorry to have to report . . ."

An experienced chief executive can choose from

among a thousand good, plausible explanations for a no-fault rationale of why the company failed to achieve the results he had promised at the beginning of the year. His report to the board and his annual report to the stockholders will be a masterpiece of cool logic and reason. He can blame the company's troubles on a downturn in the national economy, inflation, shortages in supplies, the weather, a new technology, foreign competition . . . or a combination of any of the above. In fact, most often his rationale will be irrefutable because his bottom line almost always is: "It could have been worse." He often heaps praise upon his management team for having done so well in the face of such terrible, adverse conditions. You can read such explanations in thousands of corporate annual reports each year.

However, if you believe that *management must manage,* then all those perfectly logical explanations do not count. The only thing that counts is that the desired results were achieved or that they were not achieved.

But most people do not believe that. Managers in all too many American companies do not achieve the desired results because nobody makes them do it. Explanations and rationalizations are all too readily accepted. They are even expected. Everyone knows it. The company president sets a sales goal and the sales manager and all his salesmen know that he will accept 80 percent of that figure, and that's all they will give him. In fact, if they go over that 80 percent figure, some of them will hide those sales so that they can use those figures for the next year, when they know the quotas will be raised. It happens all the time. You get what you expect to get. Seldom, if ever, do you get more.

The question of quality control in industry is a good example. In days gone by it was assumed that in a hazardous industry, one, two, or ten men would be killed and more would be injured in accidents. It was taken for granted. It happened year after year. Then the need for quality control to protect human life became imperative.

The death of even one man was not acceptable. The goal became zero defects in those operations. Lo and behold, those operations were redesigned and redesigned until deaths caused by a breakdown or a fault in the assembly line became zero. Further procedures were instituted to teach the men how to avoid human error. I remember well in the steel industry, when I was at Jones & Laughlin, the posting each day of the number of days that we had gone without a single death at the open hearths, blast furnaces, and finishing mills. As the accident-free days piled up, perhaps to 364 and 365 days, everyone grew tense, expecting the break. We had all become overly safety conscious. But if we hadn't tried, we would have had a continuation of frequent accidents.

It has taken much longer for the concept of zero defects in products to become the norm of American industry. A company turning out a million toasters a year expects a certain percentage of them to be defective or substandard—2, 3, 5 percent, or whatever. And they get what they expect. Those figures are built into the budget. Perhaps when 7 or 10 percent of the toasters, or whatever the product is, are returned as defective, the company might look into its quality control. Then it becomes management's decision: How much should they spend for how many more quality controls to achieve how many fewer defects? In high-technology products, it is far less expensive to install production-line controls than to maintain a huge maintenance staff to make costly repairs on defective products in the field. In ITT telephonic switching equipment, our standard was zero defects. We simply insisted upon it. The same is true in aircraft design and production. Faulty parts clearly are not acceptable.

When it comes to other products, however, there is a trade-off between quality control and price. General Motors, Ford, or Chrysler could build a zero-defect automobile, one that would last for twenty years, or at least I presume they could. It could be built of stainless steel and equipped with computer devices to monitor each function. But the car would probably cost $200,000 and become obsolete long before it wore out. At ITT we had a superb quality control expert named Philip Crosby who demonstrated to our line managers through cost analysis that it was cheaper to control the quality of the product on the production line than it was to repair it in the field afterwards. He insisted that a manufacturer had to set a standard of quality, set the controls to maintain that standard, and then figure the cost of those controls into the price of the product. His point was that quality control did not, per se, mean higher quality; it meant control of the quality. Thus, you could not expect a $100 piece of equipment to perform like a $400 one. But you, as management, should set the standards of quality and not accept anything less.

In quality control, you are controlling the down side. You are stipulating how many defects, how many minus numbers, are acceptable. That is only one portion of management's job, controlling the plus numbers of production. Sales and earnings should be handled precisely the same way. A manager, first of all, must set his standards of production, sales, market share, earnings, whatever, and anything short of those standards should be unacceptable to him. What should those standards be? It depends upon the industry, the products, and the manager himself. They have to be acceptable to *him*. He knows what he should be doing, if he is a manager. Certainly the industry and his competitors have set certain standards. But beyond that, he is the best judge of whether or not he is doing a good job. He sets the standards and he must manage to achieve them.

Recently I met a man who operates the jewelry concession in a number of department stores and he told me, "I don't think I'm doing my job unless I get four percent of the store's traffic."

"How do you know it's four percent you need?" I asked.

"I don't," he replied, "it just works out that way."

"Why not five percent?" I asked.

"No, just four percent," he insisted, explaining that 4 percent was more than any other counter in the department store got. Without sophisticated controls, this man had set his own standards. He couldn't sleep if he did not get that 4 percent. He would feel guilty if he did not get it. He would work through the night, he would do anything he had to, but he would get that 4 percent. I don't know precisely what he did, and perhaps 5 or 8 percent is possible, but it makes little difference. He was managing. He was an entrepreneur.

The primary difference between an entrepreneur and a professional business manager, generally speaking, is one of attitude. The entrepreneur, especially when starting out, knows that he is operating on the threshold of success or failure. A single mistake can ruin him. He can't afford that single mistake. He has to reach a certain market, make a stipulated amount of sales, and earn enough money to carry him forward. While others leave the office at five o'clock, he stays behind and works to solve those problems that beset his business. He must manage. He takes his problems home with him. He lives his business twenty-four hours a day.

The professional business manager all too often loses that sense of commitment, if he had it in the first place. All too often, he manages by the book. He relies upon the knowledge that he is working for a company large enough to absorb a number of mistakes. The professional manager does not set out to make mistakes or to succumb to a bad turn in the marketplace. He wants to succeed. Subconsciously he allows himself what he considers a reasonable margin of error. But that margin usually is far wider than that of the entrepreneur running his own business. And that margin of error is accepted! The plant manager or sales manager explains the situation to the division manager and he explains to the vice president and the president explains to the board of directors. Out come all the logical, rational excuses and they are accepted. What we have here, to my mind, is an attitude of permissiveness which allows management the luxury of not managing.

Why do boards of directors, stockholders, and financial analysts accept less than acceptable results? Because it is much more difficult to measure non-performance than performance. Performance stands out like a ton of diamonds. Non-performance can almost always be explained away. When you hear the next business report that retail sales are down across the nation because of a cold wave that is sweeping the country, you can rest assured that some retailer in Minnesota enjoyed an increase in sales and earnings that week, while another retailer in the Sunbelt suffered losses. Why? Because one was a manager, managing his business, and the other was a victim of events which he thought were beyond his control.

Judging the efficacy of management is not a subjective exercise. It can be measured at the end of the quarter or at the end of the year by the P&L statement. You look at the numbers and see what happened: Management either achieved its goal or it didn't. It managed or it did not manage. To me, everything else is nonsense. One could stretch the time limit to, say, three years, particularly in a start-up situation. Surely by that time, one should have given a clear indication of the performance of management. In an ongoing company, you can measure it by the quarter. I used to tell my management team at ITT that making the first quarter's quotas was the most important segment of the year. If you don't make your budget quota that first quarter, you probably won't make it for the year. If you make it the first quarter, then the second quarter, and then the third quarter, you probably will breeze through that fourth quarter. It always seems to work that way.

What do you do if your company or your division or your department has not made its quotas for the first quarter? First of all, you locate the problem. Then you find the cause of the problem. Then you fix it. That is why we had the comptrollers of every ITT company sending us in headquarters the figures of their companies every week. Less than satisfactory results show up in those reports very clearly. That's why our line managers "red-flagged" their major problems for immediate attention. That's why we held monthly managers meetings. We wanted to pinpoint the causes of the problems and find the best solutions as quickly as possible. If sales were down, we wanted to find out why they were down. Depending upon the cause, we might decide to increase our advertising and promotion; we might decide to change our marketing strategy, or change our distribution network, or change the packaging, or change the model of the product itself; or we might decide to reduce the cost of manufacturing the product so that we could cut its price.

We used everything available to us to get results. We used everything we had learned at school, everything we had learned from our own experience in business, everything we could learn from one another. We used our intuition. We used our brains.

"Management must manage" became our credo at ITT. It meant that we would do everything we had to do (that was honest and legal) to bring in the results we desired. If one solution to a problem did not work, we tried another. And another. Our red-flag items remained on the first page of each company's monthly report, updated for changes, every single month until they were solved. A red-flag item was like a thorn in an ITT manager's side, an embarrassment to his pride in his ability. He had to solve it. He could not merely walk into one of our meetings and announce that he still had the problem, that nothing had changed. He had to tell me and our headquarters management team and his peers what he was doing and what he proposed to do about that problem. He was not there merely to report on the situation; he was there to tell us how he was managing. If he was stumped, we would send him help, all the help he needed; *together* we would manage. But we *would* manage.

I brought this point home at a General Managers Meeting early in my reign at ITT when the man in charge of our Latin America operations reported that he had failed to sell our newest, multimillion-dollar telephone switching system to the government of Brazil. I probed for quite a while into the efforts that had been made, the presentation given, the facts of the situation. He told me of all the avenues he had explored.

"Who makes the final decision there on whether or not they buy our system?" I asked.

"President Kubitschek."

"Did you see him?"

"No."

"Why not?"

"Because _____ really makes the decision. He recommends the decision and the President follows his advice," he explained, adding, "Besides, I don't think I can get in to see Kubitschek."

"Well, why don't you try? You have everything to gain and nothing to lose."

The following month, he returned to announce with a sheepish grin on his face that he had seen the President of Brazil and had sold the ITT system. It went over quite big. The men in the room applauded him.

At a succession of General Managers Meetings in Europe, we were all stumped over a serious problem of inventory control. Our European inventory of supplies, which usually ran between $2 and $3 billion, had risen some $500 million above desired levels, and we were paying interest every month on those idle supplies. We had had checks and rechecks on that over-abundance of component parts for our telephonic and electronic manufacturing companies. Task force after task force had investigated, and month after month those inventories seemed to be rising. Finally, at one meeting, one manager suggested that he had solved his own inventory problem by placing a man at the receiving dock of each of his factories with instructions to turn back any supplies that were not needed or ordered. It was such a simple solution. And it worked. We put a staff man at the receiving dock of every one of our factories in Europe and he turned back an avalanche of supplies that were being unloaded upon us, often in advance of our own orders.

The point is, of course, that in managing you must be in control of your operations. If something goes wrong, you probe until you find the cause, and if one solution does not work, you try another, and another, and another. Managing means to manage.

Good management is more than solving problems as they arise. Good planning must include the anticipation of problems that are likely to arise and the steps to be taken to avoid them, or, if you cannot avoid them beforehand, to handle them as soon as they arise. A good manager learns from his experience and by the time he heads a company or a division he should have developed something of a sixth sense for what works and what does not work. He should have acquired the ability to analyze a situation and the problems and the people involved so that he can choose among the various alternatives the best possible course of action. Then, if he is a cautious man, he should be prepared as to his next course of action if the first one fails. That's doing your homework.

It is a discipline that is built into the credo of "Management must manage."

Part of that discipline is recognizing that the first answer you receive is not necessarily the best one. That is why I put so much emphasis upon probing for unshakable facts. They are hard to come by. The truth is that the so-called "facts" are almost always colored by the bias of the man presenting them. So you might do well to get your "facts" from a variety of sources. Salesmen will always reflect what their customers are telling them, and they tend to exaggerate the parameters either on the up or on the down side; marketing men put their faith in statistical analyses of what the market *should* be for your product, with little regard for what your customers are saying; engineers usually have an idea for a new product (which may or may not be what the market or the customers want at that time); someone else will have a dream of what *could* happen if only . . . and someone else will have a nightmare about all the things that could go wrong. The manager in charge must take the "facts" presented by each of them, strip away the biases, including his own, and try to get a true picture of what is involved. As in the childhood game of tracing the image on a coin by rubbing a pencil on the paper covering the coin, a more or less distinct image will show up with increased strokes of the pencil. As more and more different sources report the "facts" to you, the reality of the situation (or as close to it as you can come) will emerge.

Then, you as the manager must decide and take action. When you can see a situation clearly, I have found, the decision is clear and easy. The facts make the decision for you. Sometimes, when the image is vague and you cannot get enough facts, you still may have to act. But you act with some caution, aware that you don't have all the facts at hand, knowing that the situation can change suddenly and radically. Nevertheless, it is often more important to act and maintain the momentum of action because with momentum, as in a sailboat, you can still change course. Without momentum, you're dead in the water. Managing means making something happen, not studying it to death while opportunities pass you by.

Experience has taught me what I came to call the inverse ratio of time to veracity. It has long seemed to me that the lower you are in the corporate hierarchy, the more time you have to verify the facts upon which you were acting, and the less likely you are to do so; and the higher you rise and the greater your responsibilities, the less time you have to check your facts, and the more important it is to do so. As a public accountant at the beginning of my career, doing a general audit of a company, I was given all the time I needed to check the books or the inventory. I spent days counting coal bins for one company and then I certified the "fact" that there were so many filled coal bins, so many tons of coal. As I rose to comptroller, I had to rely upon the veracity of someone else's audit. When I became president of ITT, I had to rely upon hundreds and hundreds of different reports, full of "facts," and the decisions I had to make were crucial. That is why I insisted upon unshakable facts and that is why I cross-examined the men who brought me those "facts." I did not have the time to do the counting myself. I had 250 subsidiary companies to monitor, while each manager of a profit center had only one. So he had more time to check the facts than I did. And the men reporting to him had more time than he did to check the facts in their departments. But each of us was responsible, I for the whole of ITT and each of them for his own unit in the organization. Few things to my mind were more important in managing than checking the facts, bearing in mind the Law of Inverse Time-to-Veracity. Management seldom makes the wrong decisions per se. Things go wrong, and sometimes seriously wrong, when management makes the "right" decision based upon "facts" which are mistaken, misleading, or overlooked.

The most costly management mistake we made at ITT was in building a giant wood-cellulose-processing plant in Port-Cartier, Quebec, as part of our expansion plans for Rayonier, a forest-products company we acquired in 1968. In our usual exploring to develop the future potential of this new company, Rayonier's management suggested that it had long sought to build such a plant. Only the need for capital had prevented it from going ahead. Millions of acres of virgin timberland—about the size of the state of Tennessee—could be leased in Quebec Province from the Canadian government for very little money, and new technology made it feasible to build a processing plant at the edge of the timberland which could convert the wood to cellulose. The cost of the plant was estimated at $120 million. Once completed, the new modern plant would make Rayonier, which we had acquired for $293 million in ITT common and preferred stock, into the largest cellulose manufacturer in the nation.

Rayonier's plans were checked and rechecked, the risks and rewards were carefully analyzed, and we decided to go ahead. The usual gauntlet of problems showed up, but they were more or less anticipated. Then we encountered unexpected union problems at the project. To make matters worse, the new technology to recycle chemicals used to process the wood developed serious flaws. But these problems could have been managed in time, I thought. What stumped us was a fundamental miscalculation made at the outset of the project: All those lovely trees out there in the wilderness of Canada's Far North grew to no more than three inches in diameter, because of the extreme cold. The cost of harvesting and transporting them to the plant precluded the possibility of a profitable venture. We could not "manage" the size of the trees. Ten years after we had started, we had to abandon the project and take a loss of approximately $320 million. A good part of that loss was recouped when we sold off the entire Canadian subsidiary of Rayonier for $355 million. But that $320 million loss could have been averted if someone had actually gone up and looked at those trees before we had begun. Instead we had relied upon some very shaky "facts" indeed. We had seen the forest, the plant, the profits, and not the you-know-what.

Our venture into the hotel business is a good, even an extreme, example of dedication to the concept of "Management must manage." In the late 1960s, at about the same time we got involved with the problems of Rayonier, we decided to buy a hotel chain. The fundamentals of the hotel business looked good to us. In fact, we bought franchises to eight Holiday Inn motels in the Cleveland area and were negotiating to buy that chain.

The future potential of hotels and motels looked extremely promising because a good deal of the whole operation had just become computerized, particularly the reservation system. Holiday Inns had a central computer which handled all reservations for its facilities across the country with one toll-free telephone number. The computer also monitored the occupancy rate of each hotel and motel, so that the company could plan future expansions with considerable accuracy. However, negotiations to buy the Holiday Inn chain fell through. We then approached Hilton, which had sold off its European hotels to Trans World Airlines. Conrad Hilton escorted me around the Palmer House in Chicago, describing the operations of his successful hotel chain. But his price was too high. So we turned to the Sheraton Corporation of America, whose earnings on a percentage basis were the lowest in the industry. Its hotels were ancient, with an average age of thirty years, and in dire need of repairs. Even worse, the Sheraton hotels were located in depressed city core areas, and few people saw any way of improving Sheraton's overall situation. Against the advice of some of our own people, we bought the Sheraton chain in 1968. We thought we could turn it around.

Aware of the problems we would encounter, we earmarked some $700 million for renovations and the building of new Sheraton hotels. The numbers in the business seemed right to us. We had hotel building expertise within ITT and thought that we would be able to borrow almost 100 percent of the construction money needed, which could be paid back out of earnings on our new hotels. It did not work out that way. We were not that expert in building hotels, the banks would not give us 100 percent financing, and while our new hotels in South America did well, the earnings on our new hotels in Western Europe lagged seriously behind our budget forecasts. For years, the operation ran in the red. It became a blot upon the fine record we had achieved through the 1960s. As we poured more and more money into Sheraton, some security analysts thought the flow would be endless.

We tried one thing after another. Some of our own people advised me to give up, to sell Sheraton. We had task force after task force studying the management problems of Sheraton. The hotel chain was hurting our cash flow. We changed the management we had acquired with the company and put in our own man, who had been running Avis Rent-A-Car, to head Sheraton, figuring that the two businesses were not unsimilar. Avis bought cars and rented them out by the mile and later by the day; Sheraton bought rooms and beds and rented them out by the night. But our Avis man could not solve Sheraton's problems. We replaced him with one of our top financial men, hoping he could manage the money problems. But he could do no better. We replaced him with a seasoned hotel man, Howard James.

Bud James, after trying all the usual management techniques, went back to the fundamentals. Examining the common thread in our problems with Sheraton, he came up with a new, imaginative, and creative idea. James pointed out to us that ITT was a management company and not a real estate enterprise. Once we accepted that "fact," Bud recommended that we get out of the brick-and-mortar part of the hotel business altogether, and confine ourselves only to managing the hotels. We gave him our support, and he went ahead and began selling off our old hotels and ITT's ownership in our new hotels to investors who could benefit from the tax advantages in owning real estate. We would take a management fee for operating the hotels. It was a nice fit for both sides, and as Bud put it pleasantly, it would enable us to "grow with other people's money."

From the time we bought Sheraton, it took us eight years to turn the operation around. Today there are first-class ITT Sheraton hotels around the world earning some $100 million a year, after taxes. By selling off hotels and with joint ventures, ITT's capital investment in Sheraton

Hotels has been reduced to just about zero. Recently, ITT was offered well over a billion dollars for the Sheraton chain, and turned it down. That's management to be proud of.

With Sheraton, we tried one possibility after another in our quest for a solution to the hotel chain's problems. I was convinced Sheraton's woes were basically a management problem, and that we at ITT should be able to solve it. I had so much faith in that concept that in 1971, when Sheraton was still operating in the red and ITT was obliged to divest itself of $1 billion in assets as part of a settlement of the federal government's antitrust suit, I chose to keep Sheraton and to sell Avis. My reasoning was that Avis had pretty nearly fulfilled its potential; that its earnings would bring us a good price, and there was little more room for growth. Sheraton, on the other hand, had virtually unlimited potential for growth, and our management job was to make it grow.

Rayonier is an equally good, if extreme, example of another management principle that I have long held (and, as you have seen, used personally in my career decisions): If you cannot solve the problems of your environment, change your environment. We could not change those trees; that had been a fundamental miscalculation; we were stymied by the other problems at Port-Cartier. So we sold that portion of the business.

"Management must manage" does not mean that management has to be perfect, solving every problem, reaching every goal, making every business venture an outstanding success. In sports, no team, however good, wins all its games. You just have to be good enough to win most of them. In business you just have to be better than the next fellow competing with you. How much better than the next fellow depends upon the standards you set. But you must manage to achieve the results set by those standards. If you find that you cannot, that is also an acceptable answer. Then you change your environment: You sell off that business and get into something else. But you sell it off at the standards it should produce, even if they don't meet yours. You change. That is managing. What you *don't* do is go on accepting inadequate results and explaining them.

The acid test is not the explanation, however logical and reasonable. The test is whether or not you as a manager accept as satisfactory those unsatisfactory results, without doing enough about it. "Management must manage" means in reality that management must manage. It is as simple as that.

The significant difference between one manager and another is what standards each of them sets, what each establishes to meet his own requirements for satisfactory management. My real contribution to ITT as a manager was to raise those standards of management beyond what most people there thought were possible. The levels of achievement I insisted upon went right down through the ranks of the entire company. We stretched and stretched, we reached, we managed, and we achieved our goals. And we felt good about it. Conveying that concept, "Management must manage," throughout the company is, I suppose, what they call leadership. But leadership is more than managing.

SIX

Leadership

*Leadership cannot really be taught. It can only
be learned.*

LEADERSHIP is the very heart and soul of business management. No one really manages a business by shuffling the numbers or rearranging organizational charts or applying the latest business school formulas. What you manage in business is people.

Management and leadership are of course inextricably intertwined, but for the sake of clearer understanding, I think of business management as something objective: You want to accomplish an objective, to get from here to there, and your performance can be measured. You can be taught the tools of your trade in a school of business administration. In fact, if you pass all your examinations, you are rewarded with the title "Master of Business Administration." But the legion of young men and women who come out of the business schools each year, armed with calculators and computer science, are at best enlightened business administrators, not leaders. Leadership is something else again. It is purely subjective, difficult to define, virtually impossible to measure objectively, and cannot be taught in school, any more than a baseball player can learn to throw a curve ball by reading a manual. And yet it is always palpably there in every enterprise, setting the personality of each individual company, a reflection of the character and personality of the chief executive and his top management team of players. To my mind, the quality of leadership is the single most important ingredient in the recipe for business success.

Leadership, of course, is the ability to inspire other

people to work together as a team, following your lead, in order to attain a common objective, whether in business, in politics, in war, or on the football field. No one can do it all alone. Others must want to follow the leader. I don't particularly subscribe to the theory that there are natural, born leaders. Leadership is learned, although I cannot explain entirely how it is learned. The ability to lead and inspire others is far more instinctual than premeditated and it is acquired somehow through the experiences of one's everyday life, and the ultimate nature and quality of that leadership comes out of the innate character and personality of the leader himself.

My own style of leadership at ITT was not deliberately calculated to accomplish set goals. In fact, it was not calculated at all. It was much more instinctual. I established high, challenging goals for the company because that was the kind of man I was when I came to ITT. I did not even think of it in those terms at the time. But now, upon reflection, I can see that it probably goes back to my days as a student at Suffield Academy. I worked conscientiously because I liked to get good marks and it bothered me if I got a poor one. I was delighted when a teacher wrote "well done" or "interesting" on one of my papers. I learned at Suffield that I had to earn whatever I got, but I also discovered that good marks made me feel good, even proud. They stimulated me to do more. When I worked all kinds of hours to sell classified ads for the old *World-Telegram,* I did it because I was scared. I was afraid not to work hard. I did not want to fail. Out in the business world, I wanted to do as well as or better than the next fellow and I was willing to work hard for that distinction. I came to realize that the challenge the business world offered was exciting and I was positively delighted with the feeling of accomplishment when I exceeded even my own expectations in getting a particularly difficult job done.

So, at ITT I instinctively sought to instill something of the same kind of spirit into the management of the company. I had always enjoyed going to work. In fact, I never thought of it as work. It was a part of my life, a part of the environment in which I lived and breathed. I often told colleagues that business was as much fun as golf, tennis, sailing, dancing, or almost anything else you might want to name. The pleasures were different from those of eating an ice-cream sundae. Business provided intellectual challenges that stimulated and fed one's mind. They were every bit as good in their own way as the momentary pleasures of gobbling down one's dessert, and they were more durable. The sweetness lasted longer. Business could be a great adventure, a lot of fun, something to look forward to every day, and the rewards went much further than one's annual salary and bonuses.

I wanted to create that kind of an invigorating, challenging, creative atmosphere at ITT. I wanted to get the people there to reach for goals that they might think were beyond them. I wanted them to accomplish more than they thought was possible. And I wanted them to do it not only for the company and their careers but also for the fun of it. I wanted them to enjoy the process of tackling a difficult piece of business, solving it, and going on to bigger, better, and tougher challenges. I wanted them to do this, not for self-aggrandizement, but as part of a greater team effort, in which each player realized his own contribution to the team, knew that he was needed and appreciated, and took pride and self-satisfaction from playing a winning game. My job as chief executive, as I saw it, was to unlock whatever inhibitions or fears bound these people in chains of insecurity. The way to do that was to create at ITT a climate of growth and opportunity, a climate in which each fellow would want to carry his own share, and would be driven to excel not only because I pushed him but because of peer pressure and pride.

The best hope of achieving that, given my own sense of leadership, was to jump in the boat, grab an oar, and start pulling along with the other men. I suppose you might call it participatory leadership. I didn't want to be the captain sitting in the back of the boat, exhorting his men to do all the work while he sat there doing nothing. Nor did I want to be like the master of a galley, frightening his slaves half to death with the giant whip in his hands. I worked as long and as hard as any man at ITT and they knew it. I worked those twelve- and sixteen-hour days, traveled back and forth to Europe, carried briefcases of work home with me every weekend—not because I wanted to set an example. I did it because I had to do it in order to get my own work done competently. But I did set an example, an honest example, which traveled down the ranks of management and, to an extent, established a standard of performance for the whole company. After all, if I could do it, so could the next man—if he had any measure of pride in his own ability.

The rationale for the value of working extra hours is clear-cut in my mind. Consider two men of generally equal intelligence and ability: One works eight hours a day for ten years; the other works twelve hours a day for ten years. At the end of ten years, one man has ten years' experience; the other will have fifteen years' experience. Which one would you hire? Consider two rival business managers or two chief executives in a competitive situation, one working an eight-hour day, the other a ten- or twelve-hour day. Which one is more likely to become the better businessman?

On the practical side, the first obligation of any chief executive is to set the goals for his company. It is his responsibility to point his people in the direction of the goalposts, and tell them how to get there. He is the only man who can do it. That, too, will come out of his personality and character as a leader. If he is satisfied with mediocre results, that's what he will get. In a railroad company, the primary goal might be to ensure that the trains will run on time; in a utility, that the electric, gas, or telephone service will not be interrupted. At ITT, I set a much more competitive and challenging goal: a steady, stable growth of 10 to 15 percent increase in earnings per share for each and every year. Together, we set out to double our earnings in five years.

I never let up. I talked about growth, how we were going to achieve it, and I talked about more growth. In the beginning at ITT, I spent night after night talking with our management teams about what we were going to do with the company, discussing how we intended to do it. As the years went on, every time we acquired a new company we would give a welcoming dinner for the new company's management and we would talk about our goal of at least 10 percent annual growth. It did not make any difference if times were good or bad. When they were good, we should be able to make our goal easily; when they were bad, we had to work harder. But we had to make our goal each and every year. That was the message. And the new company managements believed us, because they knew that we meant what we were saying.

Now, it must be understood that we were not *ordering* these men to increase their earnings by 10 to 15 percent each year. We were telling them that we were all going to do it together, that the headquarters management team, including the chief executive, was there to help them achieve these goals. In short, we were all in the same boat, sink or survive, and we all would be rowing very hard, but in the end it would all prove to be worthwhile for all of us.

In every well-organized company there must be a sense of balance that is understood by every man and woman who works there. If you are seeking the best people available, and if you expect them to stretch beyond the ordinary, even beyond what they think are their capabilities, you have to reward them commensurately. One of the first things we did at ITT when I got there was to move onto the fast track. We set out to hire the very best people in the industry that we could find. I did not want glamorous, glib-talking men who got by on their coiffured good looks or family connections. Nor did I want geniuses who were so smart that they could not get along with the rest of us mere mortals. No, what we sought were capable, experienced men who were motivated, who wanted to achieve and to make something of their lives, and who were not afraid to work hard for what they wanted. Of course, we wanted people who were intelligent, knowledgeable, and experienced, but in choosing among candidates who had those attributes, I wanted men around me who shared my enthusiasm for work.

In order to attract and to keep these kinds of executives at ITT, we paid our people a base salary 10 percent higher than the industry averages and supplemented those salaries with generous year-end bonuses and salary increases as merited. More than that, we moved them up fast through the ranks. We gave them as much responsibility as they wanted and could handle, regardless of age or past experience, and they thrived on it. ITT became an exciting place in which to work.

Within a few years, the men who could not keep the pace and those who did not want to, for one reason or another, left ITT of their own volition or upon our request. But men still in their thirties rose to head some ITT companies; some men in their forties advanced to run groups of companies. As time went on, our management work force stabilized, and then critics or cynics began to say that I kept my people because they could not bear to give up the high pay and perks given them at ITT. Manifestly not true. Good management executives, with a proven track record, are a rare breed. They can get high pay and long limousines almost anywhere they choose to go. Those who remained with us did so because they were happy in the ITT environment, where we all worked hard, were continually challenged, were amply rewarded, and could continue to grow. They stayed, too, out of a sense of well-being and loyalty.

Of those who left ITT in the early days, most were men who did not fit in with our new pace of unremitting hard work. Later, for the most part, those who left us were men who were offered jobs that were so good that I gave them my good wishes. I would not try to stop a man or woman from accepting an extraordinary personal opportunity. To do so would be so unfair that I would have lost his or her faith and loyalty in the long run. No chief executive likes to lose a good team player for any reason. But, to my mind, the very worst reason would be losing a person because you were not paying him or her enough.

Once the right men are in place, a company's working environment becomes the most important ongoing element in the success or failure of the enterprise. The climate control is in the hands of the chief executive. He sets the temperature and quality of the air of the place. From experience, I knew that the chief executive establishes the personality of the whole company. People under him carry out his orders and tend to emulate his style. What he does and how he does it is repeated after a fashion down through the ranks of the company.

To me, the most important element in establishing a happy, prosperous atmosphere was an insistence upon open, free, and honest communications up and down the ranks of our management structure. That was the reason behind our numerous and frequent meetings: General Managers Meetings, budget review meetings, problem oriented meetings, ad hoc meetings. Every manager had a direct line to top management at headquarters We cut through layers of fat in our management ranks by putting all the people in one room so they could talk with one another, face to face, regardless of rank, and an honest assessment of any situation could be based upon the facts which emerged.

But that is only the surface of the matter. Beneath that surface was the clear understanding that we *owed* each other our honest opinions at all times. People could disagree with me or with anyone else; they could criticize me or anyone else, and no one would suffer as a consequence. I tried to welcome criticism. Naturally, no one *likes* to be criticized. One's first instinct is to be defensive and fight back. But that is the kind of defensiveness one should try to keep under control. I consciously tried to lean over backwards to avoid bridling when someone disagreed with me. I always wanted someone to point out where I might be heading for a mistake. I never batted down such a man. I listened and we exchanged views. Sometimes I was clearly wrong; sometimes he was mistaken. Not infrequently, it was a little of both. Almost always new facts and new ideas emerged and our exchange would reveal a better course of action which neither of us had envisioned before. But more important than the encounter itself was that at meetings others observed what was happening and word got around the company that one could speak his mind, disagree with the boss, and be heard. Being open to criticism usually pays unexpected dividends. People were also free to come to me or to anyone else and ask honestly for help, and they would get it, again without fear of any diminution of status, rank, or whatever. We were all in the same lifeboat, all pulling toward a single goal. That was our underlying philosophy.

In order to safeguard this policy of open and honest communications, it seemed to me that office politicking could not be tolerated in any shape or form. I announced this in unmistakable terms: If anyone tried to line up other managers to back his pet project in return for his later vote, or if anyone tried to force a man junior to him to give anything other than his honest opinion, he did so in peril of losing his job. It was dishonest. Truth went to the very heart of good management. Decisions had to be based upon an honest examination of the facts and not be swayed by one man leaning on another through rank, threat, reciprocity, friendship, or whatever. Furthermore, I wanted anyone who was so importuned in any way to report the circumstance to me privately. I promised to protect him and to take care of the situation myself privately.

It happened once that I can recall vividly. A vice president came into my office and told me in detail how a senior officer at headquarters had asked him to change his opinion and to back the senior official on one of his pet projects, saying that he would in time return the favor. The vice president, a relatively new man with us, did not know what to do. I thanked him for being honest and told him to put the matter out of his mind, to keep it confidential, and said that I would take care of it. I called the senior executive into my office and read him the riot act.

When he reached my desk, I did not ask him to sit down, as I usually did. Instead, I told him, ''Don't say a word, because if you say one word, you're fired.'' Then I repeated in detail the story I had been told, without revealing the source, for I felt sure that he had done the same thing with several men. ''Now, that's the story I've learned, and I believe it, because it rings true,'' I told him, warning him again, ''Don't say a word. I don't want an answer. I just want you to know that I know. Also, I am warning you now that if you ever do that again and I hear about it, I am going to fire you, and I am not even going to tell you why. You'll know why. Don't say a word. Just leave, and we'll never talk about this again.'' He turned on his heel and left, without saying a word.

I would like to be able to report that that man never tried such a thing again and that office politics was wiped out at ITT. But that millennium never arrived. I do believe, however, that office politics was kept to a minimum at ITT, in contrast to what goes on in the vast majority of American industrial companies, and only partly because of the dire consequences I threatened. Personal maneuvering spreads most malignantly in stagnant companies. At ITT we were expanding so fast that there was plenty of room for our management people to advance and grow with the company, without personal power plays or petty maneuvering. The important point for any management is that office politics should never be tolerated because it is a form of unfair self-aggrandizement which, if not curbed, will destroy the morale and forward thrust of any company.

The "firing line" is perhaps the most acute test of a company's leadership. Who gets fired and why and when and even how goes to the very heart of the character of a company, its management, and its leadership. Obviously, it is the responsibility of the leader, whether he be the manager of a plant, a group vice president, or the chief executive, to weed out of the system those people who are not contributing or who are impeding the general efforts of all the others. Unfortunately, there always are some people in every company who simply do not want to work. They may be lazy or disturbed or resentful or otherwise preoccupied, but, for whatever reason, they don't do their share, nor do they want to. Then there are those people with personality traits which make it difficult for them to work with their peers or their subordinates. It is easy enough to recognize such people on the assembly line in the factory. In the ranks of management, it is considerably more difficult. Nevertheless, everyone around such a person recognizes that he or she is a faker, a phony, or whatever word you might want to use. Nor will others ordinarily tell the "boss" what is going on. But they will be watching and judging. And it is the duty of the leader to recognize that kind of person and to get rid of him. It may take a bit of time before the laggard's excuses, glib talk, or downright lies catch up with him. But the alert leader will recognize the clues and will move forcefully as soon as he learns the facts. And when he does, he will earn the respect of all the others who are hardworking, imaginative, and productive and who have long resented the freeloaders in their ranks. In that sense, firing people can be a constructive role of a company's management. It clears the air and improves the climate.

Firing people is always difficult. It's the moment of truth for a business leader. You never face the problem of firing somebody without truthfully, honestly examining the question of how much you yourself have contributed to the situation. Are you firing him because the company is under pressure to cut costs, cause of general economic conditions, or because you are losing business and market share? If so, then it isn't his fault, it's yours. You were supposed to run the company so that it would be strong enough to weather bad economic conditions without laying off people and smart enough not to be caught in the crunch of new products or marketing trends.

You may be firing him because he has done a poor job. Even he knows it. But you have to ask yourself: Did he do a bad job because he was not helped? He was entitled to help. If he couldn't do the job alone, you were supposed to be smart enough to be able to help him. Maybe it's not all his fault. Maybe you failed again. Perhaps a man is failing because he inherited a tough problem that no one else can solve; or he is caught in a situation completely beyond his control.

The most difficult task of all is firing a man who *is* working hard, doing the best he can, but whose confidence in himself far outstrips his abilities. He's over his head. His judgment or lack of judgment might even be a serious danger to the whole operation. It breaks your heart to have to tell such a man that he is incompetent. After all, you probably gave him raises and promotions for ten years. It was you who put him in deep water over his head.

Or consider the man who has faithfully served the company well for twenty or thirty years, and now is in failing health and ability? He is only two or three years away from retirement. What would you do with him?

There is no simple formula for firing people. There will always be, and should be, exceptions to every rule you devise. How you handle each of the above cases, however, will determine what kind of leader you are, how much respect you command and deserve from your colleagues, and ultimately the personality and character of the company you lead. You have to take action. You have to clear the decks for all the other people who are performing up to your standards and perhaps are carrying the extra burden of those who are not. They expect it of you.

In physics it is well known that for every action there is a reaction. Every time a chief executive takes an action for or against someone in the company, either firing or promoting a man, there is a reaction throughout the company. The reaction is not simply between the boss and the man he is dealing with. The way he handles the situation involves not only the action and reaction between them. It reverberates to all the others down the line and they pass judgment upon what the boss did and the way he did it, and they react accordingly.

So you have to let all those people go—except for that last fellow so close to retirement. He has earned his right to stay on in his job, even at the expense of efficiency. Perhaps you can move him laterally somewhere, so that someone else can take over his former position. He knows the score. So do all the others around him. If you fired him, the message would be clear: It's the company policy to pay you as long as you are useful and then throw you on the junk heap when you're old and gray. Who would give loyalty to a company like that? As for the others, it is your duty to let them go, however unpleasant it may be. But you can do it as decently and as painlessly as possible. The willing but over-his-head manager can be helped to find another job for which he is better suited without destroying his self-confidence. Demoting him would do him (and the company) more harm than good.

Ultimately, a good leader should do the decent thing. He should know what the decent thing is; everyone else does. No one wants his or her leader to be tolerant of incompetence either through ignorance, indecisiveness, or weakness. No one wants to follow a weak leader. He is the worst kind. You cannot rely upon his judgment because you don't know what he will do in a difficult situation. Much more respect and loyalty is given to the tough leader, the one who is not afraid to make difficult and even unpopular decisions, just as long as he is perceived to be decent and fair and reliable in his dealings with his subordinates.

One final word on firing the man who is not pulling his oar, as such episodes apply to the crucial role of the leader. Others in the organization will not come and tell you about him. But in time, almost instinctively, a good executive will recognize the faults as well as the attributes of the men working for him. Almost always his reactions to the man will be the same as those of others who deal with him, whether he is unreliable, vacillating, or insufferably arrogant, or whatever. And when you, as the leader, give the man his walking papers, only then will the others come forward and comment. They had all been wondering how long it would take you to wake up to the reality of the situation.

By the same token, when a good person is in trouble (and it happens to the best) it is incumbent upon a leader to support and help that person as far as possible. You owe that person your loyalty because loyalty is always a two-way street. Once again, your actions will reverberate through the whole company.

As president and then chairman of ITT, I was perceived from the outside as a tough man to work for. I was often portrayed that way in the press. The stereotype of the difficult, ruthless s.o.b. driving his subordinates to early graves in his quest for quarterly profits makes good copy and sells magazines. Actually, the management team that stayed with ITT through the years, and took over when I retired, thrived on the fast pace and on the action and growth that we engendered. In recent years, since my retirement, I have received many letters from men who said that those early, growing years with ITT had been the most thrilling time of their lives.

As a matter of policy, which was stamped upon the management of all 250 profit centers of ITT, we treated every company manager as an individual entrepreneur. We were demanding, but decent. I often made the point that the facts of any given situation were making the demands upon the man, not me. I might criticize what he had done or failed to do, but my attacks were never personal. At meetings large and small, I never demeaned a man's ability or threatened him. Sarcasm or personal attacks were not countenanced at any level. I've seen more good, imaginative ideas nipped in the bud by a clever, sarcastic remark than by logical, informative criticism. Open communication meant that every man was entitled to speak his piece. I wanted my people to be as imaginative and creative as they could possibly be. When I thought a man deserved a dressing-down for something he had done or failed to do, I did it privately. I wanted *him* to know how I felt, not others.

Good ideas are hard to come by and I always felt that as chief executive it was incumbent upon me to welcome and foster imaginative thinking. The chief executive is the man in the best position to take the risk of allocating money for a seemingly wild idea. At least he should be. Those under him are too often in fear of making a mistake which might jeopardize their careers. Big companies, like ITT, with all their financial resources, can afford to take such risks. Many of our new ventures added spice and excitement to our working environment. Some succeeded beyond even our own expectations and that, in and of itself, helped build confidence in our ability to reach even further out into the unknown. Imagination and creativity are the two elements most lacking in most large American corporations.

In accord with the principle of treating each of our managers with the dignity and respect due an entrepreneur, I made it a policy never to *order* a division or company manager to do something with which he disagreed. No chief executive should. You can order a man *not* to do something: Don't burn the building down. Don't build another $500 million plant this year. But if you want him to do something with which he disagrees, you have to persuade him. If you order him to do it, you have taken over the responsibility for that decision. Then he has the right to come back to you later and say, "I did what you ordered and the whole thing fell apart, and it's not my fault." In fact, subconsciously, he was almost committed to proving that your idea would not work, and that he was right and you were wrong.

What do you do when you fail to persuade him? It happens not infrequently. Chief executives of subsidiary companies can have as much ego and self-confidence as chief executives of parent companies. You try to persuade him to take course A; he insists upon course B. He's the operating man and it is his responsibility. You tell him, "Okay, John, we [at headquarters] think you're wrong," and you tell him your reasons. "But if you still think we are wrong and you're right, then go ahead and try it."

If he turns out to have been wrong, then you hope he has learned something. The second time it happens, if he is still stubborn, you say, "Look, you're in charge, so go ahead. But we [at headquarters] are going to be kept well informed on everything you do and we are going to follow this closely, and we're going to advise you of what we think all along the way. Now, you're an intelligent guy and we expect you to sort out what we tell you, what's right and what's wrong. If you have doubts, raise them with us. If the thing is a fifty-fifty toss-up, and neither of us really knows, then you call the shot. You're the operating man. You know more about this than we do. We're not going to order you to do anything and we're not going to go behind your back. But if you go ahead, you better do your homework and know what you are doing. Don't act out of some kind of blind nonsense. If we discover that you've turned out to be wrong because you did not go far enough into the facts of the situation, then you're in trouble. With that understanding, go ahead." That's treating a man with respect. Even though you believe he is wrong, you hope he is right. The important thing is not who is right, but what is right.

Leadership is practiced not so much in words as in attitude and in actions. Everyone says he believes in team play, reciprocal loyalty, corporate decency, the dignity of labor, and fair remuneration, but when the crunch comes, how many chief executives abide by those "beliefs"? How many risk their own careers to stand up for their management team and their labor force? Or how many really are looking out for Mr. Number One? Up and down the management ladder, an executive need only double-cross a subordinate once—saying one thing and in a crunch doing something else—and he will lose that man's respect and loyalty for evermore. And the word will travel far and wide. Everyone who hears that story will think and rightly so: "If he did it once, he might do it again. He might even do it to me. He can't be trusted. I have to watch out for myself, guard my flanks, maybe think of finding another job, because this one has suddenly become insecure."

I don't think anyone can fake it. In all the companies in which I worked I invariably found that right down to the elevator boy, the maintenance man, or the floor sweeper, the people in the company carried with them a firm opinion about the character of the chief executive, the vice presidents, and their own immediate bosses. In one company I went around inquiring about our two top executives.

"What do you think of so-and-so?" I asked.

"Oh, he's a great guy."

"What do you think of so-and-so?"

"Oh, he's a real [expletive]!"

"Have you ever met either of them?"

"No, but I know . . ."

He did know. Those were his opinions based upon what he had learned and they were seldom wrong. Those men closer to the executive in question had more facts to support their opinions, but the opinions usually were the same up and down the line. And it was an accumulation of those opinions which set the tone, atmosphere, and spirit of the company. It shows up, too, in performance. Everyone knows it is a pleasure to work for someone you respect and admire, and it is hell to work grudgingly for a blankety-blank expletive.

So, as far as I can see, the best way to inspire people to superior performance is to convince them by everything you do and by your everyday attitude that you are wholeheartedly supporting them. You have got to mean it and demonstrate it. Deep down, they have to feel that support. That's the part of grabbing an oar when they are in trouble. In the beginning at ITT, the complex monitoring system that I instituted—with all the detailed reports and the meetings and the rigorous staff checks and rechecks—was resented by most if not all of our subsidiary company managers. No one likes to have someone looking over his shoulder and checking up on him. Their first reaction was fear. It took some time before they recognized and accepted the fact that our monitoring system was there so that we at headquarters could help them succeed in their line operations; and that when they succeeded, with or without our help, they would receive full credit for their achievement. They had to check me out, test my intelligence, my ability, my honesty, my character, my dependability, just as I had to check them out. But as time went on, trust and respect and a certain sense of camaraderie and loyalty set in, as well as a measure of pride in what we were accomplishing together.

The dedicated, unfailing support of a chief executive is like a lifeline or a safety net to his management team and, in fact, to the whole company. They have got to rely upon him to feel safe in their jobs so that their families and college-bound children will not suffer by a sudden notice of dismissal. Only then will they feel free to unleash their imaginations and creative energies. They have to feel free to admit to an honest mistake without fear of unfair reprisal. I've had men come into my office and admit they goofed, that the mistake cost the company several millions of dollars, but then they presented a plan by which they would rectify the situation. As long as they came in with a plan to remedy the disaster, they had my support.

As I've said, a true leader has to have a genuine open-door policy so that his people are not afraid to approach him for any reason. A man should feel free to tell his chief executive to his face, "I think you're dead wrong about such and such, and here are my reasons." A chief executive who has conquered his own ego problems listens to such criticism, for even if it is wrong, he will probably learn something. He can then set the man straight with the facts. If the man is right, the chief executive has cause to thank him profusely and then set about correcting the situation. That action will sweep down the corridors of the company and inspire others to speak their minds freely. No one, after all, has a monopoly on brains in any company.

One of the essential attributes of a good leader is enough self-confidence to be able to admit his own mistakes and know that they won't ruin him. The true test is to be able to recognize what is wrong as early as possible and then to set about rectifying the situation. I made my share of mistakes at ITT and they did not ruin me. I admitted them at General Managers Meetings, often with the expression "I guess I pushed the wrong button," and then I outlined my plan to save as much as could be saved from the situation. Usually such *mea culpas* were well received. Anyone who has goofed gets a little enjoyment out of seeing the Man up there admit to a mistake. There's nothing lost and much to be gained by admitting that you're human.

The authority vested in the chief executive of a large company is so great, so complete, and the demands made upon his time are so consuming, that most chief executives slip into authoritarian roles without realizing that the process is going on. In the vast majority of large American companies, the chief executive lives in a world of his own. He is sequestered in his luxury executive suite high up in the headquarters building. His word is law. Everyone kowtows to him. They adjust to his moods and to his idiosyncrasies. He runs the company from his inner sanctum. The people "out there" seldom catch a glimpse of him. Reports reach him through layers of management after being processed by committee after committee. He writes "yes" or "no" and initials them. He may subscribe to everything I have said about business leadership, but he cannot find the time to pay attention to those intangibles which do not show up on the profit-and-loss sheet. Subtly, he changes. It is easier and less time-consuming to be authoritarian. He has changed from a leader into a commander.

A leader leads his people; a commander commands them. There are, of course, gradations between the two, but essentially, by his attitude and by his actions, the commander is telling his people, "I want this done and by this date, and if it is not done, then heads will roll!" And he follows through. He who fails is fired; he who succeeds gets a pat, a promotion, or a bonus. His subordinates toe the line. He rules by fear. One chief executive, an old associate of mine, confided in me that as a matter of policy he visits each of his company's division managers every three months and "scares the hell" out of them. And it works. His P&L looks just fine.

To the degree that business commanders strike fear in the hearts of their management team, they have turned the American business world into a jungle in which scared people compete *within* a company for their own personal survival. In the long run, I am certain that it is counterproductive. First of all, frightened people play office politics: they won't come forward and admit their problems early enough for them to be solved. The most capable, independent people leave, not willing to work under those conditions. Good people won't want to come into such a company. Imperceptibly at first and then more and more, all these negative conditions and attitudes will feed upon one another until, in the end, the company will slide into a decline that the commanding chief executive and his board of directors will find difficult to fathom.

The person who heads a company should realize that his people are really not working for him; they are working *with him* for themselves. They have their own dreams, their own need for self-fulfillment. He has to help fill their needs as much as they do his. He has to prove to them that he is working as hard as they are, that he is competent in his own role as chief executive, that he will not lead them over the cliff and jeopardize their livelihoods, that he can be relied upon to reward them properly and fairly, that he is willing to share the risks as well as the rewards of their enterprise.

No chief executive can prove to his board of directors or shareholders how much, if anything, this leadership contributes to the bottom line in the profit-and-loss statement of the company. It is all intangible. He may have difficulties with his board in demanding seemingly high rewards and a firm support system for the men on his management team. But I am convinced that leadership is the single most important ingredient in business management, and that those attitudes of the chief executive which inspire his people to stretch and to excel contribute as much as 80 or 90 percent of a company's success.

Finally, as I said in the beginning, no one can teach you leadership. Everyone reads the same books and yet one manager will get a 40 percent effort out of his management team and the other will get 80 percent, and it will depend upon the manager himself and the hundreds of little things done every day that reveal character. There is a delicate balance that exists in the hierarchy of every company and the balance swings upon all those little things that the chief executive does instinctively, intuitively, spontaneously, or out of experiences, good and bad. Leadership, like life, can only be learned as you go along.

SEVEN

The Cluttered-Desk Executive

You can know a person by the kind of desk he keeps.

THERE ARE, arbitrarily speaking, two kinds of business executives: One has a clean desk top, and the other has a cluttered one.

Business people, especially those who have graduated from business schools, have learned to cultivate their attire, their haircuts, and their speaking voices to fit a certain mold. But if and when you catch a man at work in his office, the state and condition of his desk top is a dead giveaway. Usually, you can tell a great deal about the mentality of a person by what his or her desk looks like.

It's been my impression through the years that when I come upon a man who has a gleaming, empty, clean desk top, I am dealing with a fellow who is so far removed from the realities of his business that someone else is running it for him. Of course he is the last one to realize it. He's concentrating on long-term strategies for the company. It is his president, in charge of operations, whose desk is heaped high with reports, studies, and memorandums. If the president of the company has a clean desk, too, then it must be the executive vice president who is doing all the work. After all, *someone* in top management must be running the company.

Many disagree with me, I know. They say that a clean desk indicates an executive who has an "organized mind." All his papers are filed in their proper place, a buzz to his secretary will fetch the one he wants in a minute or two. His day is organized in specific segments so

157

that at 10 A.M. he takes up one subject, at 10:30 another, and so on through the day. I say: hogwash.

It is practically impossible for a top management man, or even middle management, to be doing the degree and level of work that he should be doing and, at the same time, have a clean desk. At any one time, dealing with even one project of moderate size, there are so many angles of that project to be considered simultaneously—past, present, and future aspects—that they cannot be rigidly relegated to a time spot in the day. The telephone rings, an important letter arrives, an emergency arises. All kinds of things impose themselves on the schedule of an executive who is really running his own show. Or important new information comes up out of its scheduled time slot. An executive, normally dealing with a great deal more than one project at a time, can retain only so much information in his head. He has to reach for that report on his desk.

If you are on the firing line with the leadership of several projects, you are going to have eighty-nine things on your desk, ten others on the floor beside you, and eight others on the credenza behind you. When the telephone rings or when you have to rush off to a meeting, you want to grab the information you need at the moment. It has to be on your desk. There's no other way you can do it. You don't want to have to stop and describe the one report, two memorandums, and whatever to your secretary. You want it *there,* at arm's reach. Your own filing system is right on top of your desk: Acquisitions are at the far right corner, budget figures in the near left corner, compensation and personnel recommendations to the right of the budget figures, and so on. And if something gets lost there, you shuffle the papers around until you find it. It is not scientific, but it works.

I kept my working files in my own office, the important ones on top of the desk, some on the floor, some behind me, some in my oversized attaché cases. I knew where everything was because I put it there. As a matter of personal practicality, at the end of each day, I put my files back in some of the fifteen or twenty attaché cases I kept on the windowsills and side tables of the office. At the end of the day or when leaving on a trip, I took three or four (sometimes more) of the cases with me. I had "containerized" my office. I could (and did) take it with me everywhere I went. Not only could I do my own homework over the weekend, I could respond to telephone inquiries at any time and any place. My office was with me. On trips to Europe and back each month, my office was the company airplane, the trusty attaché cases by my side. Work went on as usual.

My filing system was perhaps somewhat unique. Everything current was with me on my desk or in one of my attaché cases. It had to be. When I finished with a report or a set of papers, I turned that file over to my secretary. She kept it for three months. Then, automatically, she threw it away. That kept my office files down to a minimum. I didn't need anything more than ninety days old. The line and staff people reported monthly, and each report had to include an updated and fresh version of their unresolved "red flag" items of the month before. I did not have to go back and read old reports and I saw no sense in keeping them in perpetuity in dead files or in the company archives. Business to me is an ongoing, living process.

My desk was cluttered because I immersed myself in the company's ongoing business. I did myself what most executives delegate to others: I dictated my own letters rather than have my secretary or someone else write them for me. I wrote or at least outlined the speeches I would make, rather than have a professional do them. My letters and speeches were not as polished as they might have been otherwise, but they conveyed what I wanted them to say and in my own voice. My secretary did not pass on which incoming telephone calls would reach me and which would not; I was informed by intercom or with a note of each and every call. I decided which calls were urgent, important or not important. Figuratively speaking, at least, my office door was open to anyone in the company who thought he had a need to see me. He or she might have to wait until I had a free moment, but my attitude was that I was willing to listen with an open mind to whatever someone had to say. Never would I want to give the impression that anyone was intruding on my valuable time. My time *was* valuable, but I had found that most often what the person had to say was important. <u>No one in his or her right mind requests an audience with the chief executive just to pass the time or try to score personality points.</u>

The clean-desk executive undoubtedly will think all of the above constitutes a terrible waste of valuable executive time. He champions the so-called streamlined office. He delegates this and he delegates that. He delegates just about everything he can, saying that his shop is well organized and that he runs a tight ship. But I have to ask: Organized for what? Tight in what way?

If he delegates everything that crosses his desk (and leaves it clean), has he not reduced his function to that of a traffic cop? What he is really doing, whether or not he realizes it, is directing the flow of paper and giving the go-ahead or stop signal to decisions made by others. There is nothing wrong with being a traffic cop, but should he be paid the salary of a top corporate executive? One can hire a business administrator at a fraction of the salary and bonuses paid to top management.

As alluded to earlier, the man who delegates responsibilities for running the company, without knowing the intimate details of what is involved, runs the enormous risk of rendering himself superfluous. He may become what I call a three-by-five card executive. His people give him decision alternatives on a three-by-five index card and he checks off one of the multiple choices. But the people in the company know who is really making the decisions. They know whose ''recommendations'' are always adopted. They know behind which office door the power in the company sits.

The real danger in turning over responsibility and authority for a job, without knowing the details of what is involved, is that the manager who receives the responsibility might fail. If that happens, the chief executive does not know enough to rescue the situation. All he can do is to hire someone else to do the job. Therefore, beneath the façade of his title, the size of office, and the quality of his desk, he is incompetent.

On the other hand, if all his vice presidents do their own jobs superbly, it won't be long before someone discovers that they don't need him as the chief executive at all. Any one of his subordinates would be happy to take over.

It must be understood, of course, that all chief executives delegate some of their responsibilities for running the company. I did not run the 250 or so line operations of ITT. Each company manager had virtual autonomy and the responsibilities that go with it. But in delegating those responsibilities, I had to know enough of the operations involved to know what I was delegating. As chief executive, I was responsible to my board of directors for the sum total of all the ITT subsidiaries. Hence, all the reports, meetings, budget reviews, etc. To do my job, I had to get a complete rundown on every phase of our operations, from the engineering development of telephone switching equipment to the actuarial intricacies of the insurance business. Each time a new company was acquired, its management gave me and my staff a cross-section review of that business. We were then in a position to understand and pass judgment on what they were doing and, if necessary, add our own expertise to their own fund of knowledge. We were, as I have said previously, managing. We made our choices based upon in-depth knowledge rather than upon summaries contained on three-by-five index cards. All of our desks were cluttered.

In short, if you are really doing the work you are supposed to be doing, your desk has to be cluttered, because your working life is "cluttered."

I can understand the clean desk top of the man who acknowledges that he is taking it easy, semi-retired, or biding his time for one reason or another. I have known men who founded and built up successful companies, and then sat back as chairmen of their boards, allowing others to make the vital decisions. But those men are few and far between. More prevalent are the professional managers who give other reasons for their tidy desk tops. One type freely admits that he worked hard to get to the top and now, presumably safely ensconced, delights in having others do the work for him. He won't last long, in my estimation, with that false sense of security. Even more prevalent are the men who persuade themselves that they are now above the mundane, nitty-gritty aspects of the day-to-day problems of running the business. They say they have to keep their desks and minds clear for the deeper, long-range strategies that will guide their companies to new wondrous heights in the world of tomorrow. They are planning for the future, they say, looking far over the heads of the mere mortals on the operating lines of the company. They sincerely believe it, too.

The mentality and attitudes of the clean-desk executive extend far beyond the top of the desk. He insists that memorandums and reports be precise, no longer than one and a half or two pages long—no matter how complex the subject matter. He insists upon a precise agenda for his committee meetings. If an item is not on the agenda, it should not be brought up. The agenda is timed precisely: We should be at item three at 10:03, on item four at 10:13, on item five at 10:22 . . . adjournment at 11:30. Sometimes an item runs overtime, sometimes even the adjournment is delayed. The executive accepts the reality that his timetable cannot be followed exactly. But I am convinced that the very attempt to structure a meeting so precisely is counterproductive because it puts everyone at the meeting in a straitjacket. You don't need a bell that rings to cut off discussion; everyone there is aware of the time limitations set. The man who was about to say something won't even open his mouth because he knows the five or ten minutes allotted to that subject is over. You are going to lose whatever he had to say. You won't know what did not come up at the meeting. You may have lost something that could have been important. You also lost a bit of the raw material of creativity. How can you select the best gems of thought when all you hear are the first ones that happen to come up?

The cluttered-desk executive goes into his committee meeting with an agenda, too, but to him the timetable is not nearly as important as what might arise unexpectedly at the meeting. The most important item of the day could turn up at the end of the time allotted to that subject. It might be worth two hours of discussion, rather than five minutes. He might let it go on for twenty-five minutes to get the scope of it, and then assign it to someone for a follow-up the next week. But he would not cut anyone off just because the time was up. Of course, digressions, repetitions, and pontifications should be squelched unmercifully. He can and should keep control over the meeting, moving it right along. But he should know, too, when not to cut off a discussion. The truth is that no one can be certain what is important or unimportant until he begins to examine it. Then the subject should get all the time it deserves on its merits.

Those kinds of meetings will usually run late—for the same reason that the executive's desk is cluttered. It is a question of values. Which is more important: to direct a meeting so that it ends on time, or to run a meeting so that you don't kill off imagination and creative concepts or miss any opportunities that flash through the air? In a good meeting there is a momentum that comes from the spontaneous exchange of fresh ideas, while interests are high, that produces extraordinary results, and that momentum relies upon the freedom and flexibility permitted the participants. To my mind that is the essence of good management. The other course results in a treadmill approach to management, which is supposed to produce the results but produces only routine.

The price you pay for that open, flexible meeting is that you are usually, if not always, running late. That is one of my worst faults. I set up a series of meetings in my office and each one goes longer than I expect, so that by the end of the day I have a line of people, usually staff people, waiting to get in to see me. I am aware of the problem. But there is nothing I can do about it, or will do about it, as long as I feel it is more important to get the job at hand done than to keep to a rigid schedule.

Most of the men close to me understand that I am not unconcerned with the inconveniences I often cause them. They know that when I keep them waiting, I am as engrossed in business as important as theirs. They also know that once I meet with them, they, too, will have my undivided and unlimited attention.

Actually, I often become so engrossed in the subject matter at hand that I forget the time altogether and somehow it seems that the most interesting point or new idea will almost invariably come up at what should have been the end of a meeting. It does not matter if there are two or ten people in my office, just as we are breaking up someone will remark, "Oh, incidentally . . ." and the most important point of the whole meeting emerges. Only a fool would cut a man off at that point.

The clean desk top, the tight agenda, and the inflexible appointment schedule are symptoms as well as symbols of the mentality of a certain kind of business executive. He is the precise, compulsive type of fellow who often brags that he has his business down to a science. More often than not, he is a graduate from a business school, steeped in the aura of scientific management. Just as he knows where everything is in his office, he thinks he knows exactly where his business is going. That attitude permeates almost everything he does. His forte, usually self-proclaimed, is in planning scientifically for the future. It can be seen most clearly in his method of making an acquisition for his company.

He takes what is called the "rifle shot" approach: He will study the big picture of economic events, narrow it down to an industry which will prosper in those times, narrow it down further to a part of that industry, then down to a number of companies, and finally to the best company in the best industry in the best set of circumstances, and that will be the company he wants to buy. He will then take a "clean shot" at precisely what he wants.

How does he go about this? Well, first he gathers together a high-level strategy group of people and they will ask themselves, "What is the most important thing in the world at this time?" One thinker will come up with "energy." So they start with energy. What's related? Well, an energy-related business would be machine tools used in the oil fields. They go through several such industries and settle on well drilling as the best possibility. Why? Because it is not very capital-intensive, it's high-precision, and well-drilling companies generally make a lot of money.

So they get a list of well-drilling companies and, sure enough, all of them have been making money. That's no secret. They are already selling at ten to fifteen times earnings. The strategists worry about the high price, but they decide the well-drilling companies are worth that price. It is a great field with a great future and that is why their stock is selling at such a high multiple. The strategists go through the list of well-drilling companies and they pick Company X. It has a rate of growth of 20 percent a year, one of the best in its field, and that is why it is selling at fifteen times its earnings. It may take a bit longer to earn out its high price, but it is a good company in a good field and therefore is a safe acquisition. The thinking and the planning are impeccable. Every step of the way has been backed up by studies, reports, and memorandums. No one could fault them.

But when they go out to negotiate, they find that other strategists have gone through the same thinking and also have staked out Company X for acquisition. So in order to buy the one company they have decided upon, they have to pay not fifteen, but twenty times earnings. The price of Company X has gone up from $165 million to $220 million. That means it will take even longer than planned to earn out the higher purchase price. But they reason that the price is so high because everyone knows how good Company X is and that their stockholders will appreciate the high quality of this acquisition and will be willing to wait a bit longer for the earnings to overtake the interest payments on the loan they will need to make this acquisition. So they buy Company X and everyone agrees that it is a great acquisition, even if expensive.

How does it all turn out? Well, no one knows at the time of the acquisition. That's the point. All the precise, rifle-shot strategic planning in the world cannot predict and account for the vicissitudes of the future. More than likely, if everything else goes well, it may take this company more like nine years, instead of the planned five, to get into the black with its new acquisition. That would be nine years of heavy debt and no earnings. Things seldom turn out as well as planned on the strategist's drawing board. They can, in fact, turn out much worse.

Remember the worldwide shortage of oil? The acquisition strategists figured out that oil companies, especially those with untapped oil resources still in the ground, would make excellent buys. All of them did and for the same reasons. A giant chemical company bought a giant oil company, a steel company bought an oil company, an oil company bought an oil company, and they paid top dollar because everyone who could wanted to buy into the oil business. And what happened? The oil shortage disappeared. Oil became a glut on the market. Those who bought oil companies just a few years back, I would think, wish today they hadn't. It will take years for those acquisitions to pay out. The fault is not in being unable to forecast an oil scarcity or an oil glut. It is in relying so heavily upon what is supposed to be a formula for devising foolproof strategies to anticipate the unknown future. It happens all the time. It does not work because all the strategists have the same educational background, study the same information, and come to the same conclusions at the same time. Their recommendations come out like fads and fashions: The airlines bought hotels, the communications giants bought book companies, book companies bought paperback houses, everyone tried to buy computer companies, and so on . . .

In contrast to that rifle-shot approach to buying Company X in the well-drilling field, consider a certain cluttered-desk executive, a high school graduate who started off as a truck driver and built himself a machine-tool company. He sees an opportunity to buy a junkyard west of Chicago when a customer mentions to him that his dad wants to sell his junkyard so that he can retire to Florida. He never thought of buying a junkyard until the opportunity arose. But he goes out to look at it. He figures that with that junkyard he can take in scrap metal before it reaches the big market in Chicago, save $2 a ton in freight, and distribute it at a higher profit than competitors in Chicago. It makes sense to him. So he buys the junkyard. The price is reasonable because no one else has targeted the junkyard as a brilliant acquisition. What happens? He is making money from day one, and if he can improve the operation, he will make even more money than did the previous proprietor. What so many strategists often overlook is that a dollar earned from a junkyard is every bit as good as a dollar from an oil or computer company.

What this cluttered-desk executive did, in essence, was to recognize an opportunity when it came along and figure out what he was going to do with that opportunity that had not been done before. Because of his attitude, he was flexible enough to move on it promptly. What the clean-desk man did was to try to predetermine and pinpoint the precise acquisition which would give him the greatest return on his investment in the coming market. Not only did he box himself in and pay top dollar for a popular acquisition, but he probably concentrated so much of his time and effort in narrowing down his choice that he closed his mind to other acquisition opportunities that passed him by in the meantime. Don't forget, he is the same man who ran a meeting by so strict an agenda that he limited his access to any ideas, new or old, that did not fit into his time schedule.

Perhaps my examples here are extreme, but to a degree this happens all the time in the real business world. There are almost always dozens of companies up for sale or available for purchase in all sorts of fields, and some are good, some are bad, some are risky. It would seem to me that an acquiring executive should remain flexible and open to anything that comes down the pike. In judging the overall relationship of risk to reward, the most essential facts often are not written into the history of the company up for sale. What the company did before is important, of course, but not as important as your own personal judgment of what you yourself, your own management team, and your plans for the future can contribute to the acquisition. You are going to pay a certain price for the history of the company, but future profits are going to come out of *the added value* you and your own company can bring to the merger. This is frequently overlooked in the rifle-shot targeting of an acquisition. More often than not, the targeted company is acquired at the zenith of its earning performance and there is little, if anything, that the acquiring company can contribute to its value.

It is, finally, the mentality of the clean-desk executive to which I object, rather than the decor of his office or the top of his desk. The clean desk smacks of a cold adherence to scientific management, to business school formulas, to the pigeonholing of data, to the overly rigid scheduling of time, to the structured delegating of responsibilities, to an unwarranted self-confidence and complacency based upon the fallacious belief that your future will produce what you planned for. Don't you believe it.

There is one kind of clean-desk executive who might win my admiration. He's the fellow, I am told, who is thoroughly immersed in his work, his desk piled high with reports, who, the moment before you enter his office, sweeps every scrap of paper into his center drawer, and greets you with a pristine desk top, a relaxed attitude, and a ready smile on his face, and the moment you leave he dumps all the stuff back on his desk and gets back to work. I've heard of him, but I have yet to meet him.

Sometimes I've been tempted—but have always been too busy.

EIGHT

Not Alcoholism—
Egotism

The worst disease which can afflict business executives in their work is not, as popularly supposed, alcoholism; it's egotism.

OVER THE LAST TEN or fifteen years or so, one problem of the corporate executive has come out of the closet. Before that (and for as long as I can remember) the drinker who could not function or be trusted after lunch was a whispered secret among his colleagues. No one wanted to blow the whistle on him, especially if at other times he was competent, likable, and a good man. Drinking too much was viewed as a passing, personal problem that only occasionally infringed upon business affairs. His colleagues covered for him as best they could; the big boss was the last one to find out.

People still hesitate to talk about alcoholics in their midst and the human and economic problems they create in the functioning of a company. Nevertheless, industry has become increasingly aware of the pitiful problem of what to do about people with strong capabilities and character who seem to disintegrate under the influence of alcohol. They are usually very sad cases. The victim is the last one to realize what his problem is. The natural tendency of others is to treat him with compassion and to work around his drinking disability.

Among the several alcohol-related business situations that I encountered over the years, some bizarre and some rather mild, the one that stands out the most in my memory involved the head of the financial section of a large subsidiary that fell under my responsibility. The man's drinking problem had existed for years. Everybody in his

173

division was aware of it. They all knew that after lunch they dared not speak to him about anything important. His decisions could be disastrous. In fact, if you weren't careful, any meeting with him after lunch might cost you your job. People who worked with him and under him tolerated his drunken rages because in fact he was otherwise a more than competent financial man who had earned his way to the high position he occupied in that division.

I was rather new in the company at the time and the relatively poor performance of that division came to my attention. As I became aware of the uncomfortable position of all the people reporting to him, I made an issue of his drinking with him face to face, not once or twice, but three or four times. He did not or could not reform. I agonized over what to do. He had many years with the company and many good attributes. I liked him and felt sorry for him. There was always the possibility, I felt, that he could straighten himself out. But finally, in exasperation, I fired him.

What happened to him, I learned later, was typical of so many of these situations. He did not get another job. He continued to drink. His wife left him. His home life was gone. His savings were dissipated. He sank lower and lower until he recognized that he had reached bottom. That seems to be a prerequisite to recovery, because, as it turned out, he did have left within him enough discipline to pull himself together, to admit to his problem, and to seek help. He joined Alcoholics Anonymous, reconstructed his personal life with his wife and family, and came back to the company and asked for a job, any job. He wanted to work. Despite his many years of experience in the financial area, he was put in a minor job in the personnel department.

Then he came into my office to see me. He thanked me for firing him. I was astounded and embarrassed. He explained that everyone had given him so many ''second chances'' that he really never had to face the facts of his problem. My firing him was the best thing that could have happened to him, he said. His wife telephoned and thanked me, too.

Some years later this same man learned that he had terminal cancer. He stayed on the job for several months up to about two or three days before he went into a hospital, never to return. If anyone had an excuse to drink, he certainly did, but he never touched a drop of liquor through that whole period. It struck me as a curious tribute to the strength of some people whom you might otherwise write off as hopeless.

I have seen brilliant management careers cut short and ruined because of alcoholism. As they say, "some of my best friends" have fallen by the wayside because alcohol, which seemed so benign in the beginning, took hold of their lives and destroyed them. I can recall one man who was absolutely brilliant, and was in line to become chief executive of his company, who thought he was so smart that he could outwit the effects of alcohol. At crucial periods of time, he took pills to curb his taste for liquor; he came to work early in the morning so that he could get through a whole day's work before lunch; he spent his vacations drying out. In the end, alcohol won. He began to throw such fearsome temper tantrums after his three-martini lunches that he became a physical menace to anyone who approached him at the wrong time. Instead of rising to the head of his company, he was one day summarily fired.

Those cases stand out in one's mind, but no one knows how many quieter cases there have been of men who have lost their drive to achieve and to succeed because of the numbing effects of alcohol. I have seen men who walked about in a daze, who could not make decisions, who lost their self-confidence because of their hidden dependency upon alcohol. While many of them did not get fired, they ceased to count in the higher echelons of management. Alcoholism is not a black-and-white affair; its effect sometimes is so gradual that it is not recognized at all. Its victims do not always come crashing down; often they wallow in their own hidden distress.

When I became aware that alcoholism was more than an individual or isolated problem at ITT, I asked our medical director, Dr. John Lauer, an old friend whom I had brought over from Jones & Laughlin, to look into the situation and see what we could do about it. At a General Managers Meeting, Dr. Lauer recommended that we establish an in-house alcoholics treatment and referral program based upon government and medical findings that alcoholism was a treatable disease. Dr. Lauer's program for alcoholics was set up in 1973 and since then has been expanded into an Employee Assistance Program covering all sorts of personal problems such as misuse of drugs, marital and family discord, or financial difficulties. The criterion for referring someone to the program is job performance which does not respond to normal supervision, although anyone is free to seek help voluntarily. I am told that in recent years 89 percent of the men and women referred to the program have been rehabilitated and retained in their jobs rather than fired, and that the ITT assistance unit, which has served more than 6,500 employees and family members in the past ten years, now is used as a model for many other companies.

It is difficult at best to try to compute the cost to American industry of alcoholism. The federal government estimates the figure at $33 billion a year—$19 billion in lost productivity and $14 billion in increased use of health and welfare benefits. I would think it is much more. It is one thing to count the number of work hours lost to absenteeism due to alcoholism. But I am certain the government did not try to figure in the cost of bad management decisions, the opportunities that were missed, plus the cost of poor morale and job turnover due to the excesses of an alcoholic executive.

No matter how high one puts the figure, I am certain that the cost of alcoholism to American business is only a small fraction of the price companies pay for the phenomenon I think of as executive egotism. It is a problem as old as alcoholism, with probably the same roots growing out of deep personal insecurity. While egotism does not directly affect the health of the individual, it certainly can influence the well-being of the corporation, the people in it, and, by ripple effect, the productivity of an entire country. Potentially, it is much more dangerous than alcoholism to the well-being of a company. Unlike alcoholism, however, the problem of the executive egotist is *still* in the closet, a secret everyone knows, few talk about, and almost no one knows how to handle.

Whether in middle management or top management, unbridled personal egotism blindsides a man to the realities around him; more and more he comes to live in a world of his own imagination; and because he sincerely believes he can do no wrong, he becomes a menace to the men and women who have to work under his direction. Where such behavior impinges upon corporate or business affairs, the problem of how to handle an egotist is every bit as serious as that of alcoholism. The egotist may walk and talk and smile like everyone else; still, he is impaired as much by his narcissism as the alcoholic is by his martinis. He becomes unwilling to accept information which is contrary to some preconceived notion or image of himself that he is smarter than everyone else around him, that he is somehow "ordained" from on high to know the answer to everything, that he is in control and everyone else is there to serve him. To my mind, he is sick.

This kind of egotism is a far cry from the normal pride or self-esteem that resides in the heart of every man who has ever achieved anything. A good measure of self-esteem and confidence is essential to anyone who would be a leader, in corporate life or elsewhere. The corporate leader needs to exert his own personality in order to motivate people in the direction of an objective which, right or wrong, appears to him to be correct. But his leadership in getting things off dead center and moving is always subject to correction. He must be willing to admit a mistake, willing to listen to other points of view. Without trying to sound like a psychologist, it seems to me perfectly obvious that any normal person would remember his own humble beginnings, his mistakes of the past, and be open to criticism (even if he did not like it). He would want to be realistic in seeking the facts which would lead him to the best available answers. No matter how smart he thought he was, he would know that he was fallible, as well as susceptible to doubts and uncertainties. He welcomes ideas, suggestions, and information from others. He is aware and sensitive to what is going on around him. That would be normal.

Most executives I know strive not to be or to appear egotistical. Logic, purpose, objectivity are the qualities most managers seek to bring to the fore: good business is based upon those elements. The good executive screens his actions for any hint of personal prejudices and vanity. He does not become overly concerned about where he sits in a meeting or whether or not people rise when he enters a room. On the other hand, he won't allow anyone else to push his way ahead of him because he has to play the role that his position demands, lest he be seen as a soft leader. It is largely a matter of self-identity. It is one thing to know who and what you are, and quite another to go about *seeking* praise and adulation. Of course, everyone likes praise and becomes defensive when criticized. I've gone overboard on occasion in pushing my convictions upon a subordinate when I disagreed with him. But when it turns out that I was wrong, I go out of my way to make amends with that man either publicly or privately and I take corrective action for the future. Perhaps the fine line of distinction between self-identity and egotism is difficult to explain, but everyone involved can sense the difference.

It is often difficult to distinguish normal pride from egotism, particularly in the early stages of the symptoms.

That is equally true of alcoholism. A pleasant drink at lunch does not make a man an alcoholic. Do two drinks indicate that he is on the road to oblivion? Would you pin a label on the man who had three martinis at lunch? It may be the first and only time that man has had three drinks at lunch. It is not the numbers that count, but the facts behind the numbers, the pattern in the behavior.

The successful corporate executive who has worked his way up the ranks takes pride in a well-appointed office, the use of a company car or a chauffeured limousine. There's nothing wrong with that. The corporate airplane does save him valuable time and energy. He would be less than normal if he did not enjoy reading about his or his company's accomplishments in the daily press or the weekly magazines. Nothing wrong with that at all.

But I have seen grown men become absolutely distraught and almost hysterical because the color of the carpet in their office was not the right shade, or the view from their window was not the view they wanted. Some of these men were second- and third-layer management. Vanity and egotism are not confined to chief executive officers. At the top level, I've known some chief executives to compete with one another in the length and model of their limousines. In corporate aircraft, the Gulfstream III is now the status symbol, whether or not that particular plane fits the real needs of a company. The use of the Gulfstream III is defended on the grounds of "the company's image." Some companies compete for "image" with as much force and energy as they do for earnings, market share, and stock market price. That is ego gratification. I've heard a chief executive complain bitterly because another chief executive was getting better "press" than he was. I've known of men who measure the space, rather than the content, of articles given to their companies in the New York *Times*. Some corporate vice presidents of public relations earn their keep both by competing in the market for column inches and by coddling and feeding the egos of their chief executives.

One should be gratified, I suppose, if the press seeks you out for your opinions, expertise, or whatever on a current general problem in your field, or if you are invited to address a convention of your peers and to impart the wisdom of your experience. If you are the head of a large public corporation, a certain amount of public service is expected of you. You are asked to give your time—really the company's time—to this or that needy cause. We all have our obligations to the well-being of society. Those of us who can should give. But it should always be recognized that such contributions come from the corporation and its shareholders. The time you give is taken away from the time you would otherwise be spending on company business and for which you are being paid by the shareholders. Even if your speech is given during the luncheon break or after business hours, a professional manager is paid for his full time, not nine to five. A speech, a fund drive, or a civic service venture, done well, consumes considerably more time in preparation and planning than the event itself. Again, there is nothing wrong in any of this, so long as one is realistic about the cost of the contribution. It is one thing to fulfill one's service obligations to the community; it's quite another to overdo such outside activities for personal recognition and adulation.

In recent years there has been more and more competition among business executives for recognition in such ventures beyond the call of business. They become ventures in ego massage. For the sweet sound of applause, for praise and personal recognition, many business executives devote inordinate amounts of time to outside activities, delegating to others the supposedly "routine" responsibilities of their businesses. Their egos have made them blind to the reality that their first and primary responsibility is to the company that signs their paycheck.

I remember one man who headed a major corporation for about twenty years who became so enamored of his own success and the benefits of scientific management that he spent an enormous part of his time going about the country making speeches on the subject. He was quoted widely in the press as the leading spokesman on the new age of scientific management. Behind his back, however, he became a joke inside and outside of his company because while he was out making speeches, it was obvious that he was not running his own company. It got to a point where he was spending more time speaking than showing up in his office. Probably he was unaware of what was happening; his ego had taken over. The end result was that his company got rid of him. His board of directors gave other reasons for his dismissal, of course, but his case was so egregious and well known that no one was fooled.

The cost and harm of ego inflation to the companies involved go far beyond lost work hours. That is like measuring the cost of alcoholism by the rate of absenteeism. At the management level, the alcoholic can do far more harm on the job than if he slept it off at home. The same is true of the egotist. All those ego-feeding activities—the long hours in the limousine, the skylarking in the corporate jet, the collecting of press clippings, the unnecessary speeches—feed the sickness and one way or another make a corporate problem out of what had been an otherwise perfectly competent, even brilliant executive.

The real harm is that unbridled personal vanity takes over, very much the way liquor claims the alcoholic, and the man involved becomes a victim of his own egotism. He begins to believe his own press releases and the accolades arranged for him by his own public relations people. He becomes so involved with himself and his own vanity that he loses his sensitivity to the feelings of others. He loses his common sense and objectivity. He becomes a potential menace in the decision-making process. All this does not become immediately apparent around the office. The egotist does not stumble about, knocking things off his desk. He does not stammer or drool. No, instead he becomes more and more arrogant, and some people, not knowing what is underneath such an attitude, mistake his arrogance for a sense of power and self-confidence.

But he cannot fool the people around him for long. That egotistic arrogance has a corrosive effect upon everyone who has to deal with him. While people tend to pity and sympathize with the plight of the alcoholic, they have the opposite feelings about the egotistical boss in their midst. They resent the boss who is cold, aloof, and all-knowing. They ridicule him behind his back and try to work around him. They see through him and recognize that his pose does not make him the leader he pretends to be. Once that happens, the whole structure and momentum of a management team, indeed the whole company, begins to fall apart. Oftentimes, the egotistical boss will sense that something is wrong, although he will never recognize the cause; he will press harder for the respect and adulation of his subordinates, and the more he presses, the less he receives. Thus, he becomes more arrogant and demagogic in his demands. His people resent him more and more. The situation becomes worse with time. As the management team is divided into enemy camps, the head man begins to surround himself with sycophants. He can tolerate only yes men.

It does not take long for this kind of attitude to work its way down through an organization. That kind of egotism will demean and destroy the collective effort of a company's management team. People become very wary of bringing such a boss any kind of bad news. He is too likely to shoot the messenger. In turn, that will have a curdling effect upon any degree of open communications in a company. Consciously or subconsciously, no one wants to take issue, much less argue, with a boss like that. He is as likely to fly off the handle and rant and rave as the worst alcoholic. No one can be sure what he will do. He is, as they say, drunk with power. His mind is set. His attitude is that he, not you, is the chief, his is the greatest brain in the world, so it must follow that if he decides to do something it must be right. He will announce his decisions, handing down manifestos in effect: "We will do this and we are going to do that and don't tell me that it's wrong, because you people don't know beans about the situation, and I do!" Obviously, the man has become an egotistical maniac, as out of touch with reality as the alcoholic. And in business as in life, reality has a way of catching up with people.

The egotist is a much more difficult executive to deal with than an alcoholic. Perhaps on the department or even division level of management someone could step in and quash such disquieting arrogance. But in the upper corridors of power it is extremely difficult to deal with unbridled egotism. Subordinates have to cope with it by "handling" such a boss gingerly. They will stifle their own innovative ideas in order to get along with him. They will offer only the mildest debate on any issue. They will learn how to cater to his whims, agree with him, praise him. They know or suspect that his decisions are based more upon personal considerations than on realism, objectivity, or facts. Pet projects get priority. Decisions which are almost impossible to implement are passed down to the troops and no one on the line understands the reason behind those decisions. They resent it like hell. At the peer level, whether it is the chief executive officer or a member of the board of directors, people generally are aware of enormous ego problems, but they don't know how to measure or to cope with them.

One situation in which a man's ego became caught in a large merger negotiation cost his company more than $100 million. Heading a team of negotiators, this man was so arrogant and insensitive to others in his approach to the transaction that the price of purchase rose more than $100 million from what it should have been. Everyone on his team was aware of what was happening—everyone, that is, except the man himself and he was their chief executive. Yet there was no way to quantify or to certify the intangibles involved. It is very difficult to fire a man because of his ego. The man's explanation to his board of directors was reasonable: he blamed the unreasonableness of the other side. Perhaps some of the board members suspected the truth, but no one raised a question about his handling of the merger. If they had learned, on the other hand, that the man had been drunk and had lost the company $100 million, or $50 million, or even $25 million, he probably would have been fired on the spot. But could anyone question an ego?

That may seem an extreme example. But such situations occur time and time again, even in lesser degree, and somehow no one attempts to put a price tag upon the number of deals that fell through because of one man's overextended ego, the amount of business lost because outsiders chose not to deal at all with a self-styled demigod. No one has as yet devised a reasonable basis for measuring what a company should have accomplished as opposed to what it did accomplish and how much of that lost potential was caused by the blinded, closed minds of men wrapped in self-love.

Not until he is far gone does the egotist reveal plainly his overbloated opinion of himself. Like the alcoholic, he usually is adept at hiding his secret vice, covering his true thoughts by acting out the prescribed, correct behavior of executives on his level. But, as I said, reality catches up with him. Ultimately, it catches up with him in the performance of his department, his division, or his company. It cannot be otherwise, because the egotist, as a manager, is *impaired* in his judgments, in his relationships with others, in his ability to function.

I have the feeling that, generally speaking, people tend to tolerate this kind of egotism, where they would not tolerate a similar degree of alcoholism, because they have absolutely no idea of the very, very high cost it represents. I have no way of measuring it either, but from personal observations I would guess that the loss in performance, productivity, earnings in any company, division, or department subjected to the wiles and whims of an egotistical corporate executive would approach at least 40 percent. In other words, if it were not for that malfunctioning, damaging executive egotism, one might expect a 40 percent improvement across the board. The cost in lost performance is enormous.

If only people would recognize egotism as a disease, more could be done about it. But the vagueness and lack of measurement associated with a narcissistic personality have allowed this cause of mismanagement to continue as a secret loss in the business world. I suspect that it will continue to be tolerated.

Excess egotism is oftentimes based upon the utter fear of failure. Most people spend a good deal of their time developing skills to defend themselves against what they see as "failure." I don't think they really know what "failure" means, only that they want no part of it. However, it is my observation that more people and more careers are "ruined" by success than by failure. I have seen people fail at one or another point in their careers, and go on to greater success than they had ever envisioned before.

People learn from their failures. Seldom do they learn anything from success. Most people do not spend any more time defining for themselves what "success" means than they do with "failure." I've seen absolutely sound, sensible, modest people go "bananas" when suddenly elevated to heights of power not formerly experienced. Reaching the starting gate of a new position is regarded by them as having arrived at their destination. They stop moving forward and bask in the sunshine of their prominence. Unfortunately, in the business environment, the performance of a top manager cannot be determined in his first year or two, or three. Such a man can devote his time to so-called broad concepts, theories, and fancy explanations. If he is close to retirement, he knows he will be long gone before his mark on the company can be evaluated. So how can he lose? He is the only one in the race. So he sees his role as guarding his image and he begins to believe his press clippings.

On a personal, individual level, the question becomes: Can you handle success? Can you guard against the virus of personal egotism? Can you view with perspective the flattery and praise of sycophants? Can you discard the pleasant aspects of your position in the company for the more realistic problems facing you, which may be unpleasant?

Success, it seems to me, is much more difficult to deal with than failure, because only you will know how you are handling it!

NINE

The Numbers

The drudgery of the numbers will make you free.

NUMBERS ARE SYMBOLS, very much like words, with their own intrinsic simple meanings when they stand alone, and far more complex and meaningful when in the context of pertinent other numbers. A child learns the alphabet and then how to put letters together to spell words, and words together to make sentences, until he or she grows up to read or to write a book where the real meaning of the words will often be found between the lines. "Cat" can mean a kitten to a child, a Siamese or Persian to a pet owner, or a tiger to a hunter. If I tell you there are five apples in the basket on the table, what does that tell you? That there are five apples in the basket. Or, if you knew there should be six, that someone had eaten one of your apples.

In business, numbers are the symbols by which you measure the various activities of an individual enterprise or combination of enterprises which make up the parent corporation. When you add and subtract all the numbers, you come up with the well-known "bottom line" on your profit-and-loss statement. That's very simple, like spelling "cat." In managing the family's finances, such basic arithmetic might be sufficient: Did you take in more than you spent that year? Fine. But if your business shows a profit of $3 million for the year, is that good or not so good? That depends upon the context of that $3 million. Did you earn $2 million or $4 million the year before? Is it $3 million earned on sales of $40 million or $400 million?

The meaning of numbers, like that of words, can only be comprehended in relationship to one another. When I read sets of numbers, either vertically or horizontally, I automatically translate them into meaningful percentage differences. Thus, if $500 million in sales dropped by $50 million, I know that sales dropped 10 percent. If $500,000 in sales of another division decreased by $100,000, my mind's eye tells me the drop was 20 percent. Even though this division lost less money than the first, I suspect immediately that it is probably in deeper trouble than the division that lost $50 million in sales. Actually, those numbers, by way of illustration, tell me a whole lot more. They tell me that I had better look behind those numbers and find out what is happening there.

Too many people mistakenly believe that large American corporations, like ITT, are run (heartlessly) by the numbers. They make that mistake because most people read words better than they do numbers. They may understand the complex novels of Henry James or James Joyce or Marcel Proust, but they read columns of numbers as they would a vocabulary list of strange, esoteric words. As symbols of what is going on in business, numbers represent measurements, not the business activity itself. René Magritte, the surrealist artist, painted a picture of a man's pipe and on the canvas he wrote, "This is not a pipe." It wasn't. It was a picture of a pipe. So I say: The numbers are not the business; they are only pictures of the business.

Nevertheless, no business could run without them. Numbers serve as a sort of thermometer which measures the health and well-being of the enterprise. They serve as the first line of communication which informs management what is going on, and the more precise the numbers are, the more they are based upon "unshakable facts," the clearer the line of communication.

When a manager makes up a budget for the coming year, he is putting down on paper a series of expectations, expressed in numbers. They include the whole gamut of costs of the product or products—design, engineering, supplies, production, labor, plants, marketing, sales, distribution—and also anticipated income from sales based upon market share, back orders, and what have you. These figures are not pulled out of the air. Nor are they based upon whims or hopes. They are carefully garnered by the people on the firing lines of the company and they are based upon the best facts and figures available. When all the figures are pulled together for one company or one division, you have its budget. As I said, at ITT we had 250 of these profit centers and their annual budgets, replete with numbers, when lined up side by side, occupied thirty-odd feet of shelf space.

As that budget year proceeds, a similar or parallel set of numbers flows into the company, representing the day-by-day operations, and they are gathered, collated, and reported on a weekly or monthly basis. Thus the actual costs and the actual sales and the actual profit margins and earnings can be compared with the budget forecasts. Does one set of numbers match the other? Is the actuality above or below the company's expectations? If either, what are you going to do about it?

Any significant variation between your expectations and what is actually happening in the marketplace, as expressed in those numbers, is a signal for action. The sooner you see the numbers, the sooner you can take action, if needed. If one of your products is selling above expectations, you may want to increase production immediately. Or you may not. If, as happens more often, one or more of your products are not selling as well as expected, then you may have to find some way to get those sales up or begin to reduce the costs and expenses involved, and the sooner, the better. However—and this is most important—the numbers themselves will not tell you what to do. They are only a signal for action, a trigger to thinking. It is akin to the man with the divining rod who points to the spot where there is water underground. But to get the water, you have to dig for it. The key issue in business is to find out what is happening behind those numbers.

Once you start digging into the areas which the numbers represent, then you get into the guts of your business. If sales are off, is it because of the design of your product? Its cost? Marketing? Distribution? Financing? What? The search goes on not only at the top of the company but also at the operating levels. Now you get back to the importance of open communications, the honesty and integrity of the men reporting to you. These are the subjects you investigate at your meetings of managers, operating men, and staff. When you find the source of the trouble, then you must put your collective mind—you and your team of managers—to finding the very best answer to your problem. Here at this level is where you insist that management must manage. You don't want to manage the numbers; you don't want to push sales or receivables from one quarter to another, for the truth will always catch up with you. That is like treating the thermometer instead of the patient. If a thermometer registers above 98.6 degrees, it is telling you the patient has a fever; he is sick. It is not telling you *what* is wrong, only that something is wrong. You can put the thermometer in a glass of ice water or dunk the whole patient into a bathtub of cold water, and that will bring the number down. But it won't cure him. In business, you want to manage and control the elements of the business itself, not the numbers on your profit-and-loss statement. The numbers are there to reflect how well or how poorly your business is doing.

There is nothing unique or unusual about this concept. However, the difference between well-managed companies and not-so-well managed companies is the degree of attention they pay to numbers, the temperature chart of their business. How often are the numbers reported up the chain of command? How accurate are those numbers? How much variation is tolerated between budget forecasts and actual results? How soon is attention directed to and action taken on variations deemed significant? How deep does management dig for its answers?

At ITT, as should be obvious, we took our numbers very seriously indeed. Our budget reviews, which began as early as February and March and continued through the year, were drawn up very carefully. The final budget was considered a solid commitment for performance expected the following year. Our division comptrollers and staff reported weekly; our operating managers reported at least monthly. Our monthly General Managers Meetings focused upon the variations, if any, between budget forecasts and the results for that given month.

Our entire reporting system was based upon the early-warning system of our numbers. We wanted no "surprises." As soon as we discovered something amiss, or going amiss, we threw every means and every effort into solving our problems, fixing our trouble spots, innovating for a changing marketplace. As a result, we felt that we were in control. The unexpected shocks and surprises that accost everyone in life became for us manageable.

As time went on, we became more and more skilled at interpreting the numbers of our business and projecting into the future what we could do and could not do with the resources at our command. This included investments in plant, new products, increased production, all sorts of things. The skill resided in our ability to control what we were doing at the detail level, even though we were a large, complex company. That is the only way you can run a business. You cannot control an omelet: you control one egg at a time.

Many companies do not take their numbers seriously enough. Divisions may report only quarterly, which hardly provides an early-warning system. Many companies have become accustomed to operating with rather big variations between their budget projections and the actuality of the marketplace. If the numbers are down, they live on hopes and the promises of their sales force. They push harder and sometimes the numbers go back up; sometimes they do not. But oftentimes they never know the real reasons why the numbers went up or down, and when you neglect the signals it may become too late to take effective action. You find that you have lost control and that can spell disaster.

Numbers have an inherent quality to them which is as important as the digits themselves. They can be accurate or not so accurate, precise or rounded off, detailed or averaged and vague. Their quality, as reported, usually depends upon the chief executive of the company and what he expects from the men reporting to him. If he does not give much personal attention to the detailed figures, beyond ascertaining the earnings per share, no one else in his company is going to worry about them. They will round off their figures, averaging the odd numbers, perhaps shaving off a few points from the costs, adding something to boost profit margins. As the practice spreads from division to division, the accumulation of inexact, fuzzy, and then plain incorrect figures can cause havoc with decisions based upon facts which shake and tremble upon the tree of knowledge.

For example, if you are president of a company and your vice president in charge of production reports that "factory costs" for that year are $12 million, what does that tell you? You know that factory costs include payroll, materials, and overhead. But it is still too vague to be meaningful. However, if you trust your vice president, you accept his aggregate figure and go on from there. It may be a relatively small figure in the overall scheme of things and you don't think you have time to delve into such mundane details. But when things go bad and that division starts losing money and other divisions also start losing money, you're fired. A new president comes in and when he looks over those same figures, he calls in that vice president and demands to know: "What do those figures on factory costs mean? What's included there?"

"That's the payroll and overhead at the factory," explains the vice president. "We don't keep it in any more detail than that. Mostly it's payroll, that's all."

"Now wait a minute," says the new president, "that's much too high for the volume you're doing. What goes into that figure, those factory costs; that's what I want to know."

"Well, you can look at the payroll, if you want to."

"No, I don't want to read the payroll. I want to know what those guys are doing there, how much you pay them for the various jobs, how many hours they put in . . ."

"But we don't keep our records like that," says the vice president.

So the new president sets up a time-card system in which each employee category has differently coded time cards, which are punched automatically at the time clock for each shift. Now, when the new president looks over the ingredients of "factory costs," he can readily see that the payroll consists of some three hundred men on the production line, actually making the product, and another hundred are listed as supervisors and inspectors and another hundred as maintenance men.

"That's way out of line," he tells the vice president. "You go look and see what those supervisory men and those maintenance men are doing. We don't need one supervisor for every three men on the line."

That's a very simple example of getting to the facts behind the numbers. The vice president will find all sorts of things that can be corrected. He will find men in the shop sharpening tools that are no longer used, because they have to make work or lose their jobs. He will find boondoggling among the inspectors and supervisors. He will find the causes of those high factory costs and how he solves his newfound problem will reflect upon how good a manager he is.

The new president, meanwhile, will begin to look closely at all the figures that come in from all the divisions of the company, and as he delves into them, things will happen in that company that change it ever so imperceptibly into a well-managed enterprise. He will have to keep at it continually, or else things will begin to slip again. Managing a company is like writing in the snow: You have to go over and over the same words as the snow falls if you want your writing to remain legible. The reward, however, is that you get better and better at it as you repeat the same process.

Most "turnaround" situations in business involve the quality of the numbers reported to the chief executive. One man allows the numbers to slip past him because he does not care enough about financial controls, and then another chief executive comes in and begins to cut costs in order to reestablish the appropriate relationship of costs to sales, which produces that all-important margin of profit.

A new president, to continue the above example, as his first priority, will carefully go over the figures of his company, looking not at individual numbers but at the overall numbers in relation to one another. He is searching for trends and currents that tell him what is happening: numbers have a way of synthesizing the mass effects of many, many individual items which make up the whole. Once he has that mainstream in mind, however, he will begin to look into the detailed figures behind the overall averages, and he will focus on the numbers which interest him the most: sales, costs, earnings, margins, marketing, assets investment, debt and interest, whatever.

Suppose he comes up with the number 4 (which can represent $4 million, $40 million, or $400 million) for one element of one division. Breaking down that 4, he may find it does not represent $2 + 2$ or $3 + 1$. Very frequently in business a total of 4 can mean $+12$ and -8. Maybe the $+12$ should be higher, he thinks, but he focuses upon the -8 and he finds that consists of $+5$ and -13. So he delves into the -13 and perhaps he finds that represents the losses on a series of products that are terribly outmoded and not selling. By stopping production on that one line of products, he saves that loss of 13, and when he applies that saving to the bottom line of that division, the total of +4 rises to +17, a healthy gain for the new regime. Remember, he did not change the numbers; he changed what was behind the numbers.

As he moves on, reading the books of the company, he probably will find gaps in the information he needs and wants. He will then call for figures that had never been collected before and those figures will enable him to maintain a tighter control on the varied operations of the company. Obviously, the head of a company, a division, or a department wants the figures on only the elements in which he has an interest. He may want to know how many tons of coal Plant A is burning every month, but he does not care about the amount of fly ash that is coming out of the chimney. But then one day the Environmental Protection Agency imposes a fine of $1,000 for every day a company's fly ash exceeds 2 percent of the coal burned. When he finds his company is paying $30,000 a month in fines, he becomes interested in a monthly figure on fly ash. Now it is important to him.

Sometimes, however, outside events beyond the control of any individual company overtake the usual early-warning system that even good numbers provide. A sudden rise in the cost of energy, an international event of significant proportions, a plunge into recession of a whole national economy can wreak havoc with the best-laid plans. It has happened to the auto industry, the oil industry, the steel industry, and to segments of ITT.

Consider, for example, one company with $40 million in annual sales and reaping a handsome profit. It expands to $60 million in annual sales, earning even more money. It builds its sales volume to $80 million a year, and profits rise proportionally. Then the cycles change, the economy slumps, customers suddenly stop buying, annual sales slide back down to the old level of $40 million a year. But now the company is losing money on that volume. What happened? What can you do about it? No mere snipping at costs here and there will save the situation.

Some men will sit back and say, "We're waiting for the volume to come back. Look, we made lots of money at eighty million dollars and we'll make it again. We just have to wait for the economy to turn around." That's hope. Others might say, "Hell, we're in all kinds of trouble and it's hopeless. Let's sell the thing and get out from under."

At ITT, when outside events overtook us and there was nothing else we could do, we "restructured" the company so that it could cope with its new environment. To sit back and wait for the vicissitudes of the economy to help us was unacceptable as a solution. To sell off a company in times of distress ran against our grain. The numbers, which told us what was going on within that company, played a big part. We went over every relevant figure of every operation and scaled the company back down to the size it was when it was making money on annual sales of $40 million. It is simply amazing how many expenses once deemed necessary become luxuries when your company is operating at a loss. Restructuring also involved cutting back on plant and employees so that the company once again resembled its old $40 million self. At the same time, while restructuring we adopted the practice of putting forth a tremendous effort to try to increase sales a little bit, even 5 or 10 percent. We cut the company back to the $40 million structure and then tried to do $42 or $44 million in business. We called it our "one-two punch." Cannon Electric, which makes heavy-industry electrical connectors, was one ITT subsidiary which went through restructuring during an economic recession and then was built up to a point where it is now three times as big and as successful as it had ever been before. We could not have done it without a firm grasp on its numbers.

In addition to the numbers from daily operations, another complete set of numbers must be monitored carefully and regularly to ensure the well-being of any company. The figures on the "balance sheet" reflect the total assets of the company, its stockholders' investment, and its outstanding debt. These numbers will reveal as well as anything else the basic philosophy of the company, its management, and its board of directors. To the degree that a company carries debt prudently it is trying to maximize the return on its stockholders' investment.

Generally speaking, companies try to operate on as much as 30 or 40 percent debt in relationship to the equity of the company. A 30 percent debt ratio will earn a company, all other things being equal, the highest credit rate of AAA; 40 percent will reduce the rating to AA. The interest one pays on borrowed money is based upon one's credit rating. Some companies choose to operate with less debt than that, or no debt at all, even when interest rates are reasonable. That constitutes a very conservative approach to business. Growth would necessarily be limited. Obviously, the company that borrows money equal to 30 percent of its equity and invests those extra funds properly in expansion should be able to increase its capacity for production and sales 30 percent more than the company of the same size that borrowed no money. The catch is, of course, that you have to increase your earnings enough to pay the interest on the money you borrowed. That will depend upon your increased costs, sales, and earnings, the rate and amount of interest you must pay, the turnover of inventory, the turnover of your receivables, and ultimately the net amount of your cash flow. All these numbers have an intrinsic relationship to one another, and the ratio of one to the other depends upon a manager's philosophy of running his business. Should you, if you could, extend your debt to 30, 40, 50 percent of the value of your net assets to expand your business or to acquire another company? How about 55 percent? Would that be foolhardy? Or courageous? It all depends upon what you are producing and selling, the consumer demand for your products, the marketplace, the general economy, the confidence you have in yourself, in your management team, in your company, in dozens and even hundreds of variables.

No matter what course you choose, you still have to be sure of your company's ability to function in the environment in which you have placed it. You have to be certain your company has enough liquidity to meet all of its normal requirements, including its ability to borrow more and to grow next year and the year after that. The more you borrow in relation to your assets and your cash flow, the higher your expenses will be in doing business; the higher the risk, the lower your credit rating becomes, and then you must pay higher interest rates to borrow in the future or to refinance your present loans. The ability to pay or to refinance your debts as they come due is absolutely essential. The only irreparable mistake in business is to run out of cash. Almost any other mistake in business can be remedied in one way or another. But when you run out of cash, they take you out of the game.

As a concept, all this is child's play to anyone who has graduated from a business school or has run his own business for any length of time. And yet, thousands of businesses go bankrupt every year, hundreds of others merge or are taken over because they are in trouble, and the root of almost all of these troubled situations can be traced back to an inattention to the numbers involved. Someone did not get the message in time. Numbers do not stand alone on the balance sheet or in the budgets or in the weekly or monthly operating reports. They are all interrelated. Obviously, the health of your balance sheet depends upon the profits or losses shown in your operating reports, and the value of those operating reports depends upon the quality of the numbers being reported, and all the numbers are but reflections of what is happening down the line in your factories, in your sales force, in the marketplace . . . and, ultimately, the well-being of your company will depend upon the attention that is paid to all those numbers and the messages they transmit to you.

So the numbers flow in, signaling, sending their messages, and the family checkbook will tell you whether you spent more than you took in that month or vice versa, and your balance sheet will tell you just how solvent you are and will be upon your retirement. Family finances are not too different in concept from those of businesses. The professional manager, however, must cope with reams of figures covering not a single enterprise but a multitude of them, all interrelated. His skill is not just to produce a product that sells in the marketplace and yields a profit. His skill lies in how well he can do it in relation to his competition. Efficiency lies in how well he can cut his costs and maximize his profits across a broad scale of activities involving a multitude of products. That skill, in my estimation, will depend to a great extent upon his ability to understand and act upon the early-warning system provided by the numbers which flow across his desk from sources throughout the company.

The professional's grasp of the numbers is a measure of the control he has over the events that the figures represent. Through his experience, he learns to appreciate the meaning of the variables so that he can act swiftly to amend deviations from the expected; he is going to curtail the number and severity of shocks that any business is heir to; he is not going to run out of cash; he is going to command a tight ship, a well-managed company.

There is a price to pay, too, as there always is: Paying attention to the numbers is a dull, tiresome routine, a drudgery. The more you want to know about your business, the more detail you want to have, the more numbers there will be. They cannot be skimmed. They must be read, understood, and thought about and compared with other sets of numbers which you have read that day, that week, or earlier that year. And you have to do it alone, all by yourself, even when you know that it would be far more stimulating to be doing almost anything else. If you are running a well-managed company, most of the numbers will be those you expect. That makes them even more mundane and dull. But you cannot skip over them;

you dare not allow your concentration to flag. Those numbers are your controls, and you read them, on and on, until your mind reels or until you come upon one number or set of numbers which stands out from all the rest, demanding your attention, and getting it.

What you are seeking is *comprehension* of the numbers: what they mean. That will come only with constant exposure, constant repetition, retention of what you read in the past, and a familiarity with the actual activities that the numbers represent. You cannot speed up the process. Comprehension seeps into your brain by a process of osmosis and gradually you find yourself at ease with numbers and what they really represent. Saturating yourself with the numbers and the facts, no matter how remote they may seem at first, brings comprehension; somehow the pieces begin to fit together. It does not mean you are the smartest man in the business world. It is only that repetition is the secret of comprehension. When I read the figures of a given enterprise and ask questions of the manager each month and get answers, each question and answer slightly different from the month before, both the manager and I are adding to our fundamental comprehension of what is going on.

The truth is that the drudgery of the numbers will make you free. The very fact that you go over the progression of those numbers week after week, month after month, means that you have strengthened your memory and familiarity with them so that you retain in your mind a vivid, composite picture of what is going on in your company in relationship to what went on before and, even more important, what might be possible for the future. The self-confidence that you are in control, that you are aware of the significant variations from the expected, gives you the freedom to do things that you would not have been able to do otherwise. You can go ahead and build a new factory plant, finance risk-laden research, or go out and buy a company, and you can do it with assurance because you are able to sit down and figure out what that new venture will do to the total picture on your balance sheet, backed up by the expected performance of your operating divisions. Your experience and skill at working with the numbers, which came from the drudgery of all those long hours at it, will enable you to make projections into the future on paper which can be relied upon as realistic, not only by yourself but also by the banks, the security analysts, and the shareholders. When you have mastered the numbers, you will in fact no longer be reading numbers, any more than you read words when reading a book. You will be reading meanings. Your eyes may be seeing numbers, but your mind will be reading "markets," "costs," "competition," "new products." All the things you are doing and planning will stare out at you, if you will only learn to read *through* the numbers. It is an acquired, special skill perhaps, but it is the key to the mastery of any business.

On a personal note, without any undue feigned modesty, the steady and remarkable growth of ITT over a twenty-year period, in which more than three hundred companies were acquired and merged into one unified corporation that stretched across the world, was made possible largely because of ITT's earned reputation not for just the tight financial controls over our operations, but for our ability to read "through" them and to think in terms of what those numbers meant and what they called for. Our close scrutiny of the numbers freed us to act with courage. We never encountered trouble borrowing funds for expansion or acquisitions. Banks and financial institutions recognized our adherence to the real meaning of strong financial controls. We were never in danger of running out of cash. ITT grew faster and with more success than other companies of our size during the years of my presidency because we knew our numbers, and we were not afraid to move forward.

In fact, I would argue that anyone in business, if he sets up the proper kinds of controls—controls that tell him when any segment of his company is not doing what he expected, and tell him this promptly enough and in enough detail so that he can go back behind the numbers and analyze precisely where it is that he has to take action—then he (or anyone else not mentally incompetent) could run a progressive, profitable, and growth-oriented company.

That's what a good set of numbers will do for you.

TEN

Acquisitions and Growth

What is a conglomerate?

THE WORD "CONGLOMERATE" came into vogue in the late sixties and early seventies. Little understood at the start, a conglomerate was thought of as some kind of new corporate device by which certain companies, with insatiable appetites, could gobble up and swallow unrelated businesses in seemingly unending mergers. At that time, most financial analysts could see no rhyme or reason for, say, a shoe company, a bank, a lumber company, a dress company, and whatever to be housed under one corporate roof. Few people seemed to realize that many of our largest companies had been "conglomerates" for many years. General Electric made electrical generators, toasters, locomotives, refrigerators, airplane engines, and electric light bulbs. But GE did it gradually over many years. The new conglomerates were trying to do the same thing, but in a terrible hurry.

The rapidly rising stock market of the 1960s played havoc with intrinsic values, and many companies became attractive buys when the price of their stocks did not keep pace with the others. We saw more mergers than ever before. Many seemed to be made with what appeared to be tricky stock deals, some of which indeed did involve highly inflated paper values. Smaller companies took over larger companies, trading paper certificates for cash and assets. People began to get the impression that conglomerates were some kind of confidence game.

While there always are some miscreants on Wall Street looking for the quick and easy buck, and some of the conglomerates were poorly put together and of high risk, most of the mergers of the period were perfectly legitimate business moves in which good values were traded for good values, resulting in larger, stronger, well-managed companies. But all conglomerates were lumped into one stereotype and stigmatized as something, somehow, evil. Art Buchwald, the columnist, satirized public thinking in one of his columns in which conglomerates gobbled each other up until there was nothing left but one giant conglomerate and the United States government. In liberal circles, conglomerates were viewed much more seriously. I gathered that some people really did think that, unless stopped, the conglomerates would, by some sleight of hand, take over the world. Mergers, you see, were not confined to the United States; they were happening all over the industrial world.

It was precisely during this period of time that ITT emerged as the biggest conglomerate of them all. We were put up on a pedestal, praised by some and shot at by others. The truth was that ITT became a conglomerate for a very good reason: There was no other way we could grow!

In 1960, not long after I came to ITT, our highest-earning subsidiary, the Cuban Telephone Company, was expropriated by Fidel Castro. It had been the company upon which Sosthenes Behn had founded the International Telephone and Telegraph Company in 1920. We received not a cent in compensation from the Castro government. At the time it was a severe blow, but in retrospect it turned out to be a blessing in disguise. The expropriation of our property, about which we could do nothing but file a claim in the World Court in The Hague, helped crystallize our real problems at ITT.

Aside from our dismal overall earnings ($29,036,000 on sales of $765,640,000), our real problem was that some 80–85 percent of those earnings came from abroad and were subject to the particular economic conditions and political vicissitudes in those countries. We had lost six other telephone companies to the Communist bloc countries of Eastern Europe since the end of World War II. Weak currencies in Western Europe in relation to the strong American dollar threatened the value of our earnings there. And in Latin America, political sentiments of "Yanqui Go Home" made our investments there very risky. We were consistently denied the rate increases we needed to sustain our telephone services in most of those countries. In time we would indeed lose our telephone companies in Brazil, Peru, Mexico, and Chile, although some compensation was paid in those instances.

If we were to survive, it was plain that we had to increase our base of earnings in the United States. We were an American-owned company. About 90 percent of the 88,000 shareholders at the time were Americans. In order to ensure our ability to pay dividends to our shareholders, we had to achieve greater earnings within the United States. We figured that to be safe we wanted at least 50 percent—not the then current 15 percent—of ITT annual earnings to come from sales within our own borders. There simply was too much uncertainty in having to rely upon our earnings from abroad.

In describing the situation at the time, I would figuratively put myself in the shoes of a typical investor trying to decide whether or not to buy ITT stock. My imaginary investor was the trust officer of the Bank of Wichita, in Kansas. Would he invest widows' funds in a company whose business was spread about in foreign countries? I didn't think so. My job, as I saw it, was to make ITT truly "international" by bringing its business back to America. I needed to build a company whose stock that bank officer in Wichita could buy without fear for its future, a stock that he or his widows could put in the bottom of their safe-deposit boxes and sleep easy in the knowledge that ITT stock was safe and increasing in value. Our board of directors readily agreed: ITT had to grow and expand in the United States. The question before us in those early years was what acquisitions should we make to do so.

Our domestic business at the time was almost entirely in military telecommunications equipment for the Defense Department. ITT's earlier attempts to expand beyond telecommunications, before my arrival, had been disastrous. The operating people and old-time executives wanted ITT to acquire companies only within our own field of knowledge. Our first acquisitions were along this line—Jennings Radio, National Transistor, General Controls, Cannon Electric, Gilfillan. We then came within one tenth of a point of the value of our shares to merging with United Telephone, of Kansas City, the third-largest telephone company in the United States. If this merger had gone through, ITT would have become a telephone manufacturing and operating company—in effect, a utility. United wanted to trade share for share; we offered only nine tenths of an ITT share for a full share of United. When those negotiations broke down, I felt a sense of relief. I had not been too happy with the prospect of ITT becoming a telephone utility, with its high investment cost, frozen asset base, and regulated returns—all in exchange for the opportunity of competing with the Bell System, which controlled 90 percent of all the telephones in the country.

In preparing for a discussion with the board about possible areas of expansion, I prepared a one-sheet grid, listing the pros and cons of one industry in comparison to another. Along the top of the sheet of graph paper I listed such items as market, rate of returns, capital investment, ease of financing, stress on management, etc.; down the left-hand side, I listed industries. Utilities, like telephone companies, had a steady but slow increase in earnings, a fixed market, could borrow money easily, very little stress on management, and a pretty good return on investment. A utility was a legally entrenched monopoly. Our cable companies were akin to semi-monopolies, with the same pluses and minuses as the telephone companies, except that the market was open, not fixed, and the stress on management was a bit higher. Then the defense business, which was our largest in the United States, showed that the stress on management was very high: We had to bid for every single contract, and they were of limited duration, the returns were very low at that time, and the cost of labor and management was high.

I proposed to the board that we not expand our defense business. Instead, I listed another category on the grid: financial services. It had low stress on management, low capital investment, low labor costs, an open market, and was relatively free of economic cycles. What's more, its relatively high returns would always be in cash.

The first non-related acquisition I proposed to the ITT board of directors was a personal loan company—Aetna, of St. Louis. The board was aghast at the idea.

How did I pick that particular business and particular company within the field of financial services? By intuition and personal experience, more than anything else. I remembered that when I worked in Chicago I had heard of a company that had been founded by a streetcar conductor. He had started out lending money at the end of the trolley line to his fellow conductors—to be paid back with interest on the next payday. That small beginning grew into one of the biggest and most successful personal loan companies in the United States—Household Finance. So, years later, at ITT I began to look for a business like that. Aetna had been founded in St. Louis by a dentist named Charles Yallem, and was then being run by David Corwin, who thought of his Aetna as a sort of "poor man's financial consultant." Dave gave a dignity and true, honest purpose to Aetna in consolidating loans for poor people who could not borrow from banks and were prey for the many loan shark companies of that day. I liked Dave and the company and wanted him to stay on to run it for ITT.

When I proposed Aetna to the ITT board, the directors rejected it as something entirely unworthy of the good name and reputation of ITT. They put a personal loan company on a par with a pawnshop, perhaps one grade above a house of prostitution. At the next month's board meeting, I came prepared for that argument. I placed in front of each board member a copy of *Life* magazine, in which I had flagged nine prominent advertisements for the credit companies of large, very reputable corporations, such as GM Acceptance Corp., GE's credit companies, and similar installment loan institutions.

"What's the difference between what they are doing and what I propose we do, gentlemen?" I asked. After some spirited discussion, the acquisition of our first non-related company was approved. We bought Aetna Finance Co. for $39,591,000 and paid for it with ITT common and preferred stock, not cash. Since that day, Aetna never stopped growing. Last year alone it *earned* almost three times its full purchase price after taxes, which equaled the earnings of the twentieth-largest bank in the country, and its annual net income is expected to be higher in 1985.

Because Aetna was so small at the time we acquired it, we were able to buy one or two other small personal loan companies in Wisconsin. But we could not expand very much in this field because the Justice Department's interpretation of the antitrust laws forbade us from buying more than one or two companies in the same industry. So we had to search elsewhere for other acquisitions.

During one of my vacations in New England I came across the owner of a small pump company who explained to me how and why almost all pump companies were profitable. Pumps are a basic component of almost all manufacturing systems; They are always needed, new ones and rebuilt ones, as a means of getting liquids from one place to another. So at ITT I turned my attention to pump companies and found most of them were family-owned, relatively small, and not very well managed, according to modern methods. We began to acquire pump companies and then valve companies, because pumps and valves worked together as partners in industry. We built them up so that today ITT is perhaps the largest manufacturer of pumps in the world. They are hardly glamorous companies, but as my friend told me years ago in New England, they are "earners" in good times and bad. As time went on, we learned that components are often more profitable, more broadly based, and their market more secure than the end products of which they are a part. We then moved into making components for applied electronics, which became one of the fastest-growing segments in the economy.

In line with our thinking on component parts and because we needed to diversify in Europe from an overdependence on government telephone markets, in 1967 we bought Teves, a German auto parts company, for $75 million. The following year, Thompson auto parts company in the United States came to us as a subsidiary of the Sheraton hotel chain. Once again, we found that what many considered a very mundane business was in reality a stable, profitable enterprise with a growing market. Today, having built upon what we bought, our auto parts companies are a $2 billion annual business. I am told that every automobile manufactured in Europe contains at least one ITT part.

ITT, when I got there, was substantially a manufacturing company, specializing in electromechanical switching systems for telecommunications, and we grew with that field from the cumbersome electrical systems through electronics to today's sophisticated, high-speed digital systems. For a good twenty years, we poured 75 percent of our research and development budget into what our engineers and scientists envisioned as the future in telecommunications. They produced a great many advanced components in electronics for which the finished product had not yet been invented. Only now, with ITT's new System 12 for long-distance telephonic communications, have many of those early researched products come to market.

But in the sixties and early seventies, when we were still striving to build the company's earnings in the United States, we turned to the area of consumer products and service industries. That appeared to me to be the area of greatest potential growth at the time. I must say that we were early in our recognition of the swing to a service economy in the country. We proceeded almost without competition to acquire companies in the consumer field.

In picking and choosing what companies to acquire, I liked to tell people we bought what was available. Perhaps that was an oversimplification. What we did was consider companies individually that were up for sale or desirous of merging with ITT. Following no grand strategy, we looked into the rationale behind each company's business. Did it provide a product or a service that customers would buy and continue to buy? Was it a good product? Were the earnings good enough, secure enough, for the effort that went into producing them? What was the company's future potential? Was its market growing or declining? And finally, could we at ITT with our expertise in management and our access to greater financial resources *add* something significant to that particular company? Could we help it grow after we acquired it? Simple questions such as these defined for us how a particular company would fit into the ITT system of management.

Certainly, we examined the figures on the balance sheet. We formed opinions of the company's management, its current problems, the likelihood of our being able to solve those problems, and then we acted. There was nothing scientific in the process. I think our acquisitions were based largely upon intuition, experience, and a sense of confidence that we at ITT could help manage that company better than it had been managed before. In most instances, we kept on the same management and introduced the company's managers to the ITT system of business plans, detailed budgets, strict financial controls, and face-to-face General Managers Meetings. Behind all our thinking was the basic recognition that it is better to take over and build upon an existing business than to start a new one.

Moving into consumer goods and services, which represented a diversification from our reliance upon engineering and manufacturing, we acquired Avis Rent-A-Car in 1965, and APCOA airport parking lots in 1966, and Sheraton Hotels in 1968. Avis was fundamentally a good business, buying or leasing automobiles on a wholesale basis and renting them out retail by the mile or by the day; as long as one kept careful financial controls, it seemed almost impossible not to make a steady and increasing profit. We expanded Avis to the European market and it was there that its most substantial profits were to be found. Sheraton was bought on the same rationale: When more and more Americans were traveling for business and pleasure, we would build and operate more and more hotels and motels, in effect buying beds and renting them out by the night.

The acquisition of Continental Baking Company, with its immensely popular Wonder bread, Hostess cakes, and Twinkies, was a major move for us into the national consumer market. ITT products would now be sold in every grocery store across the nation. Continental was the largest baking company in America when we acquired it for $181 million worth of ITT stock in 1968. Its sales for the previous full year came to $621 million; since then, under ITT, Continental's sales more than doubled to $1.5 billion in 1982.

Along the way, we acquired a host of other small companies in consumer fields: cosmetics, light bulbs, books, hardware, and, frankly, whatever we thought would increase our earnings in the United States. One of our most promising acquisitions in the mid-sixties was Levitt & Sons, one of the leading, best-known builders of low-cost housing in this country. Founded upon the construction of an entire community of inexpensive homes called Levittown on Long Island, New York, immediately after World War II, the company was not only successful and profitable, it had imaginative plans for building large subdivisions and whole communities abroad. We thought we could provide the very high capital investment needed for Levitt's imaginative plans. With eager anticipation of future growth, we acquired Levitt for $91.6 million and it turned out to be one of our biggest mistakes. Our management philosophies did not mesh and the housing market turned down severely.

The sixties were not only the "go-go years" of the stock market, they also ranked as a period of rapid inflation and hence a steady devaluation of the dollar. To protect ourselves against this inflationary spiral, we turned to acquisitions in natural resources. Once again, we were early in recognizing that all natural resources, whether renewable or not, could only increase in value as inflation continued to rise in the United States.

Rayonier, one of the world's leading producers of wood cellulose, the basic ingredient of acetate and rayon, was our prize acquisition in natural resources. It had been a rather sluggish company with low earnings when we bought it in 1968 for $293,145,000. With the infusion of ITT capital and management and swept along with the inflationary tide, Rayonier has increased almost tenfold as an ITT asset, its present value estimated at between $2.5 and $3 billion. Two months later we acquired Pennsylvania Glass & Sand, a leading producer of silica, which is used in the manufacture of glass, and of fertilizers and pesticides, for $112.5 million. I remember that it took me no longer than twenty minutes to decide to buy that company. All the facts and figures added up to a good buy. The founders wanted to sell because they were ready to retire. One of them asked only that his son, who was then laid up because of a motorcycle accident, be permitted to return to run the company. I gave my word and Hale Andrews has been running that company ever since, and running it well. We also bought relatively small oil and gas and coal companies to round out ITT's stake in the country's natural resources.

In terms of ITT's broad future, our general objective in making all these acquisitions during the 1960s, remember, was to achieve 50 percent of our earnings within the borders of the United States. To reach this goal we not only had to grow fast, we had to grow faster than our subsidiaries were expanding in Europe. They were busy acquiring assets of their own, moving into consumer products such as television and radio sets, electronic equipment, and whatever. There were times when we were buying a company a day. In 1968 alone we acquired Levitt, Rayonier, Sheraton, PGS, and ten other companies.

We paid for our acquisitions not with cash but with shares of ITT common and preferred stock. It should be pointed out that not one of our acquisitions was made by an unfriendly tender. We bought only what was for sale. Most of the acquisition proposals, and certainly the larger ones, came to us from the investment banking firm of Lazard Frères in the person of Felix Rohatyn, a brilliant, hardworking partner in the firm, who later won considerable fame for his work in extricating New York City from the brink of bankruptcy. As a real estate broker might show a buyer a number of homes from which to choose, Rohatyn, knowing what ITT was looking for, would present to us suitable companies that were desirous of or at least interested in merging with a larger, capital-intensive company. From his proposals, we picked and chose.

When we found a company we liked, we almost always paid the price or close to the price demanded. As a result, we became known as a generous buyer. Companies came to us before going to anyone else and so we often had first choice in making an offer. I have always believed that in buying you have to offer a man what he considers his company to be worth, even if it is considerably above its book value or stock market price. Otherwise, he is not going to sell it to you. I wanted the seller to feel that he was getting more from us than he could get anywhere else. As the buyer, I had to be convinced that the future potential growth of that company made the price I was paying cheap for what I was getting. Both of us had to come away happy, because more often than not we would be working together to make the future growth of that company possible.

Some companies I bought after only a ten- or twenty-minute inspection of their books, without ever seeing the company itself. In these cases, what I was looking for was a company that was obviously doing well and that we could help do better. O.M. Scott and Sons was a prime example of this kind of acquisition. It was presented to me one night in 1971. Its principal owner, Paul Williams, recovering from an illness, had decided he wanted to sell. I looked over its balance sheet, the asking price, and within fifteen minutes I said yes. Scott, a leading producer of lawn and fertilizer products, had sales of $64 million, with net earnings of $2.7 million, for the year. The asking price was $77 million, and we paid it. Ten years later, as an ITT subsidiary, Scott's sales had increased 280 percent to $235.8 million. Its net earnings mushroomed 560 percent to $13.6 million in 1981.

Eyebrows were frequently raised on Wall Street over some of the prices we paid for our acquisitions. But we could afford to pay above the asset value of a company, if we had to, because at the time ITT stock was selling as high as twenty times earnings. So in buying a company that was selling at twelve or thirteen times its earnings, we could afford to give fourteen, fifteen, or even sixteen times earnings. The dollar value may well have been high, but once we increased the earnings of the acquisition, it fell into line with our own earnings per share. Some people looked upon our stock, and others as well, during the 1960s, as inflated. To my mind those stock prices were not so much inflated as they were representative of investor anticipation of where the value of the stock would be in the future. The value of ITT stock was solid; sellers were happy to take it in exchange for their stock. What we were really paying for our acquisitions was the value we had built up in ITT stock through hard work and good management. We were cashing in on our reputation.

From the outside, however, conglomerates in general were still viewed with skepticism, suspected of "buying" their earnings. The intimation was that those earnings could not be sustained. However, that was not the case with ITT. In 1972, *Fortune* magazine did an in-depth survey of ITT holdings and found that the earnings of our acquired companies continued to grow under ITT at about the same rate as our original holdings. "All together, the earnings of the acquired companies have had a weighted growth rate averaging 12.5 percent annually," said *Fortune,* adding, "Exactly the same growth rate turns out to apply to the 1960 'base' companies. . . . In short, ITT has shown an ability to make both its acquired and inherited companies grow at impressive rates."

I made my own survey that year, 1972, of nearly fifty corporations with $750 million or more in annual sales in 1959 and found that ITT's growth in earnings per share was second only to IBM. We were growing from within as much as from our acquisitions. After my retirement as chief executive of ITT in 1977, I totaled up our acquisitions and found that we put out some 96 million shares of ITT stock, worth, at the market value at the time, about $6 billion. Today those acquisitions have a market value of about $12 billion. Moreover, under "pooling accounting" methods used for stock acquisitions, the acquired companies went on our books at a value of roughly $4 billion, giving ITT a projected capital profit of $8 billion. Those acquired companies, which are now completely woven into the corporate tapestry, provide ITT with approximately three quarters of all its earnings today.

Of the hundreds of acquisitions we made, the acquisition decision which probably pleases me the most is the "non-acquisition" we made in the early 1960s. The road you don't take can be as important in your life as the one you do take. In the very early sixties, when computers were seen as the wave of the future, many of our engineers, particularly those in Europe, were eager to surge into this new, phenomenal field. Our German company, which was far ahead of the others in computer development, outbid IBM and won a contract to build a computerized reservation system for Air France. We lost $10 million on that contract. I called a halt to further computer development. Our engineers throughout the system complained and threatened to quit, abandoning other computer projects, unless I allowed them to continue their research and development. They wanted to learn and keep up with the state of the art. Research and development of computers was an engineer's delight from the very start, a dream of the future. To me, as a businessman, they represented a nightmare of very high investments, enormous stress on management, and ultra-high risks for any return in the far-distant future. Quite a few of our engineers did leave to join companies developing computers; computer engineers were in high demand at the time. Others continued to work on computer development for us on the sly. When I learned of this, I hired two very competent engineers and gave them a special assignment which lasted for several years: to roam at will through all our worldwide engineering and new products laboratories and to root out, stamp out, and stop all incipient general-purpose computer projects by whatever code name they were called; and if they were given any trouble, to call us at headquarters and we would stamp them out for them.

I withstood a great deal of pressure at the time to enforce my early prohibition against the development of general-purpose computers at ITT. Not only our engineers but our investment advisers favored computer development. Everyone who could was going into computers, they said. The mere announcement would send our stock up, they promised. I stood firm at the time and since then I have followed with some interest how other companies fared with computers. One of our top engineering executives pressed me with his dreams of fortunes to be made by computers which would change the world. When I refused to budge, he resigned and joined another company, which proceeded to lose some $120 million on computer development. He went from there to another company, again as head of the computer division, and that company later abandoned its computer program, losing approximately $500 million. Billions upon billions of dollars have been written off in failed computer development programs by such highly reputed firms as General Electric, RCA, Honeywell, Sperry, and others in this country, and by Siemens, Philips, and others in Europe—all because of the dreams and ambitions of engineers like the ones we encountered at ITT.

The engineers were not to blame for those gigantic losses. From their vantage point they were eminently correct in anticipating the impact that computers would have upon our lives and upon the marketplace. The fault lies with those top management people who saw themselves as grand strategists. They could sit in a room and think they could see what would happen twenty years ahead. The view was glorious. With that knowledge and their strategic thinking, they could plan how to capture a share of that computer market of the future. The trouble was, as it almost always is with grand strategies, everybody else could see what they saw and plan the very same strategies. They would all fight the leader, IBM, for a share of that enormous market. The ones who have survived thus far are still fighting IBM for a profitable share of that market, and only a few of them will survive in the long run. As I said, I derive a special sense of pleasure from our non-acquisition of general-purpose computers at ITT; that decision saved the company at least $500 million in probable losses.

The advantages of diversification and the conglomerate structure of a corporation were not recognized until the conglomerate movement was well underway. The folklore in this country had always been: "Shoemaker, stick to your trade." Anyone who dared to venture beyond his own field of expertise was asking for trouble. It followed that any company which grew rapidly in a great variety of different fields was attempting a balancing act on a tightrope over a deep chasm. It had to crash; if not today, then next year; if not next year, soon enough. That was the kind of thinking that said conglomerates were too big to be efficient, too diversified to be managed by any one man or headquarters team. Some people in the business community still believe that, although I think that they are fewer today than ever before.

Conglomerates do have a distinct and important advantage over a company (even of the same size) which sticks to one product or even several products in the same industry. The steel industry taught me that when I worked for Jones & Laughlin. When the demand for steel went down, there was nothing constructive you could do about it. You could bank the furnaces, lay off employees, wait it out, and try to survive that economic cycle. The same is true for any company or industry which essentially produces only one product. The only salvation, as I have seen it, is for a company to diversify, to produce several different products, so that when the demand for one goes down, the company can deploy its assets to the products for which there is a demand.

A multi-industry, multi-product company covering a wide span of the economic sector has a built-in insurance policy against an economic downturn. If that span is wide enough, some products of the company will still be in demand and selling well while others are in decline. There are always cycles in every business. They rise and fall like the tides, except that they are far less predictable. Thus, at ITT, when the demand for telephone switching equipment was slow, our consumer-oriented companies could be enjoying a banner year. We were able to concentrate our joint assets and efforts as one corporation in those products and industries that presented favorable opportunities. For those companies in temporary decline, we would dig in our heels, turn off the lights and pick up the paper clips, so to speak, and try to mitigate the effects of the business cycle. In other words, we would back our winners, push them to grow faster and bigger, while we dug in our heels and carried our losers. When the business cycle changed, we could redeploy our assets to back the new winners and carry any new losers. Actually, we have found that the growth in sales of a product in high demand increases at a much faster rate than the decline in products cyclically out of favor. So in pushing the expansion of your winners, you might double their sales while other company sales fall back only 25 percent. Even with the law of averages, with some of your diversified product sales going up and others going down, in a conglomerate you have an edge in your favor. In generally bad economic years, ITT's earnings still grew by 10 percent with a lot of hard work, and in good years, they grew 15 percent with half the effort.

Time, I think, has proven the skeptics wrong. Conglomerates are not abhorrent to nature. Certainly, they are manageable. One may have to work harder than the men who run single-product companies. But, once again, there are some significant advantages. In a company that has a series of autonomous profit centers, each one of them operates independently of the others and there is none of that diffused responsibility one finds in a vertically integrated company. I remember well the intense battles fought at Jones & Laughlin over fixing responsibility for something that had gone wrong, whether it was a fault of the coal mines, the coke furnaces, or the steel mills. At ITT, each company manager was responsible for everything that happened, good or bad, within his own profit center. Each new company we acquired at ITT brought with it new brainpower, a fresh viewpoint, some bit of expertise that we did not have before. In our president's office, there were no geniuses. We all worked together and we worked very hard. The management team of each new company taught us the fundamentals of that particular business, so that we at headquarters could understand and appreciate its operations. We learned something new every day about the various facets of different types of business. Since we covered a wide spectrum of the national economy, I think we became much more knowledgeable about general economic conditions all over the world. It made us, I think, better, broader businessmen than one would find in the average company on the Fortune 500 list.

While many people in the business and financial community were convinced that conglomerates were too big ever to be managed successfully, liberals in the political arena cried out that conglomerates were so big that they could not be anything but successful in competition with smaller businesses. Conglomerates were too big, growing too fast, they shouted, and bigness in business was inherently bad. It soon became a rallying cry, a buzzword or slogan, "Bigness is bad." According to the best legal opinions, there was nothing monopolistic about conglomerates as long as they did not gain control of more than 5 percent of any one market. None of the conglomerates—ITT, Textron, Litton, Ling-Temco-Vought, Gulf & Western, and others—controlled markets in a way that the law and the courts deemed monopolistic. But on the political front, the neo-populists cried out that the conglomerates would gobble up everything in sight, that they would grow bigger and bigger, more and more powerful, that somehow or other they were unfair competition to the smaller businesses. It was more an article of political faith than an accurate portrayal of the facts. In fact, most conglomerates were forging into various fields of business in which they represented but a small fraction of the market. Rather than stifling competition, they were introducing the first bit of real competition with economic clout in markets that had been dominated by companies that had grown sluggish and stagnant over the years.

* * *

ITT was to provide the testing ground for the survival of all conglomerates, first when we proposed a merger with the American Broadcasting Company in 1965 and then in 1968 when we proposed one with the Hartford Insurance Company. They became battles royal between the government and free enterprise, and they became much more political than economic in nature. That is said only in hindsight. At the time, I personally considered both mergers as strictly business propositions.

Our proposed merger with ABC started out as strictly business, a proposition based upon the fit of our two companies. Sosthenes Behn had approached ABC years before with the idea of merging, but those negotiations had fallen through. In the mid-1960s, television was still an expanding growth industry, on the verge of converting from black-and-white to color telecasts. ABC, however, was too cash poor to keep up with the new technology. The network, which ran a poor third to NBC and CBS, had been losing money on its television operations. Leonard Goldenson, its president, fearful of an unfriendly takeover, was interested in merging with a company that would preserve the integrity and autonomy of ABC.

I met with Goldenson and we worked out a merger agreement for an exchange of stock valued at about $200 million and a plan whereby he and his staff would continue to manage ABC autonomously as a wholly owned subsidiary of ITT. For ITT, it seemed like a very profitable area of expansion. We could supply the capital investment ABC needed; once that was done, ABC could become competitive with the other two networks. The merger would put us in a position similar to that of the Radio Corporation of America (RCA), which was one of our chief competitors. We had only to look at the ever-increasing cash flow that NBC provided for RCA to envision what ABC could do for ITT in the expanding field of television.

The merger, announced in December 1965, brought

forth cries of protest from anti-business groups that rever-
berated in Washington. The merger was portrayed as the
largest in broadcasting history, with intimations that because it was very big, it had to be very bad. It soon became only a question of which government agency would
investigate and pass judgment: the Federal Trade Commission, the Federal Communications Commission, or
the Antitrust Division of the Justice Department. While
the Justice Department hemmed and hawed, and our lawyers assured us that there were no antitrust implications
in competing with NBC and CBS, the FCC took jurisdic-
tion.

The FCC held hearings in 1966: Would ITT control or
manipulate the news? Was the merger in the public interest? Both Goldenson and I testified at length in favor of
the merger. We told of ABC's need for capital infusion to
modernize the network and convert to color television.
We testified as to our agreement to an arm's-length relationship between ITT and ABC news broadcasting. The
FCC approved the merger by a vote of 4–3. The anti-
business stalwarts then attacked the honesty of the FCC
hearings and demanded more time to present more evidence. So the FCC opened a second series of hearings,
which turned out to be longer and more vituperative than
the first. Once again the merger was approved, 4–3. Our
victory was short-lived. The Justice Department then
filed an antitrust suit against ITT to overturn the FCC decision and to stop the merger.

Our lawyers never could satisfactorily explain to me
the rationale of the Justice Department antitrust suit. The
only change I could see was that Nicholas Katzenbach
had been replaced as Attorney General by Ramsey Clark,
and Clark had a personal and political bent against business. Two years had passed since we first announced the
ABC merger and now our lawyers told us that an antitrust
suit might be dragged through the courts for another five
years. We would win on the law in the end, according to
our lawyers, but I could not see holding ABC in limbo for

five years, not knowing whether or not we owned the company, not being able to move forward and invest ITT money in ABC with the assurance the company was ours. Besides, the lawsuit could effectively stop us from acquiring other companies because any new acquisitions, according to our lawyers, might well prejudice the ABC case against us. So, after consulting with Leonard Goldenson, we announced on New Year's Day, 1968, that we were dropping our merger plans.

Toward the end of that year, 1968, Felix Rohatyn came to me with word that the Hartford Insurance Company, the sixth-largest in that field, might be up for sale because its management was fearful of a takeover. It had assets of almost $2 billion and income from premiums of $969 million that year, and yet it was losing money on its underwriting because of the huge claims it had been paying in the previous four or five years. Its stock price was temptingly low. Earnings throughout the fire-and-casualty industry had been depressed because of the increasing claims, jury decisions, and out-of-court settlements. When I looked at a chart of its earnings, I could see that while Hartford had been losing money on its insurance operations and the profits and losses fluctuated widely over the years, its investment of premiums was an ever-rising line of good earnings, especially in the bull market of the sixties. On my grid of good and bad businesses, I could see that Hartford had all the positive attributes of Aetna, the personal loan company which I had bought as the first step in the diversification of ITT.

When we approached the Hartford management and directors, we encountered a reluctance to a merger, based upon a general suspicion of the intentions of a conglomerate. It was still a dirty word in the eyes of conservative management. It took us almost a full year with several rounds of serious discussions to allay the fears of the men who ran Hartford. We offered $68 a share for Hartford stock, which was then selling at $47 a share, and the Hartford shareholders approved the merger overwhelmingly. We paid $1.5 billion in ITT stock for 22 million shares of Hartford stock. While the price seemed high to many people, we felt the value was there and that Hartford's stock was selling at less than the true value of the company. The merger then needed the approval of the Connecticut Insurance Commission in the person of Insurance Commissioner William Cotter, a liberal Democrat.

In the state hearings, ITT was bombarded with accusations, suspicions, and demands: ITT intended to squeeze the cash out of Hartford and leave it a shell; ITT would move the headquarters and the city would lose Hartford's support of the city's civic and social organizations; the local economy would suffer; Connecticut citizens would lose jobs, etc. The Hartford merger became a political cause célèbre, the most vocal and vituperative opposition coming from Ralph Nader, as a consumer advocate. He claimed a personal interest in this case because he had been born in Winsted, Connecticut. Wanting to come into Connecticut as friends, not as an invading army, we answered every accusation and suspicion as best we could. We offered a ten-point, written manifesto, pledging that we would invest additional money in Hartford Insurance rather than strip it out; we would ensure Hartford's autonomy, maintain its board of directors, adding only two members from ITT; we would continue the company's headquarters in Hartford and the ITT board members would travel to the city for the board meetings; we would continue to support local philanthropies, etc. The merger was given the approval of the Connecticut Insurance Commission.

Next we had to face the Antitrust Division of the Department of Justice. The new chief of the division, Richard McLaren, filed an antitrust suit against ITT to block the merger. Frankly, we were surprised. We could understand Ramsey Clark's political viewpoint, but McLaren was a Republican serving under John Mitchell, the Attorney General, who was a Republican serving under

Richard Nixon, who certainly was a Republican. To us, it seemed as though McLaren's motives were primarily self-aggrandizement, leading a political crusade against the supposed evil of big business. According to the best outside, impartial legal opinion we consulted, including that of the former head of the Antitrust Division, there was no way that a merger of ITT and Hartford would substantially lessen competition in the casualty insurance field, as prohibited by law. Even the press noted that McLaren had a weak case. But he was endeavoring to create new law or a new interpretation of the antitrust laws.

McLaren's thesis was that big business was bad for the common good, even if the big business did not control any one market. Soon after taking office, he had announced that he was going after conglomerates on the grounds that they "raise barriers to entry and discourage smaller firms from competing." Philosophically, he was entitled to his opinion, although I think his facts and opinion were wrong, but in court he would need some legal basis for that thesis. His legal brief was based upon the concept of "potential reciprocity." McLaren argued that ITT with all its other subsidiaries *could* give its Hartford insurance company an edge in getting the insurance business of all its subsidiaries, thereby creating unfair competition with other insurance companies. That was "potential reciprocity." That was like saying that a man walking down the street with a bag of golf clubs over his shoulder was a "potential murderer" because he *could* decide to hit someone over the head with a No. 2 iron and kill him. After all, almost anything can be deemed "potential."

The merits of the case were argued far and wide in legal, business, financial, and political circles. Press coverage was widespread. Suffice it to say that it turned out that President Nixon, Attorney General John Mitchell, and several other cabinet members stated publicly that it was not the policy of the Administration that mere bigness in business was bad. But they seemed to be help-less to stop the personal crusade of their chief of the Anti-trust Division. They feared political repercussions over interfering with the freedom of one of their subordinates.

While McLaren was leading his crusade to stop mer-gers of companies in the United States, it was no secret that other governments were doing just the opposite. Ja-pan helped its two biggest steel companies merge into the Nippon Steel Corp., making it the largest steel company in the world. The French combined Renault and Peugeot into one big automobile company. Germany combined twenty-six coal companies into one viable combine. The British merged five Scottish shipyards. And so it went throughout Western Europe, with governments there act-ing as marriage brokers. All this was pointed out at the time: The world was becoming one economic market in which companies would compete on an international basis, and to do that, the companies had to be big and ef-ficient. Even at that time, the United States was begin-ning to lose its edge in international competition. Our trade deficit then was some $12 billion. But ITT, with its international scope, was bringing into the United States a surplus of $1 billion a year, which was certainly a contri-bution to the well-being of the nation.

However, we failed to sway public opinion; we could not stop one man from his course of action. Once again, as with ABC, we had a legal case we could probably win in court. But we could not afford economically to remain standing on one foot in relationship to our ownership of Hartford for another five years. Three years already had gone into battle. So we reached an out-of-court settle-ment with the Antitrust Division in the spring of 1971, similar to a settlement McLaren had made previously with another conglomerate: ITT would be permitted to keep Hartford with its $1 billion annual premium in-come; in return, we would divest ourselves of other sub-sidiaries with that same amount of annual sales; ITT would also agree that for a period of ten years we would not acquire any insurance company with assets of $10 million or more, or acquire any other company in the United States with assets of $100 million or more, without the prior approval of the Justice Department. In complying with the agreement, we sold off Avis, Levitt, Canteen, and portions of Grinnell.

The settlement was not a victory for either of us, or for anyone else, as far as I can determine. I cannot see where our divestiture helped the companies we sold, or changed the marketplace or served society any better than if we had retained them. Has the public been any better off since Avis Rent-A-Car was owned by other conglomerates, Norton Simon and Esmark? By the time of the settlement, the stock market had turned down, price/earnings ratios were low, and I doubt if we would have proceeded with any more large acquisitions. Since our merger, Hartford has prospered and grown fivefold. Its sales increased from $1 billion to $5 billion in 1982; its net income from $50 million to $254 million. Today the Hartford operation represents 23 percent of all ITT revenues. What's more, its earnings produce 36 percent of all ITT profits. Since the ITT-Hartford merger we have kept every one of our pledges to the company and to the city. Harry Williams, then chairman and chief executive of Hartford, was ready to step down when we merged. I think he was surprised when we told him that we wanted him to continue and that we wanted to know his own plans for the future growth of the company so that we could invest whatever funds were necessary to make those plans work. When he retired some years later, he named his successor, Herb Scheon, and the continuity of management continued, for when Scheon reached retirement age, he named Peter Thomas as his successor. To this day, in keeping with our agreement with Hartford, ITT members of the Hartford board of directors get up extra early in the morning one day each month and fly from New York to Hartford to attend those board meetings. Among those ITT men who do this are

Rand Araskog, chairman and chief executive of ITT, and myself.

The Hartford case was a mess—politically, not managerially. Since then, however, opinion in this country has changed a great deal. No longer is the size of a company considered prima facie evidence of whether it is good or bad for the country. The years have shown that America needs the clout of big business in order to compete on the world market. The giant corporate mergers of the early 1980s, involving Du Pont, U.S. Steel, and several oil companies, ranging as high as $7 billion, dwarf the scope of the $1.5 billion ITT-Hartford merger, and have gone through without one word of protest from the current Antitrust Division of the Justice Department. When the stock market in the early eighties undervalued many companies, as it did in the sixties, the acquisitions and mergers began anew. I like to think that a good many chief executives had learned over these years the advantages of diversifying their assets and covering a wider spectrum of the marketplace.

I would like to think that the public has come to appreciate that a conglomerate, per se, is not an offense in nature. It is a diversified company, with a central management, that produces a variety of products and services that transcend any one particular industry. If a conglomerate is well managed, it will prosper and grow because it serves the needs of its customers; if it is poorly managed, it will stumble and fall of its own weight—just like any other company.

ELEVEN

Entrepreneurial Spirit

Where are the corporate entrepreneurs?

THERE is an emerging awareness of the need for a return of that old American entrepreneurial spirit to lift us out of the doldrums and to make these United States once again the envy of the industrialized world. People are talking about various ideas to single out the entrepreneurs in corporate life and to give them free rein to "do their own thing" and to earn as much money as they deserve for their ventures. Where are the Rockefellers, Carnegies, and Fords of our day? Why do our big corporations seem to be plodding along today, enmeshed in a bureaucracy of their own making, caging the free spirits in their ranks with rules and regulations that stifle the bold ventures of an age gone by? Where, people are beginning to ask, are our corporate entrepreneurs?

The answer is: There are none.

By definition, an entrepreneur is one who is in business for himself; he organizes, manages, and assumes the risks of a business enterprise. In practical terms, he's the man who bets it all, takes a big risk for a big return. He's the man who puts his company on the line or, if he does not already have a company, mortgages his house and everything he owns in order to bet that he knows something that others do not. If he wins, the rewards can be fabulous; if he loses, he is wiped out. The entrepreneurs we see today are individuals who "start up" a company, based upon a new invention or a new service, or take over a defunct, cast-off business that no one else wants and then, by dint of sheer hard work, make something of it. But most of these are all relatively small ventures, at least at the start, and they are launched outside and beyond the scope of our large corporations which have the resources to be entrepreneurial on a grand scale.

Can you imagine a chief executive of a company like General Electric or General Motors "betting his company" on the outcome of a single significant move? No, a man who heads a publicly owned company is entrusted with hundreds of millions or billions of dollars of values that belong to others. It is not his money to risk. He is cast in the role of a trustee. The people who invest their money in his company want him to give them an annual return of 10 percent or 12 percent or 15 percent. They don't want him to risk the assets of the company in an attempt to double or quadruple their investment. Can you imagine the number and size of the lawsuits which would ensue if any such corporate "gamble" were unsuccessful? A chief executive would have far more to lose than to gain by any such "calculated risk." If he were foolhardy enough to try, his board of directors, out of sheer self-preservation, would not countenance such a risk.

Some big companies try to *act* entrepreneurial, but only in a diluted sort of way. They box off areas for experimental or special development work, assign teams to work outside the mainstream of the company, all of them knowing that failure would not endanger any part of the company. The amount of money at risk is relatively so small that the chief executive's "trusteeship" is preserved even if the venture ends in total failure. He knows it and so does the group working on the project. The men on the project are not at significant risk either; they are paid their regular salaries. Even if the so-called entrepreneurial venture succeeded, it would not be large enough to influence the direction of the company. However well-meaning the motives, such "cells" of freedom from the bureaucracy of the corporation are little more than token entrepreneurism.

In truth, entrepreneurism is the very antithesis of the philosophy of large publicly owned corporations. Entrepreneurs are individuals who are innovative, independent, and willing to assume proportionately high risks for the potential of big returns. Large and successful companies are allowed to take only incremental, comparatively minor risks for comparatively minor results.

Most men who run large corporations are primarily concerned with how not to make mistakes, not even little ones. Their jobs depend upon it. In sizable corporations, where steady annual gains are expected, mistakes are not easily forgiven. A business executive on his way up will have to make at least five brilliant moves before he is considered a bright man on the fast track; one mistake along the way will plant a seed of distrust that may well destroy his career with that company. So all bets have to be covered on a personal as well as on a corporate level. Corporate managers inch their way along when handling new ideas. They rely upon a large support system of staff and outside consultants. They usually need peer support for proposing new ventures, and once their ideas are approved at a high level, they share responsibility for the new ideas with their higher-ups on the corporate ladder. The process is hardly one of going it alone. On the corporate level, fallback plans are worked out elaborately and held in readiness for a fast retreat. The spirit involved, far from being entrepreneurial, is to reduce the risk as much as possible. That does not mean that large corporations, with strong support systems, do not make big mistakes. They do! But those "big mistakes" are almost never the result of "big risks" taken deliberately in the hope of "big rewards." Invariably those "big mistakes" are unforeseen accidents which derail the best-laid plans of what had been intended to be rather safe, mundane ventures.

It is ironic—and sad—that so many companies which started out being highly entrepreneurial, usually with the introduction of a new product, and grew in size and success, lost their entrepreneurial fervor once they became investment-grade corporations. Xerox, which developed the first dry copying process, is a good example. Polaroid continued to be entrepreneurial long after the success of its instant camera, but only as long as Dr. Edward Land remained at the helm. The mystique of an inventive genius can preserve a company's innovative reputation in the minds of investors, bankers, and security analysts. With Polaroid, for example, investors had faith that another Dr. Land blockbuster was just around the corner. But when Dr. Land retired from Polaroid, much of the free, innovative spirit of the company seemed to disappear, and several of Polaroid's key people, presumably the more entrepreneurial of them, left the company, seeking, as they said, more exciting climates in which to work. Polaroid had become a more safe, staid, and stolid company. It fell into step with all the other companies of its size and scope. There is nothing wrong with this. It is just that the more successful a company becomes, the more locked in it has to be to satisfy its conservative investors.

There are exceptions, rare ones, to the rule that big corporations cannot be entrepreneurial. The most outstanding one to my mind is what Lee Iacocca did with the Chrysler Corporation. He did indeed "bet" the whole company on one model year, gambling that he could reorganize the company, cut the fat out of overhead and labor costs, oversee the production of a full line of new-model automobiles, and sell enough Chrysler automobiles to turn a profit. Even though backed by a big government loan, it was still a big bet on his part. He was permitted to make that bet only because Chrysler appeared to have no other choice. That was an entrepreneurial risk of the highest order. American Motors, faced with similar dire circumstances, took a more conservative road. It chose to sell half its stock to Renault and to reduce its production to two models of its AMC automobiles.

Shortly after I came aboard ITT in 1959, I found myself in a position to "bet the company." In my first year, Cuba was the seventh country to expropriate an ITT telephone company. While it may not have been as apparent as the Chrysler situation to the public and general stockholders, we too had a difficult choice at ITT—bet now or lose later. Some 85 percent of our earnings were derived from our companies overseas, and we were in jeopardy. So we began to bet. Cognizant of our stockholders' concern for security, we did not make one big bet; we made a series of small bets at first and then larger ones, sometimes four or five of them a week, until we had added some 350 new companies to ITT. In aggregate, we fashioned an almost entirely new company. We did it because we had to; we had no other choice.

Beyond those first few years when we were in jeopardy, however, I am not sure how "entrepreneurial" we were. But once we had melded our 350 acquisitions into 250 profit centers and our annual sales approached the $20 billion mark, and even before that high-water mark, ITT could no longer take the entrepreneurial-type risks that were taken in those early days. There was no possible way that I, for instance, could have called in the top two layers of management of ITT and told them to go all out and "bet" their companies and divisions on a brand-new market. These ITT managers conducted orderly businesses with orderly budgets, overseeing the work of some 375,000 employees. If we had tried to act like the high-technology entrepreneurs of Silicon Valley, we would have had sheer chaos through the worldwide companies of ITT. Instead of risking all our annual earnings in a new product, new company, or new field of endeavor—something in the neighborhood of $500 million or later $900 million—we would give a manager $1 million or $2 million to try something new, something "entrepreneurial." Doing this, we were not risking very much. If the entrepreneurial project failed, we would go on to something else, and still pay our expected dividend.

In recent years, as so many of our major companies carefully inched their way along in plodding stodginess and U.S. industry lost most of its competitive edge in the world market, business leaders began to search for ways of revitalizing that old entrepreneurial spirit that had once made American industry the envy of the world. If our big companies, because of their inherent structure, could not be entirely entrepreneurial, perhaps they could inculcate what everyone called "the spirit of entrepreneurism." What they sought was that old fervor of commitment that marks the entrepreneur. The man who risks everything to make a go of his own business is driven by pride, fear of failure, aspirations of success, and anticipation of large and just rewards for his efforts. It is only natural that he will outwork, outplan, outthink the corporate manager who is drawing a salary for working for someone else.

So the question becomes: How can you afford in a corporate structure to offer a self-starting, inventive employee the rewards of an entrepreneur? What can you do to stimulate entrepreneurial fervor in the corporate work force? It's really an old question. The classic case is that of the star salesman. I've heard many company presidents declare that they would put no cap on how much their star salesmen could make as long as they "created" new sales which benefited the entire company, that they would be happy even if one or two star salesmen earned more than the president himself. However, I have met only two chief executives who stuck to what they had said when salesmen actually did earn more than they did. All the rest changed the rules.

Which of them was right? I honestly don't know. Should a sales representative, no matter how good, earn more than the president of the company? The CEO has the responsibility for the design of the product, the production and marketing of the product, the financing and the management of the entire work involved in producing what the salesman sells. Does it make sense to pay him more than any of the other people who helped bring that product to market? The star salesman does have a market value, which he, uniquely, can prove by the number of his sales. The designer, production chief, and marketing man find it more difficult to single out and measure their own contributions, but they would strongly resent any salesperson whose compensation was out of line with their own. Still, the star salesperson, it seems to me, in a corporate hierarchy should be paid his or her market value so that he or she does not go elsewhere to earn more money. That market value is what some other company would be willing to pay for those sales services. But no more than that, unless you are willing to risk the happiness and loyalty of all those others contributing to the salesman's product. So much for entrepreneurism among corporate salesmen.

Some years ago, Raytheon set up one of its brilliant research engineers as the head and *part owner* of a company within Raytheon to handle a product he had developed. The idea was to spark innovations and new products from this small, independent company of engineers. When I joined Raytheon as executive vice president, I was called upon to umpire a bitter dispute between this independent development company and a sister division over the price of his product. The division wanted to buy the product, but thought his price exorbitant. He refused to reduce his price, saying that if Raytheon didn't want to pay that much, he could get that price from a competitor. He was acting like a genuine entrepreneur. Hostile charges and countercharges of ingratitude marked the meeting, and no agreement could be reached. Raytheon could not handle the entrepreneur in its midst. So Raytheon bought him out and he left the company. So much for the inventor-entrepreneur within corporate ranks.

More recently, after I retired from ITT, I had occasion to test the entrepreneurial waters of corporate America. I sought to find a corporate home for a small, talented group of men who had developed a special type of financial service. The operation was virtually without risk and had proven itself beyond its start-up phase. With only a few desks, an office, and a battery of telephones, this financial service company was already earning substantial profits. In order to expand and to double its earnings, the group wanted a home within a larger company in order to lend credibility to its short-term financing. The deal was that in return for up-front financing from a major corporation, the group would pay back the loan in three years, would give the corporation a 50 percent ownership in the operation, and at end of five years would sell its own 50 percent share to the corporation for a large sum in the millions. The corporation would make a sevenfold capital gain for its half interest in the venture.

Six different corporations looked at the deal and each agreed that the results predicted were correct, that the investment was desirable, and that the later acquisition probably would be advantageous. But the *specter* of introducing into the corporate ranks a handful of newcomers who would pocket millions of dollars at the end of five years' work was just too much for them to swallow. How would they explain the rewards involved to the other vice presidents and managers of the company, not to mention the president himself, who probably would earn only 3 or 5 percent of that amount for running the whole company? They all ducked the offer. Each decided that as good as the offer was, he would not risk wrecking his whole enterprise for one random jewel.

Corporate pay scales are delicate structures, designed to keep the workers, managers, and officers of the corporation satisfied, happy, and striving for more, while the corporation itself remains profitable. Every job in the corporation is graded and measured in medians of ranges, so that the boiler operators are made equal to the mail clerks and the division managers are equalized with the senior staff people, and with seniority each worker moves up a notch or so within his or her grade level. The essence of corporate profitability, however, is to keep taking in younger people at the lower levels and moving them up and very gradually increasing their pay. The net result is to make the employee, at some stage of his or her career, a captive of the corporation. If he is a good man, he's probably worth more than the company is paying him. If he went out on his own and if he succeeded, he might earn twice or twenty times what the company had been paying him. But by then it might be too late for him to switch jobs.

Years ago, when I started out, there was one company that rewarded its young managers with a promotion and a new title just about every week, but with no increases in pay. When these people got wise and left, the company hired new ones. Its policy was not very subtle. Today there are companies which recruit young men and women on college campuses for relatively high starting salaries and give them raises until they have been with the company long enough to make it difficult for them to fit in elsewhere. Then the raises slow down or stop and they are locked in at somewhat below their true market value. Such companies then have good help, cheap.

Most companies, however, do give reasonable promotions, pay increases, and bonuses up to the supposedly fair market value of the employee. They don't want their good employees moving over to the competitor. But their profits still come from getting these good people relatively cheap. What they give their managerial people instead of cash is security. It is a trade-off. Some men personally prefer the safety and support of the large paternal corporation to the risk of trying to go it alone, despite the greater rewards. The corporation also provides the recognition of working for a well-known, respected company. They offer their executives the comfort of plush offices, secretaries and staff, medical and dental plans, pension and savings plans, limousines, and bonuses. They give picnics and company dinners, and a gold watch upon retirement. And beneath it all, they also give their people the tacit assurance that their bosses won't be too tough on their performance. After all, everybody there is merely working for someone else—the stockholders. They cannot be expected to work as hard as the man on the outside who is working solely for himself. He's working for the toughest boss of them all.

In the search for corporate entrepreneurs, some companies, especially in the high-technology lines and most especially in the young computer companies, have tried to give freer rein to their brightest people. Recognizing that certain talented men yearn to be free of the corporate cage, these companies set up separate work groups and tell them to fly free—except that there will be a little thin string attached to one foot. So they become for a little while semi-entrepreneurs, but they are still working for the parent corporation, which will reap the real profits of their endeavors. Nor is that totally unfair. That little string keeping them from flying free also serves as a lifeline. The parent company is there behind them to back them up with financing, marketing, and whatever, and to reap the rewards of their success. A smidgeon of temporary independence from the corporate bureaucracy hardly makes them real entrepreneurs. Whether you are in a cage or flying supposedly free but tethered with a string on your foot does not make all that much difference.

Just because the structure of large corporations cannot accommodate true entrepreneurs does not mean that there are no truly creative, innovative, and hardworking individuals in corporate America. Obviously, General Electric, the Bell Laboratories of AT&T, IBM, ITT, and hundreds of other large corporations have been turning out new products and new services for years. But all this comes under the heading of Research and Development, financed by a small fraction of the company's annual budget. The digital switching system, which is revolutionizing telephonic communications throughout the world, and is worth tens of millions of dollars to ITT, was based upon pulse codes invented by Dr. Alex Reeves some years ago in ITT's laboratories in England. For his brilliant innovations in telecommunications, if I remember correctly, Dr. Reeves was rewarded with a bonus of $50,000. Actually it was more of an honorarium than a reward. If that sounds unfair, you must remember that Dr. Reeves was paid for doing that research. He had the comfort, support, and security of ITT behind him all the way.

After I left ITT, the company established an annual Harold S. Geneen Award for Management Creativity, and each year five or six people among ITT's current 300,000 employees are honored for their entrepreneurial endeavors with a dinner and a cash award of $5,000 to $10,000 each. But like Dr. Reeves and hundreds of others, they were creative but not necessarily entrepreneurial.

Why, one might ask, do such men choose to create wealth for a large, impersonal corporation rather than go out and try to do it all alone and reap all the benefits? Many of them, as I have said, when mature enough to break away, are locked in to the comfort and security the corporation provides; besides, they are hardly aware of what the outside world offers them. But more than that, I think, it is a matter of personality. Most of the corporate men I have known are satisfied with the challenges and rewards offered in corporate life and simply do not want to go it alone in the sink-or-swim environment of the entrepreneur. They work hard enough at the office, take work home on the weekends, appreciate the backup support of having every one of their decisions approved and shared by someone higher up. In short, they are not all that interested in the high risks and fabulous rewards of the man who goes into business for himself.

The entrepreneurial managers that I have known in corporate life have a completely different personality. They are not satisfied personally with "inching" their way up the corporate ladder, or with the annual 5 or 10 percent wage increases, or with the compartmentalized nature of their assignments. They are the men who love a tough assignment. I've transferred such men to ITT divisions that were in trouble, and when these men made those divisions healthy and profitable, they were rewarded with up to 20 percent salary and bonus increases. But that was not enough reward for the work and results they achieved. They knew it, and I think I knew it. But ITT could not give them 30 or 50 percent of the increased earnings they achieved for the company. I am sure this goes on in almost all of corporate America. There are would-be entrepreneurs in corporate life who work with the fervor and dedication of men possessed. But they want to fly free, with no strings attached, and no large corporate enterprise, ITT included, could allow that. So the true corporate entrepreneurs leave, as they always have, to start up or to take over an enterprise of their own, with all the responsibilities, risks, and rewards involved.

One of the more important things happening in our business environment today is the emerging understanding of the dilemma of how to harness the true entrepreneurial spirit and verve to the structure of large corporations without destroying the structure itself. What we find is increased attention to matters of morale and motivation. We find new efforts to sharpen up the management. We find companies willing to look into new products. All of these efforts are labeled entrepreneurial. But that is a different use of the word. The risks and rewards are not there, or only in a diluted, temporary form. One might say that one company is ''more entrepreneurial'' than another, but we would be talking of only minor shades of difference. Large, publicly owned corporations may devote 1 or 2 or 3 percent of their budgets to a separate ''entrepreneurial'' division or cell, but the other 97 to 99 percent of their activities will still be based upon relatively mundane growth rates of, say, 10 percent per year. It should be remembered, however, that 10 percent growth, because of the size of the large corporation, involves far, far more money, resources, and production of goods than are involved in any or all of the small entrepreneurial ventures competing in the marketplace. Every shade of difference among our large corporations in morale, leadership, efficiency, innovation, and creativity is important to the growth and well-being of American industry. Perhaps "the spirit of entrepreneurism" will help point the way. But the fact of the matter is that there are not and cannot be any real entrepreneurs in corporate life, not on a long-term basis. Entrepreneurs stay with large companies long enough to gain experience. Then they leave to get the cash.

The wave of the future in American business, it seems to me, is with the entrepreneurs! In the past few years there has been an amazing new and broader acceptance of the role of the entrepreneur in our society. The business, financial, and investment communities have come to recognize that the man, the woman, and the group who want to go out and do it all themselves can indeed create new wealth and market value by their endeavors. They are worth investing in. And what one is investing in most often is not a better mousetrap or new computer, but in the fresh, fervid burst of energy, commitment, and hard work that entrepreneurs themselves invest in their own enterprises. The entrepreneur cannot do otherwise. He is betting his company: he succeeds or he goes under and loses everything.

The most successful and most common of our new entrepreneurs are not necessarily those who invent or design something new. They are the individuals who borrow money to buy a discarded, unprofitable division from a large corporation and then turn it around and make it profitable. Often they are the same men who ran that unprofitable division in the first place and then decided to go it on their own. At ITT, we had a company in Cleveland that made little terminals for the electronics business. We couldn't make money on it. So we agreed to sell it to a couple of employees there. They asked us to do one thing: to close down the plant and fire all the employees before selling it to them. We did that. They turned around and hired back about half of them and they started making profits the very next day. ITT could not have done that without incurring a strike there and perhaps in other plants as well. But the new owners could run the same production with half the labor costs.

Two men I know had a computer company sold out from under them, and instead of going along to work for someone else, they started their own little computer company in Minneapolis. With the backing of a small investment group they put up $3 million, borrowed considerably more from a bank, and produced their own specialized computer, which luckily found a ready market. They had lured away a number of key people from the old company; everyone worked like hell and was paid more in stock options than in salary, and three years later that company was worth in the neighborhood of $300 million.

The risks are particularly high in the start-up of a new business and especially in the volatile computer industry, but the rewards are commensurate with the risks, as they should be. The Osborne Computer Corporation was a wild success for two years or so, reaching $90 million in annual sales of its portable computer. Then it went bankrupt. But entrepreneurial ventures are not limited to technological innovations. I know men who in recent years started up or took over companies operating restaurant chains, retail jewelry stores, a machine-retooling factory, financial services, women's apparel, medical technology. All of them worked harder than they ever had before and made fortunes for themselves and their investors.

The most promising entrepreneurial ventures are those which involve experienced men or women taking over established businesses which they know well, and running them as entrepreneurs. The risks are not eliminated, but they are minimized; the rewards may not be as spectacular, but the chances of success are greater. It is these kinds of ventures which are becoming increasingly prevalent and acceptable in the business world today. They are launched with what is called a leveraged buy-out. In simple, general terms, a leveraged buy-out works like this:

In times of recession when earnings are down, when stocks are selling at a low price/earnings ratio, when interest rates and debt service are high, or a combination of the above, large companies may decide to "streamline" their operation, tighten their belts, and sell off divisions. They do so for any number of reasons: the divisions are losing money, or not earning enough profits to justify the headaches they cause, or they simply do not "fit" into the new corporate strategy. So a division or a company is put up for sale, usually at a bargain price near or at its book value. Let's say the company for sale is earning $10 million a year before taxes, or $5 million after taxes. It is not a dog. But it is not good enough for the big corporation for one reason or another. The corporation puts a price tag on it: $40 million, which is approximately its book value.

Now, we have one or two or five people who are the key executives of that division. They would like to take it over and run it themselves. They know they can improve upon its performance. But they have no money.

So they go to a venture capital group with the facts and figures of their balance sheet, their P&L statement, and their plans and strategies, their hopes and aspirations. If everything adds up and makes sense, the venture capital group will undertake to put together a deal by which these managers can become owners or part owners of their own company. The venture capital group will put up seed money, say $2 million. The management group may be asked to put up "some" money to guarantee its commitment to the venture. The managers may have to go out and borrow money against their homes for the project. That "some" money may be all the money they can lay their hands on. They also agree to give the venture capital group a share in the new company.

Next, the venture capital group finds an investor, a group of investors, an insurance company, or some institution willing to take a risk in the new venture for a generous return, if it is successful. He, she, or it will buy $8 million of debentures or preferred stock in the new company and in return will also receive, say, 40 percent of the common stock of the new company.

With $10 million in hand, the venture capital group approaches a bank with all the facts and figures of this particular situation and persuades the bank to take a calculated risk. The detailed business plans of the new company, listing expected expenditures, income, and earnings year by year, could be as thick as a book. The new wrinkle on the American business scene, as I have seen it, is the growing willingness of major banks to take such risks. To compete in the marketplace, they have become more willing to take somewhat greater risks for larger returns. The bank will examine the loan proposal very carefully. It will scrutinize not only the facts and figures but also the human element, the men and women involved in the new venture, and if it all adds up to a worthwhile risk, the bank will authorize a loan of $30 million for a set period of time, say five years, usually at a variable rate of interest that is 1.5 or 2 percent above the prime rate. That provides a handsome profit for the bank, and its $30 million loan is secured by the $40 million book value of the company. If the new company defaults, the bank has first call on all of its assets; before the other $10 million in debentures, preferred or common stock is paid off.

Once the deal is consummated and the company bought, we have in effect the same company producing the same products with the same management team at the top. But the situation is entirely different. Before, the division manager worked for the big corporation. Now he is president of the company, working for himself, owning perhaps 10 percent of the company, with his other key managers sharing another 10 percent ownership.

Now he is living the dream of a lifetime: that 10 percent is worth $4 million or more, if he succeeds. Now his very survival is at stake. If he fails, his name, his reputation, his pride, his hopes for the future, all will go down the drain with the company. While he may not have put up any of his own money (although some do), he invested his "sweat equity" into the project. He will work now as he never worked before to make this enterprise a smashing success.

The new company will strive to cut labor costs, overhead, luxuries, and inefficiencies out of the operation, while increasing sales and production; it will pay no dividends, no bonuses; it will direct almost all of its earnings back into the company and into paying off the bank loan. Whereas the old corporation paid $5 million in taxes on its earnings of $10 million, the new company will pay $4 million in interest to the bank, leaving only $3 million to be paid in taxes (if that money cannot be apportioned elsewhere), and leaving another $3 million to pay off the principal of the loan. But in all likelihood, the new company ought to increase earnings by at least 14 percent, bringing earnings to $11.5 million the first year, and $12.8 million the next year, and perhaps $14.2 million the following year. The loan will be reduced annually, bringing down the yearly interest to be paid, until it is paid off in total or refinanced, very much as a home mortgage is reduced over the years. The new company will have an edge in reduced taxes on the same amount of earnings.

Nevertheless, during this five-year period, no matter how experienced and hardworking the management may be, no matter how much careful thinking and planning went into the new venture, the new entrepreneurs will be operating at considerable risk. At any time, the economy might go into a tailspin, their product might become obsolete or be overtaken by a competitor, an unexpected strike or a flood could halt production. They do not have the leeway that a big corporation has. They have the burden of that $4 million interest payment to the bank each year. If their earnings dip below $4 million, they are in trouble. They have to run to the bank and plead for more time. Most banks, I have found, are willing to work something out with honest borrowers who become over-extended because of misfortunes beyond their control. They foreclose only on helpless or hopeless situations or downright frauds.

Depending on all kinds of circumstances and how well the new company performs, the entrepreneurs will be able to amortize the bank loan in four or five or eight years to a point where they can refinance a long-term loan, with bank payments more to their liking. At that point, pre-tax earnings might be up to $20 million, $10 million after taxes, and the company worth $70 million. Everyone has come out ahead—the company managers who became owners, the venture capital team who put the deal together, the initial investor who risked his wealth, and the bank which had returned to its old true role as a financial partner in launching new businesses. And well they should, for together in a creative effort they have produced out of nothing $70 million worth of new wealth. The old big corporation was paid $40 million for the value of the original company and presumably put that money to some other use. The bank was paid back its loan. The investors got their money back, plus handsome rewards. And the new company has added something significant to the economy of its community by employing, say, 800 workers, and giving work indirectly to another 800 who work for suppliers, who, in turn, support another 3,200 dependents. The new company is thus sustaining 4,800 men, women, and children in our economy.

This is the way our economic system is supposed to work. It is part of our folklore. Stockholders may and do object to a professional manager earning $500,000 a year, but no one objects to a man who started a business, built it up, and is rewarded with $5 million or $50 million. He created something new for everyone and deserves whatever rewards come to him. So, out of the adversity of international competition and the stagnation of many of our large corporations, the new entrepreneurs in our midst have emerged to become the real cutting edge of our industrial efficiency. The entrepreneurs, in their fervor to succeed, have managed overall to improve the usage of assets at their command and have produced a dynamic upsurge of productivity. Everyone gains.

The day of the true entrepreneur seems to have arrived. Still, they are only a very small segment of our economy. But that $70 million company in our example should be worth $140 million or so in another five years, and at the end of ten years, it may be worth $200 or $300 million.

In time, it will perhaps grow into a large, multi-divisional corporation listed among the Fortune 500 top industrial companies. The Fortune 500 list is constantly changing. And while the founder of our example company remains at the helm, he may still be allowed to "bet his company" and function like an entrepreneur. But when he and his entrepreneurial colleagues are gone and the company is listed on the New York Stock Exchange and in *Fortune* and *Forbes*, the headstrong mavericks and entrepreneurs there will not be allowed or able to fly free without a string attached to their feet, and the cycle will begin all over again.

TWELVE

The Board
of Directors

What shall we do about the board of directors?

THE ORGANIZATIONAL STRUCTURE of any of the top five hundred industrial corporations in America is formed and is seen, traditionally, in the shape of a giant pyramid, with the broad base of workers on the bottom and the narrowing layers of management reaching up to the apex, where the chief executive officer sits in the solitary seat of ultimate corporate power. That, as it happens, is only half the picture. Above the exalted chief executive, if you look closely, is a large, amorphous mass, representing the owners of the corporation, the stockholders, who more often than not far outnumber all the employees. And if you look even more closely, you will see that the mass of owners is connected to the corporate pyramid by an archaic, creaking contraption at the top called the *board of directors*.

Great honor and homage is bestowed upon the august members of the board. They are pillars of the community, usually business executives, lawyers, bankers, who have demonstrated by their careers that they are men and women of integrity and accomplishment. They are wined, dined, and catered to with all the social graces and limousines and airplanes at the company's command. Once a month, they gather at the company headquarters to sit in judgment upon the management of the company on behalf of the stockholders.

Have you ever seen the Board Room of a large or even medium-sized company? Typically, it is the most exquisitely expensive, awesome room in the building, hidden behind closed doors, hushed in silent splendor, like a

257

Mayan temple in the middle of a jungle, representing the inner soul and spirit of a bustling corporation. The walls, if not adorned with modern art, carry the somber portraits of departed souls who once ruled there, looking over the shoulders of the present keepers of the flame and leaders of the tribe. You can count the number of board members by the empty chairs around the great polished table. The table is oval, of course, so that all who sit there can be deemed equal. At one end of the room stands the lectern and projection screen like an altar exuding an aura of sacred profundity. The thin china coffee cups from which the members sip may be stacked on a sideboard in readiness. But when you see all of this, as an outsider, the board room will be empty; these important people use it only twelves times a year.

The first Tuesday or the second Thursday of every month, the members show up for a board meeting. Upon entering the room, each is handed a sealed envelope. Soon, the minutes of the previous meeting are read and approved. Perhaps at that point they adjourn temporarily so that the executive committee of the board can meet separately to discuss management salaries and changes in company personnel. When the whole board reconvenes, the chief executive presents an overall view of the company's activities and results of the month. The chief executive, if he is so inclined, may go into details or he may turn that task over to his financial vice president, or the production vice president, or the marketing man, or the corporation counsel. They explain what's happening in the company. Someone will describe the company's latest product, or its newest plan of expansion or acquisition, the new market demand for an old product, or whatever. The company's problems will be explained away in the most positive light. Whatever the results, management always reports, in effect, how good they have been and are and will be, despite whatever intolerable conditions hover over the economy or the marketplace. They never tell you that they've done a lousy job or that they were beaten by a more efficient or smarter competitor. Never? Well, hardly ever.

What can an outside director do? He can ask a question about what troubles him. It will be answered logically, if not in any great detail. If the director questions the answer, he will be given more detail. He will be told that management's answer comes not from the chief executive alone but also from those in the company, right down to the division involved in the problem. They know more than he does about anything concerning the company. They live with it day by day; they have given the problem considerably more thought than he has. The management team has reviewed and rehearsed what they are going to say so that they can make orderly, coherent presentations to the board, putting the best possible face on the facts. Directors come in only once a month. What do they know? What have they got to back them up—intuition, feelings, gossip overheard, or a report read in the media? If one stubborn director continues, he is likely to be embarrassed by what he doesn't know. If he persists, he is casting himself in the role of a troublemaker, and no one likes a troublemaker. So what to do, except sit back in his chair, taste his cold coffee, and desist?

A board of directors meeting is mostly a one-way line of communication. Management does 90 to 95 percent of the talking. Outside board members, who are not part of the management, sit there and listen; then they go to lunch, and then they go home and open the envelope which contains their fee.

They are all honorable men with the best of intentions. Chief executives and their vice presidents do not lie or intentionally distort the facts presented to the board. They merely present the rosiest picture possible, covering over the warts, wounds, and scars. The outside board members might endeavor to study and to understand the strategies, planning, and performance of the company's management. Is the company doing well? Fine and good.

It is doing well because of the chief executive and his management team. You don't need a board of directors at all. It is a rubber stamp. But if the company is not doing well, or as well as it could, then what? What can the board of directors do about it? How do they know that the company is not living up to its potential? All they can learn is what they are taught from that selfsame management team; all they can get is what they are given. Perhaps that is the fundamental reason so many American companies of late have meandered on through a maze of mediocrity. Of the top five hundred American industiral companies, I would estimate that approximately 95 percent of their boards of directors are not fully doing what they are legally, morally, and ethically supposed to do. They are not doing their jobs. And they couldn't, even if they wanted to.

The board of directors of any company is supposed to represent and advocate the best interests of the owners—the shareholders of the company. The board's primary function is to oversee and evaluate the performance of management in running the company, and if that performance is not adequate or satisfactory, to do something about it. That does not mean the board is supposed to run the company. The professional managers have been hired to do that job. The board was elected to act in the place of the owners. The board's responsibility is to sit in judgment on the management, especially on the performance of the chief executive, and to reward, punish, or replace the management as the board, in its wisdom, sees fit. That is what is supposed to happen. That is what may appear to happen. But it doesn't.

Polite lip service is always given to the concept of the primacy of the stockholders in the corporate setup, but there is an internal arrogance on the part of professional managers and longtime (professional) board members that leaves uninformed stockholders out in the cold. How independent are those outside directors? Nominally, they are elected by the stockholders; actually, in most instances they serve at the pleasure of the chief executive. They are nominated by a committee of the outside board members, but the nominations have to pass the scrutiny of the chief executive. If he says, ''I cannot work with that man,'' that man will not be nominated. If there ever is a direct conflict and confrontation between a board member and the chief executive, who stays and who goes? It is well known and accepted that only those men and women who can ''get along'' are nominated and elected to the board as the management's slate of nominees.

One might also ask how independent can board members be if they accept all the perks heaped upon them by the management which they are to judge. Isn't there a fundamental conflict of interest involved here? Certainly the board would object if the company's purchasing agent accepted free dinners and trips abroad from suppliers. Maybe the board members, in order to preserve their independence and integrity, should pay for those five-course luncheons given in executive dining rooms. Perhaps the fees paid to board members should be reexamined. If a board member is dependent upon those fees, how can he act independently? I have a feeling that most board fees are too high for the work done to earn them, and too low for the work that should be done.

If the board of directors is really there to represent the interests of the stockholders, what is the chief executive doing on the board? Doesn't *he* have a conflict of interest? He's the professional manager. He cannot represent the shareholders and impartially sit in judgment on himself. He should not. Nevertheless, in every corporation that I know of, the chief executive is a member of the board. In more than three quarters of the Fortune 500 corporations, the chief executive sits also as chairman of the board. As chairman, he is not only running the company, he is also running the board. I wore both hats in my day at ITT, and it felt great: chief executive officer and chairman of the board. No crime was involved. But it was not fair to the interests of the stockholders. It was not a suitable structure, nor did it go to the purpose of the board of directors. The unfairness goes deeper. The chief executive is not alone on the board of directors; ordinarily he is backed up by his top management team. So, in most companies, the chief executive really needs to persuade only one or two outside directors to obtain a majority. Certainly, none of the inside directors would substantially challenge his boss in the board room.

That is not to say that the chief executive does not have the best interest of the stockholders in his heart or mind. Generally he does, but conflicts of interest can arise. The point is that, as things are presently constituted, there are few, if any, real checks or balances upon the power of the chief executive within our large public corporations. That's the presumed job of the board of directors, and it is not doing it.

Oh, yes, the board sets the salary, bonuses, and fringe benefits of the chief executive, and it can also fire him. But how often have you heard of a board removing a chief executive for being inadequate? I doubt if more than a handful of the Fortune 500 chief executives have been removed from office in any one given year. Have they all been performing so marvelously well over these past years of declining American industrial production that so few have been found, for one reason or another, wanting? I doubt it. When has a board ever cut a chief executive's salary? When disaster strikes, when the ground heaves, the walls buckle, and the roof caves in, when the wreckage is all around them, then the board, if it survives, sits up and acts. I suspect they take action, not out of concern for the stockholder, but because of a sudden awakening of self-interest: as fiduciaries, they themselves may be in legal jeopardy. Even so, how many companies have gone belly-up without their boards of directors having attempted any semblance of remedial action? Too often the board has no idea of the trouble the company is in, or finds out about it too late.

The fault lies not so much with the individual directors; the structure and the traditional operation of our corporate boards make it virtually impossible for any individual director to fulfill his responsibilities adequately. A board of directors can and occasionally does say no to a specific management request, if and when it disagrees with a particular expansion plan, a research project, or a merger. But suppose some members of the board come to the conclusion that the chief executive is inadequate for the job, or that he is competent but not as good as someone else might be. First of all, that is a difficult, complex decision to reach: there are no set standards of measurement to which they can turn with assurance. How can they form a fair judgment if nearly all their information comes from the chief executive himself? He does not readily tell them about his mistakes, his bad decisions, the opportunities missed, the potential lost. No chief executive would tolerate board members going behind his back and seeking information from his subordinates. Company structure and tradition prohibit such freewheeling, not to mention the danger to any subordinate who dares to speak behind his boss's back.

Nevertheless, suppose several outside directors come to the conclusion that on a scale of one to ten their man is only a four. He has not done anything outrageously wrong. It is simply that he is mediocre. The directors have the power to fire him, to pay him three months' or three years' salary according to his contract, and to go out and find someone better to head the company. It would be cheap at the price. But they hesitate to confront management and destroy the harmony of the board's relationship to the chief executive. They are concerned, too, with the "talk" it will cause among security analysts, the banks and lending institutions, and investors. The "talk" will get around that there is something very wrong with the company, "internal problems," you know, dissension in the ranks, something being hidden, and as a result the company's reputation and stock price will suffer far out of proportion to the need of replacing an inadequate executive. The outside world seldom knows he is inadequate. Undoubtedly he has friends and believers in the business and financial world. Replacing him will create enemies for the company, and they will talk.

Even if they want to go ahead with their proposed action, dissident directors cannot have a formal discussion of the problem with the whole board. The chief executive is the chairman. In order to act, they have to form a conspiracy against him. They would have to phone other outside members, and invite them, perhaps one by one, to lunch at the club or to a secret meeting in a hotel room in order to talk about their chief executive behind his back. If they fail to persuade others, they can expect retribution. He would act to remove them from the board. They must wonder if the possible result is worth the definite risk. In the end, the dissident board members might rationalize that it might be better to allow their dissatisfactions to ride—perhaps a little longer. After all, management is promising that things will get better. Now the directors have joined in a conspiracy of mediocrity with the management, at the expense of the shareholders.

In most large corporations, the board of directors has also given up its real prerogatives on determining the pay of top management. Outside compensation consulting firms are routinely called in and they set the parameters of corporate salaries. Their yardstick is not performance but rather the size of the company and what the fellow down the street is paying in a similar or parallel situation. Boards of directors accept those recommendations almost without fail. It is their form of no-fault insurance. Then each year, when it comes time to give salary increases, the board turns over its only real tool for controlling management to a small committee of board members— usually three or five of their most senior men—and these "old boys" of the compensation committee meet separately and discuss what kind of compensation is due the CEO and his key men this year. The discussion might take no more than three minutes or thirty minutes; it is all cut-and-dried. It's usually a friendly discussion; the old boys know each other so well.

If the company is not in trouble, top management automatically gets, say, a 10 percent salary increase. If one man did particularly well, he gets 15 percent. Hardly a year goes by without increases for top management. Healthy stock options are handed out almost traditionally. They are geared not to the performance of the company, as they once were, but to the Standard & Poor's or the Dow Jones Index. When the stock market goes up, everyone cashes in; when it goes down, the board issues new options at lower prices. But except if a company is upon or over the threshold of bankruptcy, when have you ever heard of a chief executive whose salary was reduced? In a recent survey of one hundred corporations, fifty-five of them had declining profits in 1982, but the chief executives of nearly half of those with declining profits received increases in compensation. In 1984, when the U.S. auto industry recovered from a disastrous recession, but still was in trouble from Japanese competition, the top U.S. auto executives rewarded themselves with bonuses and stock options so generous that it brought forth a public outcry. All those rewards had to be approved by the boards of the big three auto firms.

One of the auto chiefs defended the huge bonus which was added to his large salary for 1983 by citing his company's profits for that year and pointing out that his personal compensation amounted to only a small fraction of those profits and a small fraction of the price when applied to all of the automobiles sold by his company that year. Besides, he said, he had worked twenty-five years to reach the chief executive's chair in his company. All true. What he did not answer was, to my mind, the key question: What did he do individually, what did he personally contribute to bring about those increased earnings and to warrant such a bonus? The amount of compensation does not disturb me, as it does some people. Rock stars, baseball players, and movie personalities are paid large sums of money, but in those cases it is clear that they earn what they are paid. It is their individual outstanding performances that draw in those paying crowds. Their contribution to earnings are measurable. Personally, I believe that anyone who creates something new or valuable, or builds something to a height not attained by others, is entitled to very high rewards. Businessmen, too. But the key question that should be addressed to all business executives, not only those in the auto industry, is: What real personal contribution did he make that was sufficiently outstanding to earn that level of compensation? Bonuses should not be linked solely to a turnaround in the market or to what is being paid down the street.

The chief executive himself handles compensation matters within management ranks quite differently. He and his top managers hold long, intense meetings, reviewing the performance of the men who report to him. Targets have been set and results are measured against those targets. As a result, men in the company are kept on their toes, in fact toeing the line. Inadequate managers are weeded out to make room for men who can bring in results. Salary increases and promotions are meted out with great care and concern. It is an ever-ongoing progress in the ranks of management. But at the very top, at the level of the board of directors, there are no such performance reviews of the men who are running the company. There is no slot on the board's agenda to consider the quality of the chief executive's contribution to earnings. This primary function of the board is delegated to a committee, whose *pro forma* decision is routinely confirmed by the whole board.

All in all, the boards of directors of U.S. industry include numerous first-rate people doing what amounts to a second-rate job, primarily because there is a very fuzzy connection between the authority of the owners and any standard of performance of its chief executive and management. Under present conditions, shareholders, whether individuals or institutions, have virtually no way of knowing whether or not they are getting their money's worth from the men hired to manage their company. Shareholders can read newspapers, magazines, security analysts' reports, but such material is prepared and written by *outsiders*, who are not privy to what is really going on inside the company. Boards of directors are in a position to learn, and they have the legal authority to find out anything that they want to know, and they can act if and when they so desire. But over the years they have grown so soft and so ineffectual that most often they are a captive of management, rather than effective representatives of the company owners.

Furthermore, the declining thrust and productivity of American industry in recent years can be attributed, at least partially, to what these board of directors could have done and did not do. The stakes are enormous. The Fortune 500 corporations, after all, comprise the overwhelming share of the industrial output of this nation, and the archaic old-boy network no longer serves the true needs of the greatest industrial power in the world.

Every diligent board of directors should address itself on behalf of the shareholders to this key issue: *What is the standard of performance of its company's management—not what the company earned last year or this year, but what the company should have earned.* Hardly any board is aware of the company's lost potential, the opportunities missed, the heights not reached, the time lost, the change of direction not taken.

Today's boards of directors are ineffectual because they really don't know the answer to those questions. They may think they know. They have opinions based upon what they have been told by the company's management. But individually, not one of them would invest his own money or his bank's money on the basis of what somebody told him. He would go out and do his own checking. That's due diligence, and by law if they don't exercise that due diligence, they are liable.

If a board of directors as a whole is to do its duty, it seems to me, the directors should regain their objectivity in viewing its management's performance. Objectivity as well as productivity has dwindled away over the years. In a company where the founder or majority stock owner is chairman of the board, you will find that kind of objectivity and scrutiny. Whenever their own money is involved, board members will not hesitate to ask all sorts of questions of the top managers running their company, and they won't be satisfied if performance does not come up to their expectations. That, to my mind, should be the attitude of every diligent board in every publicly owned corporation.

Just how a board of directors regains its objectivity vis-à-vis the company's management is something for each individual board to work out for itself, depending upon its situation. The problem will be how to free itself from its dependence upon the one-sided flow of information from the company's management, how to get independent information about the company's activities by which they can check on what management tells them, how to set standards of performance by which they can judge the company's management. In short, what would the board members do if they really owned the company.

One way for a board of directors to regain its independence would be to take all the internal management members off the board! The chief executive, too!

The chief executive and his management team would continue to attend board meetings, but they would be there to report and to explain to the board what they did and why in managing the company, as they did before. The board would have the clear responsibility to see that the management was doing a satisfactory job. Each group—board and management—would then have separate and distinct responsibilities.

The board's function, as I would like to see it, still would not be to run the company or even to instruct the chief executive in how he should run it. When they take positions contrary to those of the management, it would have to be on the grounds that the chief executive is not running things well, or that his recommendations do not make sense to them, or that his proposed level of expenditures may be exorbitant, or whatever. Then they can contribute to his knowledge and judgment by explaining to him their views as to why he should recommend something different.

The chief executive's role becomes one of convincing the board that his recommendations are solid and should be supported on their merits. That is his present and traditional role, and one with which no able chief executive would have much trouble. He is still running the company. He still has an intimate, firsthand, in-depth knowledge of the company unequaled by any of the outside members of the board. If he's a good man and his judgments are sound, he should have no difficulty in persuading his board of directors to support him. If an honest difference of opinion arises, then the advocacy system of putting forth all the facts, opinions, feelings of everyone in the board room should result in an agreement on the best answer available to them.

That is the way it is meant to work now. In general, it does not. To make the necessary changes, we would have to make boards of directors genuinely independent of the managements they are there to judge. Remember, the prime function of a board of directors is to form continuous judgments on whether or not the chief executive and his management team are running things properly and well. The board should represent the owners and only the owners, even as they support valid positions of the management to the stockholders. Board members should take pains not to be beholden or even appear to be beholden to the management for any perks or privileges. They can do that simply by eschewing all the traditional perks and privileges. They, not the chief executive, for instance, should set their own fees, subject to public scrutiny. Some companies may want full-time or part-time working directors to oversee management. Such directors should be paid substantial fees, depending upon how well and actively they do their work. Other companies may want their directors to be staffed independently by experienced men who will "audit" the performance of their company's management and report their findings to the board. Or, better still, some boards may choose to hire outside management consulting firms to do independent studies of specific areas of the company for the benefit of the board of directors. The mere separating of the board from the management may bring the necessary measure of independence to the board room.

I can hear the loud cries of protest in the corporate jungle: No chief executive wants someone looking over his shoulder all the time! Of course he doesn't. But the board already calls for an independent accounting auditor to check management's figures—so why shouldn't the board also hire an independent management "auditor" to check management's policies and performance? It's the board's primary function. Whoever did such auditing would have no power to tell the chief executive or anyone else in management what to do. He would be there purely to audit. Obviously he would have to guard his own professional independence from the good-fellow camaraderie and favors of management. His loyalty would have to be to the board. He would report his findings to the board, just as Price Waterhouse or Arthur Andersen submit their audits. It would be for the board to use that information and to take whatever action it sees fit. However, now the board would have its much needed, independent source of information. In fact I would guess that such a professional adviser would have to say very little at a board meeting. His just being there "in the know" would oblige the chief executive to be more objective in his presentations to the board.

I am certain of one thing, however: With an informed board, led by one of its outside members as chairman, the quality and intensity of board meetings would rise to a level that has not been seen for many years. The board need not and should not take outside audits of management at face value. Certainly the company's management would be given every opportunity to respond to whatever comments, charges, or complaints are brought out. Nor would the board be hostile to management. Its purpose is to be objective and helpful. The board and the management both want the same thing for the company and for the stockholders, but they may at times have different points of view on how best to obtain it. No one has a lock on the truth or on the sure road to success or the best way to solve a particular problem. But the best way ever devised for seeking the truth in any given situation is advocacy: presenting the pros and cons from different, informed points of view and digging down deep into the facts and coming up with the best answer available.

If a company wanted to go a step further, perhaps the board should be telling management how well it expects the company to perform for the year ahead, rather than the other way around. Why should the hired managers set the targets and goals of the company? Why shouldn't the directors, as representatives of the owners, at least be taken into the process? That kind of advocacy would do a lot more for the company than just an evaluation of past performance. If a board reviewed with a chief executive what the board, as representative of the shareholders, expected of management *before* a fiscal year started, not after it, what do you think would happen? It would create for the board a role it does not have today, and it would lead to a much better evaluation of the short- and long-term objectives of the company. Again the board would not be trying to run the company or to tell the chief executive what to do. It would be giving him an evaluation of what they think his performance should be to satisfy their view of the interests of the shareholders. My guess would be that that chief executive might go back to his management team and say, ''Look, fellows, the board thinks we ought to do better. They think we ought to do 10 percent better and I can tell you their reasons. Maybe their assumptions will prove to be wrong; maybe ours will. But we're just going to have to stretch ourselves to try to make 10 percent.'' Management must manage. That's the message, and it can come from the board.

If the directors of American industry were to do that kind of job and do it properly, more than a handful of men would change jobs as chief executive each year. But I can guarantee that those who get $500,000- or $1,000,000-a-year salaries and bonuses will be earning them.

If I am correct in detecting the beginning of a trend toward the appointment of younger men to head large corporations, then our boards of directors are, without being aware of it, taking on an added responsibility in monitoring the operations of those companies. The idea seems to be that men in their forties and younger can act with the vigor and boldness of youth in correcting the shortfalls of their elders.

There is nothing wrong with appointing a youthful chief executive, so long as the board recognizes that his intelligence, quick mind, and audacity are not tempered with the maturity of experience. It's a question of odds. A man in his late thirties or early forties may be every bit as mature and stable as a man in his late fifties or early sixties. But the odds are against it. And of course he would be the last to know it. I have nothing against young men in positions of authority. I was young once myself. At the time I was very confident in my strongly held opinions. Age and experience helped me smooth out my rough edges.

I also promoted many young men because of their ability to head divisions of ITT long before their age or years in the company warranted it, but I monitored them very closely. That is the responsibility today's boards of directors are taking upon themselves when they appoint youthful chief executives. The inherent danger is that when a young chief executive makes a mistake, it is likely to be an audacious, bizarre one, with dire consequences. Again it is a matter of odds. But the point is that the board must be that much more careful in monitoring young chief executives. The board's responsibility is akin to that of a parent in raising a child through adolescence to maturity. The board should consider itself a parent, wise with the maturity of its years, at peace with its own fallibility, standing ready to check the extreme opinions of the teenager who is so sure he or she is smarter than his or her parents. I would go so far as to say that a good board, like a good parent, should exercise a measure of control in "bringing up" its chief executive officer. The board cannot allow him to take over the house.

An independent, informed board would be able to do the job it was created to do. When such a board met, common sense would tell its members what kind of information they needed to make a rational evaluation of the company. They would seek information not only from management, but from outside sources and from their own independent studies. Then, when they sit down with management again, the board meetings will be substantially different from what they are today. There would be two-way communications in the board room.

What are the dangers of giving so much added power to the board? As long as the board's actions are open to the scrutiny of the shareholders and its actions reported in the company's annual report, I do not foresee problems which cannot be overcome. The chief executive does not have to accept the advice of the board. If it comes to an impasse and showdown with an unreasonable board, he can offer to resign and issue a statement on their dispute. He would be protected from an unreasonable board by his contract guarantees of a healthy severance pay schedule, plus public opinion. I see little room for an independent board to abuse its powers. It might perpetuate itself beyond the years of normal retirement of its individual members. But those members would be getting nothing more than their fees for doing their jobs, and those fees could be reviewed at annual stockholders' meetings, where *both* factions report to the shareholders.

Those chief executives who are running their companies well, producing results that can be measured, and who are confident in their positions would have nothing to fear from independent boards of directors. It would relieve them of that burden of loneliness of the long-distance runner. An independent board, free from even the appearance of collusion with management, would be in a better position to reward a chief executive generously for exemplary results. The shareholders, receiving their portion of increased company earnings, would be reassured that their company's officers were earning every cent of their compensation.

If I have succeeded in defining the problems that exist in the intermingled relations between boards of directors and company managements, I am satisfied. The solutions offered here may seem extreme to some people, if they are applied to all of corporate America. But extreme examples make people think. Solutions will then become a question of degree, depending upon circumstances in different companies. The goal, however, should be the same: to find a way in which the directors of a company, representing the stockholders, can deal with that company's professional managers at the oval table in the board room at arm's length.

The impact of a free and independent board of directors upon a company's management would be profound. Its ultimate effect upon the productivity of this country would be enormous.

THIRTEEN

On Caring:
A Summing Up

The key element in good business management is emotional attitude.

I CARE! That's why this book was written. I have a great belief and faith in American business. But as I look around, I see—as others do—American preeminence in business being overtaken by other countries. I get the impression that big business, once so very vital and growth-oriented, is now befuddled and bewildered. I see what I consider mediocre performance all around me, not so much in the small, entrepreneurial new companies as in our largest industrial corporations, which are the wellsprings of our economy. The vitality and juices seem to have seeped out of the top layer of management, and are being replaced by dry rot and procedures that smack of plodding bureaucracy. So many of our major corporations seem mired in a swamp of laws, customs, procedures, public relations, buck passing, and personal attitudes of playing it safe.

There is, I am sorry to say, a horrendous amount of flabbiness in American industry. Blame is often placed on labor, and labor can be part of it, but unfortunately flabbiness starts at the top layers of management and works its way down. If it is to be cured, the remedies must first be applied there at the top. I am afraid that too many business executives have been taken in by their environment. They have learned how to "play the game," to say the right thing, to make the right motions, to go along with the crowd, to follow the advice of their PR men. Where are the gutsy businessmen of bygone years, the men who made waves, the men who were recognized as "stand-up" individuals? "Guts" is an ugly-sounding word, but a true one. It is the appropriate word to best convey what I think has gone out of the main line of American business management today.

The key, essential element in all good business management is emotional attitude. The rest is mechanics. As I use the term, management is not a collection of boxes with names and titles on the organizational chart. Management is a *living force*. It is the force that gets things done to acceptable standards—high standards, if you will. You either have it in a company or you don't. Management must have a purpose, a dedication, and that dedication must be an emotional commitment. It must be built in as a vital part of the personality of anyone who truly is a manager. He or she is the one who understands that management must manage.

The attitude is a self-fulfilling one, too. The man who says, "I must do this," will stay at his task until all hours, trying again and again and again, until he finds a satisfactory answer. The answer must be, above all, satisfactory to him. And he will know it. There may be seventy-eight ways to do something and only ten of them with satisfactorily good answers. The manager will continue to probe and to seek for one of those ten answers. It may not be the best of all answers. But he won't settle for anything lower than one of those ten. The next time he will strive for yet a better answer, higher on the list, learning something new all the time, and achieving better results as he goes along. He will work this way because of his emotional attitude, more than anything else, and that attitude inevitably will be emulated by those who work with him, so that it becomes a way of life in that organization. The urge to do what must be done is powered by deep-seated emotion, not logic. He might not be able to explain why he works the way he does, or why he makes this choice and not the other one. He does it because he "feels" that it is right. That feeling is transmitted to others who work for him or with him. They know his emotional commitment includes them as well as the goals of the enterprise. They are willing to follow his lead because of that "feeling" which makes him the kind of person he is.

No matter if you are managing a business, a church, a scout troop, a career, or your home life, I believe that the test of management is whether or not it achieves the goals it sets for itself; the higher the goals, the better the management. In fact, if the level of goals is too low, I wouldn't call it management at all; anyone can do it. A marathon runner is someone who can run twenty-six miles 385 yards *in a given amount of time,* whether the standard is two and a half, three, or three and a half hours. But what about the fellow who runs it in ten hours? He's not a marathon runner; he's a guy wearing short pants and a pair of running shoes who is out getting some fresh air. We are defining the runner in terms of his *performance.* So do we define a corporate manager.

If the manager is to accomplish his objectives, he absolutely has to get the information necessary to make the right decisions. The steps along the way define themselves as he goes toward his objectives. To surmount each step, he needs solid facts so that he can recognize the realities of situations. His decisions, if based realistically upon reliable information, will not be all that difficult. Facts are power. They are crucial to good management. In order to get the straight facts in any situation, the manager must ask straight questions, and to do that he must do his homework so that he has a deep understanding of what he is encountering. If he has a good record of making the right decisions, he can help people around him to be effective and successful in their own areas, so that their total accomplishment is greater than the sum of their individual parts. That is leadership. And if the leadership is successful, it creates a momentum in the enterprise which enriches the participants with such a feeling of pride and energy that they produce results, short-term and long-term results, which they themselves never thought possible. I've separated the elements here, but in practice they all move along together, en masse, nourishing each other like the fusion in a nuclear reactor, creating the fire, the pressure, and the power which produce energy. All this is the critical emotional content of good management.

This is the emotional horsepower that drives people to do things, drives them to keep at it because they feel they *must* get the answer, drives them to push on until they get results that are satisfactory to them. Of course, you don't always succeed in every effort. But then you recognize it early on, and you get out of that situation. You cut your losses and go on to something else. If you are a manager, you don't drift.

That's what we did at ITT. People have said ITT grew because of our rapid acquisition program. But we spent 90 percent of our time managing the company, including the acquisitions, so that it would grow internally, which enabled us to trade our stock for the assets of other companies. We spent only about 10 percent of our time in making acquisitions. Much more significantly, from the beginning we fired and hired executives until we achieved a team of managers who fit our definition of managers. When we reached that "critical mass," we blasted off. We had the emotional firepower to achieve the progress and growth which we had set as our goals.

The "mechanics" of management enable you to stay on the rails so that your emotional firepower does not drive you over the cliffs of bankruptcy. The mechanics consist of the structure and organization of your company, the communications network handling the flow of information, the financial controls, the schedule of meetings, the elements of production, quality control, marketing, distribution, et al. The mechanics of management are very important; companies have gone off the tracks and failed because of neglecting them. I have carped about our nation's business schools and perhaps denigrated the value of MBA degrees more than I should. So I should point out that I do not think business schools are wrong in teaching what they do, but I do think their emphasis is lopsided. Too much attention is being paid in those schools to the mechanics and not enough to the emotional values of good business management.

Not until our MBA graduates learn the value of the emotional components of management and the price they must pay to achieve them will they become managers by my definition. If and when we have a nation of business managers of that type, American industry will surge so far ahead of our international competition that we will once again become the envy of the world. The world has always been short of top-notch managers. There is plenty of room in the top executive suites of the United States today for young men and women who grasp the managerial concepts of emotional attitude and the mechanics and can continually differentiate one from the other.

Some time ago, speaking at the Wharton School of Business Administration, I was asked how one should go about succeeding in a business career. I told the students that one should move around and gain experience in his or her early years and then settle down to a chosen career at age thirty or thirty-five. That would give a person a career of some thirty or thirty-five years. In that time, the top management of a company is likely to turn over three or four times. So there would always be room for a good manager. All a young person has to do was to pick his or her job and start working toward it. As I said about *all* management, including the management of one's life: Decide what it is you want to do, and start doing it.

If I were to amend that answer today and try to sum up what I have come to believe over a long career in business, I would put forth these personal precepts on how to manage:

—You must play by the rules, going through the channels of the company structure, taking no shortcuts; but you don't have to *think* by the rules. It would be a great mistake to confine your imagination to the way things have always been done. In fact, it would consign you to the mediocrity of the marketplace.

—Avoid all pretensions. Doing things for "show" will backfire on you and turn the whole flavor of your enterprise rancid. Avoid ego trips, office politics, and acting a part that is not really you.

—Remember: Facts from paper are not the same as facts from people. The reliability of the person giving you the facts is as important as the facts themselves. Keep in mind that facts are seldom facts, but what people think are facts, heavily tinged with assumptions.

—You must find out everything essential by yourself. As a manager, you are entitled to a straight answer to a straight question, and you will usually get it when your question is right. The right question comes from many sources and must be assembled in your own head, perhaps for the first time.

—The good guys in your organization want you to ask the right question, because they can and want to answer it. Then you can all move forward together.

—Only the phonies will squirm when confronted by questions that go straight to the heart of the matter, and it is your job as a manager to recognize the phonies and to get rid of them. The good guys will expect it of you.

—No one is going to tell you the answer or solution to any problem in advance of your questioning. It is the nature of organization and the interaction of the hierarchy that usually stop a bright man from breaking the code of getting along with his peers.

—When you are the man or woman in charge, you and only you must make the decisions, particularly the close ones. That's what you are being paid for, whether you head a task force, a department, or a whole company. Your decisions should be based upon the facts of the situation. The facts are the authority. Because you are in charge, *you* are entitled to be right or wrong, but it must be you. Your commands will be honored and respected, but they must be *your* commands. You are not entitled to announce decisions or give commands by proxy, by allowing someone else to speak for you.

There is a price to pay for all this, personally. Ask yourself: How much of your life are you willing to devote to becoming a manager who succeeds in achieving superior results? The flabbiness in American industry today is due in large measure to the men who have made it to the top enjoying the perquisites of position rather than devoting the time and effort required to prepare them to manage. It is all too easy to delegate the crucial decision-making to others, while you go out acting the part of a company president or vice president at lunches, dinners, and conferences.

Ask yourself: Do you have the resolve and the kind of high standards of performance to put aside a lot of pleasurable aspects of your life to make yourself into a manager who "must" succeed? Are you willing to work long, late hours, forgoing much of your social life, in order to achieve superior results that will make your reputation? If you think you can work at it half-heartedly or at a half pace, then you probably are not going to become a true manager, for there are others who will outstrip you in the race to the top. If you are willing to make such personal sacrifices, then make them and don't complain. You wanted the job; no one forced you to take it.

If you become that successful manager, you will face the truth of the required personal sacrifice every day at 5 P.M. Your working day belongs to others. You have to be available to all those in your organization who have a need to communicate with you. Meetings, informal conferences, one-on-one conversations with your peers and subordinates will be an endless strain. People will bring to you their needs, their complaints, their problems—all from within the company. From the outside, there will be the demands of people you have to see, people you want to see, people you don't want to see but must, and then there are the lunches you simply cannot avoid.

But at five o'clock, the day people and their demands upon you are gone. You can sit at your desk, alone, and realize that you now can do what *you* want to do. The buzzer on your desk will bring in one of your two secretaries. Your limousine and chauffeur await below. The plane is at the nearby airport. You can go anywhere you want. Perhaps you have a computer terminal on your desk. You can check out the winning scores on the stock market for that day, or you can check the theater shows in New York or London. There is almost always a dinner invitation you could accept. But there is, also, that "homework" on your desk.

This is the time, when all the others are gone, when you can do your own work, your own thinking. You don't have to do it. The company will go on if you don't do it. There are many eager beavers ready to make your decisions for you. You could rely upon them, and to all appearances you would still be in charge. You would still issue the orders and they would be obeyed. But there would be a difference. They would not be *your* orders or *your* decisions. They would come from others to be mouthed by you. And you would know it, and so would the others in your organization. And you would lose something called the respect and confidence of your people. Your leadership would turn into a bureaucracy and the vitality of the company go stale. It would all happen so gradually that only the most perceptive of people would notice the change. But you, in your heart of hearts, would know it. That's the choice. Do you want to do your homework late into the night, or pack up and go home and let someone else do the nitty-gritty work?

I faced that choice at the end of every normal working day at ITT. Perhaps with a sigh, I would call home and say I'd be working late. I'd take off my suit jacket, loosen my tie, put on an old black sweater, and settle in to do my homework. Dinner would be sent in, to be eaten at a small table in the office. My wife would know not to expect me home until 11:30, or perhaps later. This was my time to work on all those reports until the figures and the words blurred. This was my time to think and to reflect and to make decisions. There were occasions when I used to wonder if I was being foolish putting in this much time and effort, whether or not I was overdoing it. But I always concluded that there was no substitute for it. I have never met a man who was a true leader, and not a captive of his environment, who did not do his own homework, no matter what the cost. There really was no other way.

But one does not have to be monolithic in his devotion to a business career in order to succeed. I know that is a popular conception. But there is plenty of time in a week to devote to family, recreation, hobbies, and rest, if one makes conscious choices. I set a pattern early in my career that I carried through all my years with ITT. I lived near where I worked and did not commute to the suburbs. I devoted as much time as necessary to my work, often late into the night, five days a week. On the weekends I got away from it all. Or, if I still had work to do, I took it with me and gave part of the weekend to it. I've never been one to seek the club championship at golf or to make other serious commitments to my hobbies or sports. They were for me a matter of unwinding, of leisure and enjoyment.

Perhaps my earliest avocations, which have lived with me through my life, were fishing and hunting. These took me outdoors and away from papers and books, and from the cities, of which I'd already had too much in my youth.

I caught my first fish when I was about eight years old, at summer camp. It was a beautiful yellow perch. I can close my eyes and still visualize coming up through the water the wonderful colors of that perch. That was a great many years ago. At that point I was more hooked by fishing than the fish. I have long had an affection for the water—be it oceans, lakes, rivers, or trout streams. I've been avid at all kinds of fishing, whether fly-casting in small trout streams or trolling the offshore waters of oceans for bigger specimens. I've fished around the world when I traveled. It's a great pastime and ever fascinating. Nor did my interest stop there. Still following the attraction of water, as time went by and I could afford it, I built and owned and operated just about every kind of boat, from rowboats and skiffs to racing shells and to large sport fishing boats with towers and fighting chairs. Perhaps it all goes back to the day when I was nine months old and my mother, as she told me, dug a hole in the sand at Bournemouth and dunked me into the small pool of sea water because it was "good for me." Maybe I sense it, if I can't remember it.

Hunting was something I took up later in life, when I moved to the Middle West. Like fishing, it took me out of doors and usually in good company. There wasn't much hunting to be found in New York City, but pheasant-shooting in the prairies, duck-shooting on the rivers, quail- and duck-hunting in the South engrossed me. I never felt comfortable about shooting animals. We have them on our farm in New Hampshire. Deer and bear both are quite safe from me there. But bird-shooting and shotguns have been a different matter. I became fairly good at trapshooting—all right at skeet. I would argue that shotguns are a great investment, or perhaps that is just an excuse for the enjoyment of their intrinsic beauty of workmanship. I own several.

In the course of my time at ITT, I tried to pass some of these feelings on to others, something to be added to the breadth of the people who worked for and with me. ITT had a fishing camp on the Canadian border with twenty miles of trout streams and five sizable lakes. We had a fishing camp in the Florida Keys, with a converted houseboat that would allow eight or ten people to fish the shallow flats. We had a hunting camp in Georgia with fifteen thousand acres of land devoted to both timber and wild quail.

Yes, we had these things and we tried to share such interests and feelings with our people. We used to invite board members who liked to shoot to spend a week in the spring at our Georgia camp, and we would send our top management executives there on a rotation basis so that they all had a chance to meet and get to know the ITT directors under such conditions. I wanted them to experience something that I had found so desirable in my life.

Of course, there was also a business side to it. These same people learned to use the facilities to entertain our dealers and customers. There is no better way you can get to know your customer, or he you, and, as I've said, knowing the man is the essence of salesmanship. George Brown, an ITT director of many years' standing, showed me the way. He often invited me to his hunting camp in southern Texas, where I would meet and mix with heads of corporations and occasionally meet some of the more prominent public officials of the country. Another director, Alan Kirby, widely known for his fortune but actually a quiet and retiring man, talked wisely and at length of serious matters while fishing with me on a river on the Gaspé Peninsula in New Brunswick. These are among the special memories that one does not easily forget. It was this "something" gained from being a part of nature that I wanted to pass on to our people.

Lest some stockholder become concerned about the expense of all this, let me assure you that it cost the company nothing. After I stepped down from ITT, the new management had different values and sold off all these properties. I believe our original investment was about $12 million for those many acres of productive timberland. They were sold for something more than $30 million, for a clear profit of about $20 million. But that was not the real profit to ITT. The gain was in the new and invigorating thoughts and spirit that nature inspired, and the feeling of all those who enjoyed the wilderness that the company for which they worked so hard could go out of its way to add something unforgettable to their lives, something aside from business which would live on with them. That was the true reward. I also built a golf course and clubhouse in Bolton, Massachusetts, which offer similar rewards, but in a different way. It is one of the top one hundred golf courses in the United States and, with 8,300 yards from the back tees, one of the longest. It is still in use for ITT customers.

Among the other participatory sports I enjoyed was tennis, which I began playing back in prep school and continued as long as my legs held up. Golf, a later avocation, still frustrates me, as it does others, but I particularly appreciate now how golf helps one work off other frustrations and how it accommodates itself so gracefully through the years to age—my age. One thing that never interested me greatly was spectator sports. Somehow I'd rather be a poor but active player than sit and watch the greats.

Hobbies have always engaged my intellectual curiosity—extensive reading beyond business, and, in my earlier days, extensive writing. I still play at the piano. I say "at" because I would not want to even intimate any mastery which I do not possess. I play at other musical instruments well enough to amaze myself—the guitar, banjo, and accordion. I like jazz, swing, and Dixie, and have a wall-size collection of such records. I enjoy the theater (a heritage from my mother, I guess) but, please, no messages. All in all, I like to learn and be learning. I am a constant accumulator of information. I subscribe to and read about twenty magazines and three daily newspapers.

How does one do this and put in the work hours? The answer resides in what I *don't* do. I don't attend a lot of purely social occasions—the luncheons, cocktail parties, and dinner gatherings—except for very special ones given by friends or where duty absolutely calls. It's never been my idea of fun to stand around and make small conversation. I make enough social contacts in my business life. You don't need prior social contacts to reach people. All you have to do is pick up the phone and call. You'd be surprised how well that works. To my way of thinking, eschewing social gatherings has been a fair trade-off for the time it gives me to spend with out-of-doors sports and my hobbies.

One is always asked the question, or maybe one asks it of one's self: Would you do it differently, if you had it to do over? I think not. Looking back on it all now, I can very well say that I enjoyed all those years in business. I liked the hard work. I enjoyed the time spent with my associates. I shared with them many periods of exhilaration, topped perhaps by certain peak experiences in which we all felt we had achieved something in creative business management, or, more simply put, in our own personal performances.

Throughout all of this, I always felt that I was learning and growing year after year, along with a great team of managers at ITT. As a group we were gratified and fulfilled with our high standard of performance and our record of progress and achievement, which made a significant contribution to the lives of so many people. Probing more deeply, I am certain that this sense of achievement and of making a contribution sustained the pace and dedication we gave to our work. We were doing something that we felt had not been done before and we were reaching out to do it.

I don't know that one could ask for a lot more. I enjoy a game of golf, as long as I have a job to go back to. I guess that means two things: that I enjoy the golf and I need or at least enjoy the work as much as the golf.

FOURTEEN

Envoi!

AL MOSCOW did not think this chapter was needed in the book. But I did. Besides, I did not want to wind up the book with a Chapter Thirteen. So, we agreed to put it in.

This will be the shortest chapter in the book, and perhaps the most important.

I think it is an immutable law in business that words are words, explanations are explanations, promises are promises—but only performance is reality. Performance alone is the best measure of your confidence, competence, and courage. Only performance gives you the freedom to grow as yourself.

Just remember that: *Performance is your reality.* Forget everything else. That is why my definition of a manager is what it is: one who turns in the performance. No alibis to others or to one's self will change that. And when you have performed well, the world will remember it, when everything else is forgotten. And, most importantly, so will you.

Good luck—and good performance!

Harold Geneen
June 4, 1984

INDEX

A

Adams, Charles Francis, 36, 77–81
Administrative assistants, 93
Aetna Finance Co., 211–12
Air Force, 40
Air France, 220
Alcoholism and managing, 173–76
Allied Chemical Corp., 12, 77
American Broadcasting Co., 225, 226–27
American Can Co., 66–71
American Motors Corp., 238
Amertorp, 66
Andinger, Gerhard, 12
Andrews, Hale, 216
APCOA airport parking lots, 245
Araskog, Rand, 11, 94, 232
Atlas Corp. of Journal Square, 65
Attitude
  and leadership, 148
  of manager vs. entrepreneur, 118
Avis Rent-A-Car, 2, 128, 215, 231

B

Bailey, Glenn, 12
Barrett Division, Allied Chemical, 77
Baruch, Bernard, 58
Behn, Sosthenes, 2, 37, 38, 39, 41, 208, 225
Bell & Howell, 37, 71–74
Bell System, 210
Bennett, Richard, 94
Bergerac, Michel, 12
Board of directors, 257–74
Bottom line, 43–48, 189
Bouvier, Jack, 58
Brown, George, 287
Brussels, ITT-Europe set up in, 47–48
Buchwald, Art, 208
Budgeting, 190–93
  time spent on, 106
Buy-out, leveraged, 249–53

C

Cannon Electric, 198, 210
Canteen, 231
Caring, and managing, 277–89
Cash cows, 26–27

Cash flow, cash cows, stars, and dogs, 26–27
Castro, Fidel, 208
Chicago *Tribune,* 61
Chief executive officer, and board of directors, 261–72
Chrysler Corp., 238–39
Clark, Ramsey, 226, 228
Clean-desk executive, 157–69
Climate
  and leadership, 135
  and success or failure of enterprise, 139
Cluttered desk vs. clean desk, 157–69
Colt Industries, 12
Columbia Broadcasting System, 12, 225
Commanding vs. leading, 151–52
Commitment, of entrepreneur vs. manager, 118–19
Communication(s)
  military contracts, 40
  and office politics, 140–41
  open, 88–90, 139–40, 149–50
Company, structure of, 85–90, 95
Compensation. *See* Salary
Computers, rejected as ITT project, 219–21
Conglomerates, 207–8
  advantages of, over one-industry company, 222–24
  as stereotype, 208
  testing ground for survival of, 225–32

Connecticut Insurance Commission, 228
Continental Baking Co., 2, 215
Control
  and delegating, 18–19, 160–62
  and ITT size, 94–95
  of numbers, 189–204
  of quality, 115–17
Corporations, and entrepreneurial spirit, 235–45
Corwin, David, 211
Cotter, William, 228
Criticism, and interchange of opinions, 139–40
Crosby, Philip, 117
Crucible Steel, 12
Cuban Telephone Co., 208
Curtis, Richard, 6

D

Datamatic, 78
Day & Zimmerman, 54
Debt-equity ratio, 199–200
Decision making, and facts, 101–2
Defense Department, 210
Delegating
  and clean-desk executive, 160–62
  and losing control, 18–19
Dogs, 26–27
Dow Chemical Corp., 3
Dunleavy, Tim, 11, 94
Du Pont, 232

E

Earnings
  domestic, 46–47

growth during Geneen's
ITT tenure, 5, 44, 45–46
Eastman Kodak Co., 3
Egotism, and managing,
18–19, 177–86
Employee Assistance
Program, 176
Entrepreneur
company manager as,
145–47
vs. manager, 117–18
spirit of, 235–53
Environment
changing, 70–71
and problem solving, 128
and success or failure of
enterprise, 139
Esmark, 231
Esterline, 12
Europe, meetings with
executives in. *See*
General Managers
Meetings
Executives
attracting and hiring top
people, 46, 137–38
clean-desk vs. cluttered-
desk, 157–69
and entrepreneurial
spirit, 235–40

F

Facts
and decision making,
101–3
unshakable, 99–103,
122–25
Farago, Catherine, 6
Federal Communications
Commission, 226

Federal Trade Commission,
226
Filing system, 158–59
Financial reports, sent
directly to headquarters,
90–93
Firing line, 142–45
Flanagan, Robert M., 12
Formal structure vs. open
communication, 85–88
Fortune magazine, 219

G

Geneen, Harold S.
at American Can Co.,
66–71
at Bell & Howell, 36–37,
71–74
as door-to-door book
salesman, 60–61
and early days at ITT,
38–50, 81
early years of, 33–38
filing system of, 158–59
hired by ITT, 34–38
at ITT, 1–13
at Jones & Laughlin,
74–77
leadership style of,
134–37
at Lybrand Brothers,
64–66
at Mayflower Associates,
64
at New York Stock
Exchange, 58–60, 64
at Raytheon, 36, 77–81
sells classified ads for
New York *World-
Telegram,* 62–63

See also General Managers Meetings; International Telephone and Telegraph Co.

Geneen Award for Management Creativity, 245

General Controls, 210

General Electric Co., 3, 94, 207, 212, 221

General Managers Meetings, 7–8, 9, 103–6
  in Europe, 42–43, 96–98, 103, 105
  and focus on numbers, 193
  problem solving in, 120–22
  as think tank, 106

General Motors Acceptance Corp., 212

General Motors Corp., 1, 3, 76, 94

Gilfillan, 210

Goldenson, Leonard, 225, 226

Government and industry, adversary relationship of, 23–24

Grinnell, 231

Growth, 203
  and acquisitions, 207–32
  domestic, 209–13, 214–18, 239
  and information flow, 94–95
  and leadership, 137
  stretch target for, 44–48

Gulf & Western, 224

H

Hamilton, Lyman, 94

Harriman National Bank, 60

Hartford Insurance Co., 2, 225, 227–32

Harvard Business School, 77

Hawkins, Norval, 62

Hennessy, Edward L., Jr., 12

Hilton, Conrad, 126

Holiday Inn chain, 125–26

Honeywell, 78, 221

Hoopingarner, Professor, 53–54, 81

Household Finance, 211

I

Iacocca, Lee, 238

Industry and government, adversary relationship, 23–24

Inefficiencies, rooting out, 9, 98

Information flow, 90–92
  and organization structure, 86–88

International Business Machines Corp., 3, 94, 219, 221

International Telephone and Telegraph Co. (ITT)
  acquisitions and growth of, 2–4, 46–47, 203, 207–32
  domestic growth of, 209–13, 214–18, 239
  earnings of, 5, 44–47
  entrepreneurial spirit and growth of, 239–40
  Fortune survey of holdings, 219
  Geneen at, 1–13

Geneen's early days at,
    38–50, 81
and hiring of Geneen,
    34–38
management at, 29–30
open communication at,
    88–90
planning at, 92–93
and rejection of computers
    as corporate project,
    219–21
size of, and control, 94–95
stretch target set for, 44–48
Inventory control, 121–22
Ireland, Charles, 12
Irving Trust Co., 12
ITT-Europe, 12, 47–48
    monitoring operations of,
    49

J

James, Howard (Bud), 127
Japan, management in, 19–23
Jennings Radio, 210
Joint venture
    of Honeywell and Ray-
        theon, 78
    with Sheraton Hotels, 127–28
Jones & Laughlin, 74–77,
    116, 176, 223
Justice Department, 212, 228
    Antitrust Division of, 226,
    230, 232

K

Katzenbach, Nicholas, 226
Keene Corp., 12
Kirby, Alan, 287
Kirk, Robert L., 12
Knortz, Herbert, 23, 93

L

Land, Edward, 238
Landsberg Brothers, 60
Lauer, John, 176
Law of Inverse Time-to-
    Veracity, 124
Lazard Frères, 217
Leadership, 133–53, 279
Leavey, Edmund, 37–38
Lenhart, Norman, 64–65
Lester, James, 94
Leveraged buy-out, 249–53
Levitt & Sons, 215–16, 217,
    231
Ling, James, 77
Ling-Temco-Vought, 224
Litton Industries, 224
Lobb, John C., 12
Loft Candy Co., 60
Lombardi, Vince, 12
Louisiana Land and
    Exploration Co., 64
Lybrand Brothers, 64–66

M

McConnell, Joseph, 64
McGregor, Douglas, 19
McKinsey and Co., 46
McLaren, Richard, 228–29,
    230
McNab, Joseph, 71–73
Magritte, René, 190
Maintenance men, pooling
    of, 76
Management
    as living force, 278
    by objectives, 5–6
    performance in judging,
    35–36

scientific, 25–26, 28–29, 164–65, 181

Manager
vs. entrepreneur, 117–18
as entrepreneur, 145–47
performance of, as board concern, 267–74
product line, 89–90, 93

Managerial positions, categorizing personnel for, 27

Managing, 111–15
and alcoholism, 173–76
and caring, 277–89
cluttered-desk executive's approach to, 167–68
and commitment, 118–19
and control of numbers, 189–204
and egotism, 177–86
from end to beginning, 50
guidelines for, 281–82
at ITT, 29–30
Japanese style of, 19–23
and leadership, 133–53
and performance, 35, 279
and quality control, 115–17
rifle shot approach to, 165–67
sales and earnings, 117
according to Theory X and Theory Y, 19–21
according to Theory Z, 19, 21
See also Problem solving

Margolis, David, 12

Massachusetts institute of Technology, 19

Mayflower Associates, 64

Meetings
flexible vs. rigidly scheduled, 162–64
and open communication, 138
time spent on, 106
See also General Managers Meetings

Mentality of clean-desk executive, 162–63

Mistakes, admitting, 150

Mitchell, John, 228, 229

Moreel, Ben, 75

Moscow, Al, 293

N

Nader, Ralph, 228

National Broadcasting Co., 225

National Transistor, 210

New York Graphic, 61

New York Stock Exchange, 58–60, 64

New York Telegram, 61

New York University, 53, 63–64

New York World-Telegram, 62–63, 134

Nippon Steel Corp., 230

Nixon, Richard, 229

Norton Simon Industries, 231

Numbers, managing and control of, 189–204

O

Odlum, Floyd, 65

Office of president, 93–94

Office of Price Administration, 72

Office politics, 39, 140–41

Open-door policy, 150, 160
Operating reports. *See* Reports, monthly
Opinions, interchange of, 139–40
Organization structure, 85–87, 95
and open communication, 88–90
Osborne Computer Corp., 248

P

Palmer House, Chicago, 126
Parsons, Eugene, 61
Participatory leadership, 135–36
Paternalism, 21
Pearl Harbor, 66
Pennsylvania Glass & Sand, 216, 217
Percy, Charles, 71–73
Performance, 293
in judging management, 35–36
and managing, 279
target, 44–45
Personnel, categorizing, 27
Peugeot, 230
Philips, 47, 221
Pick Your Job and Land It, 70
Planning, 92–93
and managing from end to beginning, 50
time spent on, 106
See also Problem solving
Polaroid Corp., 238
Politics, office, 39, 140–41
Preiss, C. G., 67–68
President, office of, 93–94

Press, misunderstanding ITT stretch target, 44–45
Prince of Wales, British dreadnought, 67
Problem solving, 120
and deciding what business a business is in, 126–27
and environment, 128
at General Managers Meetings, 96–98, 105–6
and monthly reports, 98–100
and planning, 122
Procter & Gamble, 3
Productivity, and alcoholism, 176
Product line
managers, 89–90, 93
Strategy and Action Board decisions on, 48
Profit and loss statement, as measure of results, 119
Profit centers, 96

Q

Quality control, 115–17

R

Radio Corporation of America. *See* RCA Corp.
Rayonier, 124–25, 128, 216, 217
Raytheon Co., 36, 77–81, 241
RCA Corp., 3, 44, 221, 225
Reeves, Alex, 244–45
Relaxation, 285–89
Renault, 230

Reports, monthly, 9, 93, 96
  problems highlighted in,
  99–100
Research and development,
  and entrepreneurial
  spirit, 244–45
Revlon, 12
Revson, Charles, 12
Rice, Joseph A., 12
Rifle shot approach to
  managing, 165–67
Rohatyn, Felix, 217, 227

S

Salary
  at American Can, 69–70
  at Bell & Howell,
  70–73
  as classified ad salesman,
  62, 63
  as door-to-door book
  salesman, 60–61
  and entrepreneurial spirit,
  242–43
  and hiring top people, 138
  at ITT, 81
  at Lybrand Brothers, 64
  at Raytheon, 78
Sales and earnings, 117
Scheon, Herb, 231
Scientific management,
  25–26, 28–29, 164–65,
  181
Scott (O.M.) and Sons, 217
Scudder, Henry, 40, 41
The Selling Process: A
  Handbook of
  Salesmanship Principles
  (Hawkins), 62–63
Serio, Marie, 6
Shareholders, 91

Sheraton Corporation of
  America, 2, 126–28,
  213, 215, 217
Siemens, 47, 221
Silver's, cafeteria, 61
Sloan, Alfred P., Jr., 1, 76
Sperry, 221
Stanton, Frank, 12
Stars, 26–27
Strategic Air Command, 40
Strategy and Action Boards,
  48
Strichman, George A., 12
Structure of company, 85–87
  and open communication,
  88–90
  organizational, 88–107
Suffield Academy, 7, 56–58,
  134

T

Taylor, Wellington, 58
Team spirit, at General Man-
  agers Meetings, 104–5
Teves auto parts, 213
Textron, 224
Theory X and Theory Y,
  19–21
Theory Z, 19, 21, 24
Think tank, General
  Managers Meetings as,
  106
Thomas, Peter, 231
Thompson auto parts, 213
Three-by-five card executive,
  160–61
Time, and veracity, inverse
  ratio of, 123–24
Time-motion studies, 25–26
Trans World Airlines, 126
Truman, Harry, 75

U

Union Carbide Corp., 3
U.S. Steel Corp., 3, 77, 232
United Steel Workers Union, 75
United Telephone, 210

V

Venture capital group, and leveraged buy-out, 250–52
Veracity and time, inverse ratio of, 123–24
Vought Corp., 12

W

Wall Street, and ITT, 5, 44, 218

Western Union, 12
Westinghouse Electric Corp., 3, 44
Wharton School of Business Administration, 281
Whitney, Richard, 58
Williams, Harry, 231
Williams, Paul, 216
World Court, 208

X

Xerox Corp., 237–38

Y

Yallem, Charles, 211

Z

Zero defects, 116–17